CultureShock!
A Survival Guide to Customs and Etiquette

Venezuela

Kitt Baguley

Marshall Cavendish
Editions

This edition published in 2008 by:
Marshall Cavendish Corporation
99 White Plains Road
Tarrytown, NY 10591-9001
www.marshallcavendish.us

Other Marshall Cavendish Offices:
Marshall Cavendish International (Asia) Private Limited. 1 New Industrial Road,
Singapore 536196 ■ Marshall Cavendish Ltd. 5th Floor, 32–38 Saffron Hill,
London EC1N 8FH, UK ■ Marshall Cavendish International (Thailand) Co Ltd.
253 Asoke, 12th Flr, Sukhumvit 21 Road, Klongtoey Nua, Wattana, Bangkok
10110, Thailand ■ Marshall Cavendish (Malaysia) Sdn Bhd, Times Subang,
Lot 46, Subang Hi-Tech Industrial Park, Batu Tiga, 40000 Shah Alam, Selangor
Darul Ehsan, Malaysia

Marshall Cavendish is a trademark of Times Publishing Limited

ISBN 10: 0-7614-5569-8
ISBN 13: 978-0-7614-5569-1

Please contact the publisher for the Library of Congress catalog number

Printed in China by Everbest Printing Co Ltd

Photo Credits:
All black and white photos by the author except pages 20–21, 120-121,
130-131, 164-165 (Photolibrary). All colour photos from Photolibrary.
■ Cover photo: Reuters.

All illustrations by TRIGG

ABOUT THE SERIES

Culture shock is a state of disorientation that can come over anyone who has been thrust into unknown surroundings, away from one's comfort zone. *CultureShock!* is a series of trusted and reputed guides which has, for decades, been helping expatriates and long-term visitors to cushion the impact of culture shock whenever they move to a new country.

Written by people who have lived in the country and experienced culture shock themselves, the authors share all the information necessary for anyone to cope with these feelings of disorientation more effectively. The guides are written in a style that is easy to read and covers a range of topics that will arm readers with enough advice, hints and tips to make their lives as normal as possible again.

Each book is structured in the same manner. It begins with the first impressions that visitors will have of that city or country. To understand a culture, one must first understand the people—where they came from, who they are, the values and traditions they live by, as well as their customs and etiquette. This is covered in the first half of the book.

Then on with the practical aspects—how to settle in with the greatest of ease. Authors walk readers through how to find accommodation, get the utilities and telecommunications up and running, enrol the children in school and keep in the pink of health. But that's not all. Once the essentials are out of the way, venture out and try the food, enjoy more of the culture and travel to other areas. Then be immersed in the language of the country before discovering more about the business side of things.

To round off, snippets of basic information are offered before readers are 'tested' on customs and etiquette of the country. Useful words and phrases, a comprehensive resource guide and list of books for further research are also included for easy reference.

CONTENTS

When people think of Venezuela, what often comes to mind is Miss World and coffee. A little reflection usually recalls its powerful oil industry and the name Simón Bolívar, but what lies beyond that?

To most people, the South American continent is a dark mass dappled with odd patches of light. The fiestas with their pulsating Latin rhythms. Political instability, guerrillas and military coups. Countries rich in natural resources and teeming with wildlife. Venezuela has, or has had, it all. It is a country of contrasts, not least between its proud foundation and its contemporary obsession with the culture of the United States. This book aims to provide anyone intending to spend some time or settle in Venezuela with an up-to-date and accurate portrayal of this diverse and deeply fascinating country.

CULTURE SHOCK

There can be no better way to begin this book than with an explanation of its title and the rationale behind it. When you live in a new country, there is a process of adaptation that cannot be avoided. This is obvious. The most surprising thing about this process is the psychological effect that it has. Your personality changes. Maybe not in any profound sense; you won't necessarily become more sophisticated, wise or cultured just by living in a foreign country. You won't be freed from your own cultural values merely by being able to compare two or more cultures. You won't be able to step out and separate yourself from culture entirely and become an individual capable of adapting to any and every situation. However, this doesn't preclude gaining valuable insights into your own culture.

Culture shock may involve disorientation, fear, helplessness, a sense of instability and insecurity and mild panic. This might sound exaggerated but if you look at your own experiences you may have a sense of recognition. You might have had to adapt to a change of town and a change of school in your childhood with all its initially attendant miseries. Do not forget that children are more adaptable than adults, although less secure emotionally.

For adults, culture shock presents other problems. You can lose confidence in yourself as you find that you simply cannot function as well as you are used to. Misunderstandings and misreadings of situations are bound to happen. You cannot help but suffer an emotional reaction to all of this. You will feel frustrated and quite possibly react in anger due to that frustration. You may direct this anger at yourself, although you are blameless for not knowing what you can only learn by experience (yours or someone else's). You may be angry at your new hosts for not understanding you or even for not trying to understand you. You may withdraw and defend yourself vigorously. You may feel that your beliefs, your way of life and your personality are under threat. You may feel spurned, left out, unwanted and rejected just because you are not like them. Not only is the new country a bewildering feast for the senses but there are new rules to be learned, most of which are, unfortunately, unspoken.

A mild sense of paranoia can occur when you feel that the people around you are all pressing for you to change and become like them. "Why can't they accept me as I am?" you mutter to yourself. You may find that the difference between them and you leads you to cling onto whatever is at hand to remind you of home. Something as insignificant as a sports report torn from a newspaper may take on the appearance of a lifeline. You may develop a siege mentality and decide to reproduce the conditions of your environment 'back home' as much as possible. This will allow you to involve yourself slowly and on your terms.

Patience and understanding are the key words here. Remember that many of the host people do not have the experience needed to relate to what you are going through. Take, for example, your struggle to learn a foreign language. You may well feel that your hosts are pressurising you too much and demanding more than you are capable of. Clamming up and being uncooperative will only cause offence. This can be a test of your social skills. Make it clear when you cannot follow a conversation and need people to repeat things for you. Causing conversations to slow down to run at your speed may make you feel you are dominating the whole conversation and preventing people from speaking freely and enjoying themselves, but if you are beginning to learn a language this can't be helped. On the other hand, you may revel in being the centre of attention while you keep trying to make your needs known.

However, if a turn in the spotlight is not for you, or you feel uncomfortable with such a dictatorial approach, you can monopolise just one person (bring a friend) and use that person as a crutch. Ask him or her for explanations and to repeat what has just been said. Venezuelans with a good knowledge of English would be ideal. Those who have studied English will also understand the problems you face and be more likely to sympathise with your plight. Quicker and less cumbersome than a dictionary, you can use them to help compose what you want to say. You must be firm and say it, or the moment may be gone. This is why it is really best to have the attention of the whole group, so that the conversation flows at a pace you are comfortable with.

I have taught foreign students in England. Many of them find that the experience of living in another culture allows them to value more some facets of their own society. They are grateful, if only for that reason, that they have experienced another culture. They also feel that it teaches independence. Those students spend only nine months in England. You will presumably be spending more time than that in a new society and need all the help you can get to make the process of culture shock as comfortable as possible. That is where this book comes in. By giving you as much background as I can on what the experience of living in Venezuela is like for a foreigner, you can build up your own picture of the country, its culture and people. When you are there, you will feel more at ease in new situations as you will have the knowledge you need to deal with them. You will also be able to predict how people will act in given situations and what their expectations are of you. Hopefully this book will also stimulate your interest in a beautiful and fascinating country.

ACKNOWLEDGEMENTS

I dedicate this book to my wife, Sofia, for her support and love over the two years I took writing this book.

An enormous debt of gratitude is also due to my stepfather Ian for his expertise and my mother-in-law Sofia Valdes for her invaluable help in securing photographs and information. My mother, father and brother have also been more than helpful. Thanks for information to Pedro Mailat and family.

A huge 'gracias' to my best friend and No.1 Venezuelan, Pedro Luis Rojas.

MAP OF VENEZUELA

CARIBBEAN
SEA

TRINIDAD
AND TOBAGO

CARACAS

VENEZUELA

GUYANA

COLOMBIA

BRAZIL

FIRST IMPRESSIONS

'I found some of the most beautiful country in the world.'
—Christopher Colombus

FIRST IMPRESSIONS OF VENEZUELA

First impressions are lasting impressions, but as you get to know a country there are so many first impressions that what I would like to do in this chapter is to give the reader an impression of my first impressions, a flavour of things dealt with in more detail through the book. If they are but fleeting impressions, I hope they serve to stimulate the imagination and whet the appetite.

Caracas has been called the Gateway to South America, so it is no surprise that I arrived like millions of others via Simon Bolivar International Airport at Maiquetia. I noticed the potted palms, Burger King, varnished piranhas for sale and felt disappointed that it wasn't more different. Outside, the quality of the sunlight impressed itself on me immediately with its raw power. The curiously desolate nature of the hillsides, with a few small succulents and shrubs surviving in the hard earth, was always a contrast to the beauty of almost all the other landscapes in Venezuela.

Driving into Caracas, the first thing I saw were the ramshackle brick shanty houses tumbling down the hillside and growing organically, one piling on top of another. Not far away were the impressive detached *quintas*, houses built to the wealthy owners' specifications, but always carefully walled and gated away from the public. This was stark evidence that the cliché that Venezuela was a land of contrasts was very true.

As we drove into the city, the crush of traffic and the modern cityscape of tall office buildings and apartments was apparent, along with the occasional bloated dog carcass. Caracas seemed a busy, fairly dirty, youthful and vibrant city. It has been said that Caracas is a city that is hard to fall in love with, but within a couple of days it was obvious there was plenty to do, whether going to the cinema to watch dubbed Hollywood films, going to a jazz concert at the Teatro Teresa Carreño, a gig with a rising Venezuelan pop star at a country club, or a jazz club where the waiter whisked your ashtray away and replaced it with a clean one every time ash was flicked into it.

The private beaches were stunning and the ease with which people chatted to me on the bus, at work, outside our flat and made extravagant plans to fly to Los Roques or spend the weekend partying on the beach at Choroní, (most of which fell through) was surprising. The love of food, especially meats, and barbecues (*parilla*) and whisky and dancing at private parties and the eagerness for the

The first time I walked the streets of Caracas, I was struck by the beauty of the people, the extreme glamour of the young women and the stately bearing of the señoras, the mix of skin tones from tan to dark brown, the way even soldiers smelled of cologne. There was an overt sense of sensuality; as girls walked down the street, men threw remarks and stares their way for hundreds of yards.

weekend and for any chance to take more days off was easy to become accustomed to.

The way a scratch game of soccer took forever to get started, or how waiting for a date to turn up took hours, or the impossibility of getting reliable information or doing any business at all over the phone and the need to have more than one face-to-face meeting to establish a rapport. The mix of modern and old, with beautiful young people in the latest European or US fashions hurrying along with men in *liqui-liquis* and straw hats.

The occasional flash of natural beauty amidst the city reminded me that I was in a country rich with wildlife. There might be a pair of gargantuan iguanas in the branches of a small tree overlooking the highway, or parrots bursting over an apartment block with a flash of green and raucous cries, or vultures circling slowly overhead in search of carrion.

Noticeably different was the poor quality bread (except bread fresh from the *panaderías*) and the even worse printed paper (except for the coffee-table books in the best shops). There was also the extreme comfort and luxury of the shops and restaurants in the malls and the variety of delicatessen foods in the *panederías*, everything that gave the impression that a fabulous lifestyle was within easier reach than in Europe or the USA. The contrast were the street children begging outside and inside restaurants, the beggars missing limbs or with elephantiasis or other extreme disfigurements.

The bombastic style of TV presentation, the love of glamour and showmanship, the strange value placed on blonde hair and light skin that predominated in television presenters and actors. The telenovelas with beautiful people and terrible acting, but loads of glamour and ostentation.

The kindness shown to strangers and warmth of hospitality but the indifference to ambulances struggling through the traffic or a man lying bleeding profusely in the street. The gun crime and mistrust of the heavily-armed police or lighter-armed army. I heard shots fired in anger for the first time in Venezuela and saw a staggering variety of guns carried by police and soldiers. Policemen holding machetes over the heads of party-goers after a night of revelry at a university party.

The frenetic energy of the traffic and pressures of trying to get around the city to do business against the relatively relaxed nature of most work and people's lack of interest in public service. In a bank, girls chatting and doing their nails while you waited for them to serve you. The demands of people to talk, get to know you, enjoy your company, go out and have fun and talk some more. The ancient and unlovely cars and the endless workshops that kept them going. Maturín seemed to be a city composed solely of car workshops.

The calm of the countryside and small towns and villages, the sense of tranquillity and awareness of the natural world, the scents of trees and plants and bird calls and the clarity of the intrusion of man-made sounds, such as the clanking of pots. People just doing nothing for hours on end, awaiting the next meal or for the next thing to happen.

The physical extremes of Venezuela, from the humidity of the Amazon rainforests and the tea-brown Orinoco, teeming with ants and anacondas and red howler monkeys. The Amerindians, traditionally dressed or in Disney T-shirts, living a rural life much the same as anyone else's, or an unenviable urban existence or rarely a traditional lifestyle that excites the imagination of Westerners. The dramatic flight through the Andes to Merida and the almost cathedral quiet of the small towns with wedding-cake coloured houses and churches, the mountain landscape with the semi-cactus succulent squashy frailejones. The surprising sand dunes of Coro and architecture of the ancient capital, the tourist-trap beaches of Puerto La Cruz, Margarita and Los Roques with incredibly good restaurants everywhere. The tepuis, rainbows and falls of Roraima, La Gran Sabana and the endless, merciless plains of Los Llanos, dusty and intensely beautiful in the sunset. The cloud forest in Monagas, haunting and transcendental, a place of quiet stasis, closer to Nirvana than Limbo.

It is a beautiful country, with beautiful and extremely hospitable people. There are many difficulties and frustrations to living in Venezuela, but its best moments are unforgettable and time spent there is sure to enrich your life immensely.

OVERVIEW OF LAND AND HISTORY

CHAPTER 2

'Now is when Venezuelans will
listen to me speak of Bolívar.'
—Hugo Chávez

THIS CHAPTER PRESENTS THE GEOGRAPHY of the country as a guide to its physical and cultural diversity. Its aim is to give you a regional orientation so you will gain a general feel for places encountered in conversation or in the media. Hopefully it will also inspire you to travel and experience all of the totally distinct areas of the country. In my two years in Venezuela, I travelled whenever I could but there are still places I deeply regret not having seen and intend to visit one day. Venezuela is a country with an extremely diverse variety of environments, many of which are preserved in national parks, and a rich history. To appreciate the country, you must travel around it and experience the way people live in these varying environments. To live exclusively in a big city like Caracas or Maracaibo is to miss out on much of what is best about the country. In the largest cities, you could almost be in any big city in the world.

It was always a huge relief to get out of the city and head for the countryside, even though I never felt that I disliked the city. The much gentler pace of life and the feeling of being close to the limitless natural beauty of the countryside was immensely soothing. The truth is that the cities and the countryside are like chalk and cheese. This chapter also gives you the background on Venezuela's rural depopulation and catalogues the development of the cities at the expense of the small towns. The totally different pace of development has meant that the normal rural/urban differences are highly exaggerated, so much so that they could be two different countries. The only link between the two are the *barrios*, where people perpetuate rural lifestyles at the fringes of the city.

It is no coincidence that the cities are located along the coast. The coastal region has always held the key to Venezuela's wealth, whether in pearls, fish or oil. The only rival is the plantation-rich Andean region. The rest of the country is referred to as el Interior, making it seem unknown, mysterious and wild. El Interior is where you will find the cultural wealth of the country, unclouded by the current global superculture (mainly derived from the United States) and the Latin entertainment industry that seems to be centred in Miami. Both Venezuelas are real, but only one is still in touch with its roots.

There are 22 states in Venezuela and a Distrito Federal. In this chapter we will sweep across the country from west to east. Environmental characteristics will be discussed, and the states and their major towns briefly described. The states are: Amazonas, Anzoátegui, Apure, Aragua, Barinas, Bolívar, Carabobo, Cojedes, Delta Amacuro, Falcón, Guárico, Lara, Mérida, Miranda, Monagas, Nueva Esparta, Portuguesa, Sucre, Táchira, Trujillo, Yaracuy and Zulia. Along the way, we'll go through the Andes, Los Llanos and La Gran Sabana.

FROM THE ANDES TO THE CARIBBEAN
Zulia

In the far north-west corner of Venezuela, Zulia's pincers stretch around the fount of the country's riches, Lake Maracaibo (Lago de Maracaibo). It is from Zulia that the greatest wealth of the country springs, for this is Venezuela's oil country besides being a significant producer of milk and beef. Zulia is the home of the *gaitas*, music that is played only at Christmas in Caracas but all year round here. *Gaitas* bands include players of *cuatro* (four stringed-guitar), maracas and *furrucos*, as well as vocalists. The lyrics are either religious (played at Christmas) or political in tone.

It was in the waters of the Gulf of Venezuela (Golfo de Venezuela) and Lake Maracaibo that Amerigo Vespucci (Américo Vespucio) saw the Parajuano Indian *palafitos*, the palm leaf huts on stilts that inspired him to name the region

Pequeña Venecia (little Venice), which of course became Venezuela. You can still see traditional Parajuano *palafitos* at Sinamaico Lagoon.

Zulia's population is more than three million. Agriculturally, it is the country's top producer of cassava and plantain. Here are the national parks of Sierra de Perijá and Ciénagas del Catatumbo. This is a scorchingly hot state, with temperatures even Venezuelans find uncomfortable. The humidity level is 80 per cent plus. You have been warned!

Maracaibo

Home of the Maracuchos, as its residents are called, Venezuela's second largest city (population almost two million) enjoys strong rivalry with Caracas, seen at its fiercest during baseball games. Maracuchos have a reputation for being tough and straight-talking, blunt to the point of rudeness. The fast Maracucho accent is easy to pick out.

Maracaibo experienced many problems in its early development. It was ransacked by pirates entering the lake and destroyed by the local Indians until the missionaries finally pacified them. Today the city retains a strong *guajiro* presence, highly visible due to the traditional *mantas* (caftans) and pompommed sandals that some women wear. *Guajiros—* cattle ranchers—recognise no authority but their own. They have their own laws and do not have to carry *cédulas* (identification cards).

Having a Siesta

Due to the heat, Maracaibo is a city where the siesta is observed, from noon until 2:00 pm or longer. The streets come alive again later in the day, when people turn out to enjoy the relative cool of the evening.

Cabimas

Cabimas (population 210,000) is the petrol town of Venezuela and is consequently heavily industrial.

Ciudad Ojeda

Ciudad Ojeda might create a sensation of *déjà vu* for some visitors as it was built to the same plans as Washington D.C. under the orders of President Eleazar López Contreras. It is now an important oil town of 88,000 inhabitants.

Falcón

Falcón is on the western Caribbean coast of Venezuela. The cape of San Román reaches out into the Caribbean, carrying the Paraguaná Peninsula, an expanse of hot earth broken by cacti and scrub. This is a familiar landscape along the coast and its inhospitable and desolate nature contrasts with the beauty of the Caribbean.

Falcón was named after General Juan Crisóstomo Falcón in 1901. It contains possibly the most unlikely and therefore incredible environment in Venezuela as its capital, Coro, is surrounded by desert complete with wide expanses of rolling dunes (*médanos*) and camels. This region is included in the Parque Nacional Médanos de Coro. Added to this is the Parque Nacional Morrocoy: tiny islands scattered over the Caribbean, with the mangrove trees that are nesting sites for spectacular bird species. With the incredible vivid blue of the Caribbean and the abundance of fish, the national park is a diver's paradise.

Falcón's Economy

Falcón's economy is diverse and includes livestock (cattle and goats), cheese, petroleum, tourism, cement production and agriculture (beans, corn, tobacco, bananas and tomatoes). Off the coast sit the Netherlands Antilles of Aruba, Bonaire and Curaçao (the ABC islands), of which Aruba is a famous holiday destination.

Coro

In the language of the Arawak Indians, *coro* means 'wind', as it is blessed with an easterly breeze that ameliorates the effect of the blistering heat. In the past, Coro was frequently the site of insurrections and it also used to carry on a brisk smuggling trade with the Netherlands Antilles. Coro was the original capital of the province of Venezuela. The town (population 169,000) has been blessed with the grandiose titles of Monumento Nacional and Patrimonio Histórico de la Humanidad for its preservation of colonial architecture, particularly the mansions, which, along with the numerous parks, give it a genteel air.

Chichiriviche

This small town in eastern Falcón must be seen solely on account of the large flock of flamingos and other bird life nearby. Tourism is building up in this beautiful part of the national park.

Yaracuy

Yaracuy is a western state that almost touches the Caribbean. This fertile state produces cattle, goats, pigs, timber and an immense variety of fruit. The state has a touch of mystery and magic. It is the home of the witch-goddess Maria Lionza. The national park of the state is called Yurubí.

San Felipe

A small capital for a small state, San Felipe has only 79,000 residents. It was founded in 1729 to be the region's administrative centre. It was the home of the Caracas Company (also known as the Compañía Guipuzcoana). In 1812, the city was levelled by an earthquake. What you see today was built to the north of the old San Felipe, thus it has no trace of its colonial past.

Aroa

Aroa (population 37,000) was the site of copper mines owned by Simón Bolívar's family. It has since fallen from its exalted position of a major industrial town. It had a *teleférico* (cable car) and the first railway line in Venezuela, the Ferrocarril Bolívar.

Nirgua

The Minas Real de San Felipe de Buría of Nirgua were special mines—they were the first gold mines discovered in Venezuela. The mining settlements came under constant attack from the Jirajara Indians and they were forced to close several times before finally being abandoned. Now Nirgua grows corn, cassava and *auyama*, a Venezuelan variety of pumpkin.

Carabobo

This state owes its name to the decisive battle in the War of Independence. Despite being a small state, Carabobo is an economic powerhouse and has experienced rapid population growth (now 1.2 million). It touches the Caribbean coast and lies to the west of Caracas. The region produces beans and yam for the country. The house of José Antonio Páez, Venezuela's first president, is located here. There is also the Parque Nacional de San Esteban.

Valencia

Valencia (population 1.4 million) is heavily industrialised and has an industrial park where 500 Venezuelan companies are located. It was founded by Alonso Díaz Moreno as Nueva Valencia del Rey in 1555, the first Spanish settlement in the centre of the country. Valencia has been rebuilt many times, having suffered destruction from a variety of causes, including the Spanish adventurer Lope de Aguirre, local Caribe Indians, French pirates and the earthquake of 1812.

Puerto Cabello

Puerto Cabello (population 165,000) is a port with great economic importance for the country. Despite the nearby oil refinery of El Palito and cargo activity, Puerto Cabello has pleasant streets and an interesting history, including the controversial Caracas Company and the city's liberation from the Spaniards by Páez.

Aragua

Aragua is named after a tribe of Indians who settled in the area before the Spanish Conquest. Located close to Caracas, it is the site of industrial and housing centres for the capital, although agriculture and industry live side by side in this state. The population is almost 1.5 million.

Aragua's Parque Nacional Henri Pittier is named after the Swiss naturalist who catalogued over 30,000 plant species in the area and pushed for the creation of national parks. Its cloud forest draws naturalists to observe its enormous diversity of animal and bird life; there are over 500 bird species in the national park.

The best beaches in Venezuela can be found in Aragua. As well as Choroní (described below), there are Cata, Cuayagua

The landscape near the beach at Choroní is dramatic.

and Chuao, wonderful beaches that retain a tranquil local feel, free from the trappings of tourism. The only drawback is the strength of the waves at these beaches.

Maracay

Maracay has been called the Ciudad Jardín (Garden City). The original Maracay was an Indian *cacique* (chief) of the Aragua tribe. Its population is half a million and growing. Despite its industrialisation, it retains a colonial feel. Petroglyphs, in the form of concentric circles, can be seen at La Pedrera.

Choroní and Puerto Colombia

Many Caraqueños brave the four-hour climb over a cloud forest range to get to Choroní. This used to be a centre for coffee and cacao haciendas and it is still a lovely town with whitewashed colonial houses, wooden shuttered-windows and iron grilles. Choroní itself is not the attraction; it is Puerto Colombia on the seafront with its small hotels, the scene of nightly revels and the rhythm of drums. There is a constantly changing variety of restaurants by the beach and a fleet of small brightly painted fishing boats in the harbour. It is hard to believe that such a small town was once a noteworthy

Cata, one of the most spectacular beaches on Venezuela's east coast.

centre for the export of the region's produce of cacao, coffee and sugar.

Colonia Tovar

Colonia Tovar is a small and surprising town hidden in mountains near Caracas. The surprise is not just the appearance of a Black Forest town from a bygone era but the apparently traditional Germanic lifestyles of the inhabitants. Colonia Tovar is a genuine town although many of its traditions have been preserved as a tourist attraction. It was settled by a group of German immigrants who were invited to work the land of a creole, Martín Tovar. As they had smallpox, the Caraqueños moved them to Tovar's lands and they have kept themselves separate until recent times. The population is only 7,000 and the Germanic blood is now mixed with Venezuelan. German food and handicrafts are found here.

Distrito Federal

The Federal District is the political and economic centre of the country. In many ways it *is* the country and it is sometimes hard not to see *caraqueño* culture as being Venezuelan culture. There are around four million people here, nearly all crammed in the small valley in which Caracas is located. When you consider that the second largest city, Maracaibo, has only 1.5 million people, the third largest, Valencia, has less than a million, and no city other than Barquisimeto reaches the half million mark, it is easy to understand the dominance of the capital. The Federal District is somewhat confusingly organised. It is composed of two municipal areas, Libertador and Vargas. Libertador, along with the municipal areas of Baruta, Chacao, El Hatillo and Sucre, form the Área Metropolitana de Caracas.

Caracas

Santiago de León de Caracas is known as the 'gateway to South America'. The capital has many of the characteristic features of major cities: pollution, traffic congestion and high-rise buildings. It is unique in many other ways however, one being El Avila, the mountain that looms over the city and provides a useful reference point wherever you are in Caracas. On the other side of El Avila is El Litoral, the coastal region with beaches where many Caraqueños spend the weekend. It also has Puerto La Guaira, the most important port in the country, and Simón Bolívar International Airport at nearby Maiquetía (you can't name too many things after El Libertador).

Caracas is a city full of contrasts. The first contrast is with the rest of the country. Caracas exudes sophistication in both its modern buildings and the glamorous people who walk its streets. The buildings are unvaryingly modern and most of the citizens live in apartments that run the entire range of quality but are usually well kept, with a concierge, working lifts and sometimes an armed guard. There are also large *quintas* (luxurious houses with their own compound) in zones protected by high-level security and ramshackle *barrios* built on the hills, sometimes rubbing shoulders with the poshest country club areas. The *barrios* have grown rapidly with the influx of migrants from Colombia, Ecuador, Perú and other South American and Caribbean countries. Some are firmly established, with electricity and water and even Metro lines

The modern buildings of Caracas contrast with the natural beauty of the Avila mountain.

that run up to their bustling market areas, such as Plaza Catia. The street markets are full of life and noticeably cheaper than the stores, but at night they are hazardous.

Caracas has all the international restaurants you could hope for and some of the largest shopping centres in the continent. As you walk the streets you can sometimes see, through the haze of pollution, bright green parakeets or scarlet ibis flying overhead. The people look far better than the city does. The Guaire River that runs through the city is tarnished by multi-coloured pollutants that are pumped into it by the plants situated at its edge. The river swells with a cargo of rubbish in the rainy season and may deposit a tasty morsel such as a dead dog for the plentiful vultures to feast on.

Modern Caracas was built on oil money, and the get-rich-quick mentality still spurs a fast pace and a sometimes cynical and callous attitude in the city. I have seen injured people lying unattended in the streets and nobody moving to let the private ambulance through. The people say they use their sirens just to get home quickly and that those who stop to help may find themselves the victims of a trap. Crime is a problem, especially in the *barrios* where the death toll is always high. Carjacking is common in the city, as is theft at gun or knifepoint. Only good money or insurance will get you a high quality of medical care at the best clinicas.

Despite this, Caraqueños themselves are extremely hospitable and friendly. Caracas is not one of those cities where people keep to themselves. You can make friends—on the streets, on the buses, absolutely anywhere. Neighbours will feel insulted if you do not pop in and hang around at least once every day.

Caraqueños are inclined to be both young and female, famously so in the British film *Gregory's Girl*, where two boys attempt to hitchhike to Caracas, having heard that it had the highest female-to-male ratio in the world. They are renowned jokers, style-conscious and addicted to entertainment. Cinemas are cheap and always busy, as are restaurants. Even fast food joints selling burgers or pizza are trendy. Shopping malls are the places to hang out with your friends. Clubs and bars are popular but English pubs are unknown. In bars you may have to buy a bottle of whisky if you want to sit at a table, as people really come to dance and talk rather than drink. There are clubs to cater for most tastes and live music is usually played, especially in the popular jazz bars.

PUB... PUB

Caracas is the only city in Venezuela with an underground train system (el Metro), which is the pride of the city. Caraqueños may throw half-eaten burgers out of bus windows but don't dare drop even a gum wrapper in the Metro. It is spotlessly clean and wonderfully efficient. While up above traffic may be almost constantly gridlocked, the Metro rushes swiftly along its two lines. Security is good and if you step too close to the edge, a voice over the PA system will ask you to step back. I once suffered this humiliation when I did not realise I was being referred to until everybody was staring at me and the voice boomed, "Will the man in the black trousers PLEASE STEP BACK!" The trains are also spotless, as are the hygiene-conscious and heavily perfumed Caraqueños.

Above-ground each station is linked to the Metrobuses, which, while efficient, are not frequent enough to prevent lengthy queues and congestion. Being on a crowded Metrobus in the rainy season is to invite asphyxiation, as the windows are all kept firmly shut. Aside from the Metrobuses, there are the plentiful and highly colourful *carritos* (small buses).

Public transport aside, Caracas is a city where the car is king. The cars are generally old and make the city look like the legendary graveyard of the American motor. Even in the wealthier zones, you may still be awakened every morning by the wheezing of motors being not so gently coaxed into life. People love to drive, despite the constantly heavy traffic and the high quality of the Metro and Metrobuses. The truth is that not only is the city too small for its population, it is also too small for the cars. The inadequacies of the transport system mean that Caracas appears much bigger than it actually is. You can expect to spend around two hours a day travelling, or even double that if you have to visit different parts of the city. In some spots, the pollution can make you choke and make it nearly impossible for you to walk around with eyes open. On the other hand, there are some delightful public areas denied to traffic and the wealthy suburbs are peacefully congestion-free.

Caracas possesses some fine art collections and museums. Perhaps the most compelling reason for visitors to spend time in Caracas is the impressive variety of museums. There

Bustling streets and skyscrapers in modern Caracas. Known as the 'gateway to South America', Caracas is the capital of Venezuela and is the only city in the country with an underground train system.

is the the Capitolio, the Casa Natál of Simón Bolívar, Quinta Anauco (a restored hacienda owner's home, with colonial art and furniture), the Children's Museum (Museo de los Niños), Museo de Arte Contemporáneo (Venezuelan and international artists, including Picasso and Matisse), Museo de Bellas Artes (including Diego Rivera and Botero), Galería de Arte Nacional (as its name suggests, art by Venezuelans, such as the studies of Simón Bolívar by Tito Salas) and Museo de Ciencias Naturales. Large kinetic sculptures by Venezuelans Jesús Soto and Alejandro Otero dot the city.

Exploring El Hatillo

El Hatillo is a small, colourful, touristy town just outside Caracas. It is a popular evening and weekend haunt for Caraqueños, who gather there to sample the idiosyncratic restaurants and clubs. For tourists, there are a large number of shops and traditional events such as open-air concerts, dances, processions and *patinatas Decembrinas*, the Christmas ritual of roller-skating around the church.

La Guaira

Named Huaira by the Tarma Indians, San Pedro de la Guaira is a contrast between the modern port buildings and the colonial houses of the town proper. It has three castles left from those built in the 17th and 18th centuries to ward off the unwanted attentions of pirates. It may look small, but La Guaira is Venezuela's principal port.

El Litoral

The beaches along El Litoral are extremely popular and include the resorts of Macuto, Caraballeda and Naiguatá.

Los Roques

Los Roques Islands are worth mentioning for their exceptional beauty and the fact that they are the largest group of coral *cayos* (cays) belonging to Venezuela. Get there by plane or yacht to enjoy the white sands, pretty mountains of pink conch shells and plentiful wildlife.

Miranda

Miranda, east of Distrito Federal, was named after the famous and revered precursor of independence, Francisco de Miranda. It contains several dormitory towns for Caracas and the region of Barlovento, where plantations and slave towns once dominated. This region now grows cacao, beans and plantain. Tourism on the Caribbean coast and industry in the valle de Caracas drive the economy of the state.

Los Teques

The state capital was founded in 1703. The name comes from the Caribbean Aractoeques Indians.

Guarenas

This dormitory town for Caracas can take some time to reach due to traffic congestion, although many folk brave the bus ride—over two hours one way.

Higuerote

If you spend time in Caracas, it won't be long before you hear Higuerote mentioned. This small port has long been an attraction for holidaymakers from the metropolis and serves as a launching pad for the exploration of small islands off the coast. Higuerote was the site of slave-worked cacao plantations and retains an African influence, seen for instance in their *tambores* (drums) and wild dancing.

San Francisco de Yare

This town is home to the devil dancers of Yare (Los Diablos Danzantes de Yare), a visual spectacle with roots in Spanish, Indian and African traditions. The festival happens every Jueves de Corpus Cristi, in May or June.

Anzoátegui

Anzoátegui has some of the most attractive tourist areas on the Caribbean coast, as well as being known for oil production. It also contains the beautiful Mochima National Park. There are over a million inhabitants in this state, which gets its name from General José Antonio Anzoátegui, a local hero of the War of Independence.

Barcelona and Puerto La Cruz

These two cities together with Lecherías (combined population about 500,000) form a conurbation along the Caribbean coast with the largest number of hotel rooms in the country. Barcelona, the state capital, still retains a traditional flavour with its colonial architecture and many fishing zones intact. It gets its name from the Catalan origin of its founders. The Paseo Colón is a wonderful place to stroll along in the sea breezes and take in the smells of the restaurants that line it. Barcelona is dominated by the tourist industry.

Puerto la Cruz was built up around its oil refinery, which you will see if you take a small boat out to one of the tiny islands nearby. The city becomes busier as tourism grows, but is a lively and pleasant town, entertaining but without the congestion of Caracas.

Sucre

Sucre proudly carries the name of Mariscal Antonio José de Sucre, who was seen as successor to El Libertador himself.

Puerto La Cruz, a view from one of the many Caribbean islands.

Another source of local pride is the fact that Sucre was the first Venezuelan land to be touched by Christopher Columbus.

Sucre has less than a million inhabitants. It is the second most important state for fishing and cacao. Crops grown are coffee, tobacco, tomatoes and sugarcane. Its two peninsulas extend into the Caribbean: the dry Araya Peninsula in the west and the humid tropical rainforest of the Paria Peninsula in the east. Paria Peninsula is reputed to have the best beaches in the country, including Playa Arepita, Playa Colorada and the best-developed beach outside Distrito Federal, Playa San Luis.

Cumaná

Cumaná is the first city to be built in South America, in 1521. Cumaná means 'river and coast' in the tongue of the Cumanagotos Indians, who were pearl divers pressed into the service of the Spanish. Cumaná retains some colonial character, although the *terremotos* (earthquakes) of 1684, 1765 and 1929 did considerable damage. It has some beaches and is a fishing centre. Despite a population of nearly 300,000 it still has an empty, slumbering air in the afternoons as people take their siesta. The Castillo de San Antonio is the oldest Spanish fort in South America and has a terrific view of the city from its vantage point.

Nueva Esparta

Nueva Esparta consists of the island of Margarita and the smaller islands of Cubagua and Coche. Margarita is possibly the best-known place in Venezuela after Caracas, as it has been developed to its full tourism potential. The wealth of Margarita extends back to colonial times when it was known for its pearls. It was originally the land of the Caribe, Arawak and Guaiqueríe Indians, then later had to ward off pirate assaults to defend the rich harvest of its pearl beds. It was the site of occupation by both royalist and republican forces during the War of Independence. Today Margarita is a free port and extremely popular with tourists, as much for its colonial ambience as for the many beaches. Margarita is small enough to be explored in one day.

La Asunción

The capital of Margarita has a population of 24,000 and is the seat of government for the islands.

Porlamar

This busy urban centre of the island is where the majority of people gather to eat, shop and socialise.

Coche and Cubagua

Coche is a developing tourist location although it is far smaller and quieter than Margarita. Cubagua is the location of the historic city of Nueva Cádiz.

The Andes

In the far west, the Venezuelan Andes represent the northernmost point of the mighty mountain range before it falls into the Caribbean. Due to their relative isolation in the mountains, the people of this region have more in common with their Andean neighbours in Colombia than with the rest of Venezuela; their culture and lifestyles are quite distinct from the rest of the country. Andeans are said to be reserved, traditional, conservative, religious, hardworking and unfailingly polite and friendly. The cobbled streets, picturesque houses, culture and Indian names of the towns all indicate accurately that the pace of life is genteel and strong ties with the past are maintained.

The Andes are the only part of Venezuela where it is genuinely cold with more than just a morning chill; the weather is usually damp and windy. The region and its environs are part of the Parque Nacional Sierra Nevada. Below the steep mountainsides with their vertiginous roads and plots of land are the *páramo* (high plain), which is bleak and very scrubby, although it does contain a surprisingly wide variety of bird species. There are even cloud forests alive with hummingbirds, pine forests and glacial lagoons. You can fish in the Black Lagoon (Laguna Negra).

Mérida

Mérida, one of the three Andean states, lies along the southern edge of Lake Maracaibo. Coffee, tobacco and corn are grown here and tourism is vitally important. The highest peak in the country, Pico Bolívar, is here, alongside Pico Espejo, which has the longest and highest *teleférico* in the world; unfortunately it often breaks down. The national parks are Sierra Nevada and Sierra de La Culata.

Mérida

Santiago de los Caballeros de Mérida, the state capital, is a peaceful and calm city of about 240,000 inhabitants. The second oldest university in Venezuela is here, the Universidad de los Andes.

Trujillo

The climb of the Andes northwards ends in Trujillo. Trujillo's landscape is of mountains, valleys and *llanos* (plains). Trujillo is unusual in that it has two rainy seasons. The state is the second most important for coffee and also produces pineapple and garlic. There is a monument in Trujillo known as the Virgin of Peace (La Virgen de la Paz), which is truly awesome in size.

Trujillo

This state capital (population 36,000) climbs bravely up a mountain valley (Valle de los Cedros). It was finally settled after moving seven times in its history. Like other Andean towns, Trujillo maintains a slow pace as well as its colonial architecture.

Táchira

A succession of presidents have made their way from their birthplace of Táchira down to Caracas. This Andean state bordering Colombia has one million inhabitants. Coffee is its main product. The Táchirenses make handwoven cloth, earthenware jugs and ceramics. Its national park has the impressive name of Juan Pablo Peñaloza Paramos Batallón y La Negra.

San Cristóbal

The state capital, on the bank of the Torbes, is a friendly and tranquil town of less than 275,000 inhabitants.

Lara

Lara lies east of Zulia and south of Falcón. For a small state, its population is large, reaching 1.5 million. Agriculture is strong due to excellent irrigation from the area's rivers. It produces coffee, sugarcane, potatoes, tomatoes, onions, black beans, corn, bananas, grapes and pineapples. Livestock is also a major source of revenue, and cheese is produced. Lara is the state of art and music and it has also produced several of Venezuela's poets and intellectuals. The artistry of the state is on display in the towns of Tintorero, Cubiro, Sanare and Carora. There is also a reconstructed Indian village at Quíbor. Lara's several national parks include Cerro Saroche, Dinira, El Guache, Terepaima and Yacambú.

Barquisimeto

Industry and commerce are major concerns of the state capital (population 900,000). Barquisimeto means 'river of ash' in the language of the Indians who defended the region with such vigour that the city had to be rebuilt twice.

El Tocuyo

As with many Venezuelan towns, the original name has been shortened for convenience from the effusive and keenly religious Nuestra Señora de la Pura y Limpia Concepción de El Tocuyo. It was built in 1545 and served briefly as a capital. After an earthquake, it was rebuilt under the order of Marcos Pérez Jiménez and the original colonial buildings were lost. On 13 June, El Tocuyo celebrates the dramatic fiesta of San Antonio de Padua.

Los Llanos

South of the coastland lies a deep and broad swathe of country that contains the llanos or plains of Venezuela. This region makes up an entire third of the country.

The plains are divided into the high and low llanos. The high llanos are close to the north and the mountains, including the Andes. The low llanos are influenced by the rivers, which flood in the rainy season. The plains people (llaneros) build on river banks (*bancos*). Flood areas are called

Life on the open plains where children care for the cattle.

bajíos and marshes are *esteros*. *Galeras*, the hills built up from flood deposits, are named after the Spanish galleons they resemble. *Chaparales* are clumps of trees that exist among the grass.

The llanos are great, open expanses that dwarf and intimidate visitors with their sheer vastness. There are, however, significant differences between the llanos of different states. In Anzoátegui and Monagas, flat hills known as *mesas* break up the prairie. The llanos of Guárico and Cojedes have hills and low mountains. In Portuguesa, Barinas and Apure, the plains are flat.

The temperature is very high during the rainy season and this combines with high humidity to create an oppressive atmosphere. The rainy season begins sometime in May and ends sometime in November. In the dry season, the small lakes dry up to almost nothing and the amazingly diverse animal life of the region clusters around them. The llanos include species such as scarlet ibis, capybara, freshwater dolphins, manatee, hoatzin, jaribu stork, howler monkeys, caiman and turtles. The atmosphere is hot but bearable in the dry season.

Llaneros speak a dialect that mixes Indian and African phrases with Spanish, reflecting their diverse origins. They wear woollen ponchos and straw hats, and are thought

A different kind of family life on the llanos, capybara.

of as astute, honest, independent, liberal and introverted. Many towns in the llanos began as mission settlements, and llaneros from tribes including the Caquetios, Achaguas and Otomacos were led into the War of Independence by their Indian *caciques*. As the seasons change, these tough cowboys round up cattle and break wild horses. The nasal singing typical of the region is accompanied by small harps called *arpas*, cuatros, maracas and *bandolas* (mandolins). This music is called *golpe* and *joropo* and is the national music which has now mutated into the modern *joropopop*. Lyrics are written to the verse forms known as *décimas*, *corridos* and *coplas*. Cockfighting, bull catching (*coleos*) and *bolas criollas* are popular traditional pastimes. Less traditional but more fun is fishing for piranha, whose scant flesh you can eat with a delicious feeling of revenge.

Portuguesa

The breadbasket of the country is named for the river that crosses it. Portuguesa lies in the west and is landlocked with the Andean range (*cordillera andina*) running down the western side. It also has high and low llanos. The state grows rice, corn, sesame, sorghum, beans, sugarcane and cotton.

Guanare

The patron saint of Venezuela, Nuestra Señora de la Coromoto, has her basilica in this state so Guanare (population 135,000) is regarded as the spiritual capital of the country. Typical llanero festivals are held here, featuring music, theatre, puppet shows and traditional dances.

Cojedes

Cojedes, whose name was taken from the river Cojedes, is a small state sitting in the heart of the country, south of Carabobo and Yaracuy. The coastal cordillera rises to the north and the llanos stretch away into the south. It used to be the llanos of Caracas until 1864, when General Juan Crisóstomo Falcón created the state. The llanos are of course the home of cattle. There is also forestry and crops including rice, corn and sugarcane.

San Carlos

San Carlos (population 70,000) was founded by Friar Pedro de Berja in 1678 and named after Saint Charles of Austria. After the earthquake that ended the First Republic, the people of Caracas fled here. San Carlos is also where Bolívar gathered his forces before the Battle of Carabobo. The popular caudillo Ezequiel Zamora died here, fighting government forces.

Guárico

Guárico, a central state south of Caracas, is an agricultural heartland for Venezuela, growing rice, corn, tomatoes, cotton, cassava and beans. Livestock is also significant and some of the bitumen fields of the Orinoco extend into the state. Guárico means *cacique* in the language of the Caribe Indians. The llanos here contain great diversity in wildlife, particularly bird species. Nightfall over this state in the central llanos is quite movingly beautiful.

San Juan de los Morros

The state capital (population 83,000) was named after Saint John the Baptist. Its attractions include limestone rock formations and thermal springs, and its economy is based on industry and business.

Monagas

Monagas carries the name of General José Gregorio Monagas. It lies in the east, next to Delta Amacuro. Its llanos has a very wide variety of wildlife. Livestock, agriculture (corn, sorghum, cassava and sugarcane) and forestry (pine plantations) play an important part in the state's economy. Petroleum is another rich resource, with some of the bitumen of the Orinoco. There is a statue of the famous German naturalist Alexander von Humboldt outside the cave of the oilbirds (Cueva del Guácharo), which he explored. Guácharos are blind, nocturnal oilbirds found only in one or two other places in the world and are an attraction well worth seeing. The beautiful and

A monument to Alexander von Humboldt outside the oilbirds' cave.

tranquil forest region is preserved as Parque Nacional del Guácharo. The state has over half a million inhabitants.

Maturín

The state capital was named after a *cacique* who died fighting the Spanish invaders. Maturín (population 300,000) is a rather industrial town. It was founded by the Capuchin friar Lucas de Zaragoza in 1760 but does not have the prettiness of other towns of its age.

Caripe

Caripe is a small, extremely picturesque town known as the Eastern Garden of Venezuela. It is surrounded by coffee fields over which low clouds drift soothingly.

Barinas

Barinas runs from the Cordillera de Mérida in the west to the low llanos in central Venezuela. Livestock, agriculture and petroleum provide income. There is a wide variety of fish. More than half a million people live in the state.

Barinas

The state capital, a commercial city of 220,000 people, is the site of several battles in the War of Independence. It has attracted foreign companies and as a consequence has become industrialised and has been marked as a centre of future growth.

Apure

Apure, south of Barinas and bordering Colombia, is a large state with vast, sparsely populated, flat llanos. The plains are fed by the Orinoco, Meta, Apure and other major rivers. Livestock provides a livelihood for most of the population; there is also agriculture and forestry. Passing through the state, you will see a limitless expanse of scrub scattered with trees and thin cattle. The land's flatness lends the sky an imposing vastness that has the effect of making you feel extremely small. The heat increases the sensation of vulnerability. There are two national parks here, Cinaruco-Capanaparo and Río Viejo.

San Fernando de Apure

The state capital (population 197,000) is a great place to hear llanero music. The wide, dusty streets are largely empty, except in the evening when the young come out to meet and play. San Fernando has some nice restaurants, but is not otherwise a vibrant place.

La Gran Sabana

The landscape of La Gran Sabana is dominated by savannah and flat-topped mountains called *tepuis*—'mountain' in the local Pemón Indian language—which are part of the Macizo Guayanés, one of the oldest rock formations on earth. The region is also home to Mount Roraima, the largest of the tepuis, made famous by the novelists Rómulo Gallegos and Sir Arthur Conan Doyle, who used it as an inspiration for the novel *The Lost World*.

The inaccessible nature of the *tepuis* means that many species have evolved here in isolation, although none are surely as harmful as the spiders supposedly taken from this region in the film *Arachnophobia*. There are also diamond mines and the highest waterfall in the world, Angel Falls (Salta Angel), named after the American pilot who stumbled upon it while on a gold-hunting expedition. There are many other waterfalls cascading from the sides of the ancient and mist-shrouded *tepuis*.

Canaima and Kavak

Canaima, the tourist heart of Parque Nacional Canaima, offers accommodation from where travellers can set out on walking or more ambitious camping expeditions to explore the striking landscape of *tepuis* and waterfalls. This village is accessible by plane.

Kavak, a traditional Pemón village built for the benefit of tourists, offers a rare chance to see traditional Pemón life at first hand.

Bolívar

Bolívar, the largest of all the states, is in the east, sandwiched between Guyana, Brazil and the northern states. This land of natural splendour contains the national parks of Gran Sabana and Canaima. Its inhabitants include Indian tribes that have lived there for over 10,000 years. Bolívar is rich in resources, including bauxite, natural gas, hydroelectric power, petrol, diamonds, gold and iron ore. The country's largest rivers pass through this state.

Ciudad Bolívar

The state capital's present name is considerably shorter than its original name of Santo Tomé de Guayana de Angostura de Orinoco. In time it became known more conveniently as Angostura, famous for Angostura bitters. It is also famous as the site of Simon Bolívar's Congress of Angostura (Congreso de Angostura), which declared the creation of Gran Colombia, placing Angostura at the heart of Bolívar's grand design for the liberation of the continent. In honour of its distinguished history, Ciudad Bolívar was renamed in 1846 and preserved in its colonial splendour. Its population is 350,000.

Ciudad Guayana

This thriving town (population 603,000) situated on the river Caroní emcompasses Puerto Ordaz and San Félix and the steel, aluminium and iron plants at Matanzas. In contrast to the tranquil pace of life in the state capital, Ciudad Guayana is a hive of industrial activity.

San Tomé

San Tomé is a remote town of considerable historic interest. It is not only the first Spanish settlement in the region, but is also where Walter Raleigh saw his son die in battle with the Spanish. Raleigh burnt the town and killed its governor in his quest for El Dorado. The fabled town of gold claimed another victim when Raleigh was executed by James I to restore trade relations with Spain.

Delta Amacuro

Delta Amacuro, Venezuela's newest state, formed in 1991, was surprisingly named after the Amacuro and not the Orinoco, the largest river in the country. It lies at the easternmost fringe of the country next to the Atlantic Ocean, journey's end for Venezuela's great rivers.

This state is frighteningly hot and humid. It is wild and untamed but also the site of bitumen and petroleum exploitation. It is one of the world's largest deltas and, apart from the very wide Orinoco, it is a network of small channels (*canos*) that can only be navigated by small launches or canoes. It is therefore a perfect place for wildlife to flourish and for discovery by canoe. The region is mostly impenetrable jungle and mangrove swamps. In fact, the Orinoco is stained a deep brown by tannins leached from the jungle trees. Orinoco is 'father of our land' in the language of the Warao Indians. The Warao live in *palafitos* connected by walkways and fish from dugout canoes, called *curiaras*. One of the greatest adventurers of all, Sir Walter Raleigh, came here to the tiny capital of Tucupita, which he called Cutupity Village.

Tucupita

The name of the state capital supposedly originates from the name of a *cacique*, Tucu, who blew his whistle for help when he found himself lost in the jungle: *pita* is the sound of a whistle in Spanish. Tucupita still has that middle-of-nowhere feeling, with only a restaurant or two and a couple of small hotels. It is hard to believe that the population is 60,000, as the town is dreamily quiet and seems largely empty. Indigenous culture has a noticeable presence here. It is easy to pick up a guide who will lead you into the Orinoco and its channels via a launch.

Amazonas

Amazonas is the southernmost state and pushes the land southwards between Colombia and Brazil. This is the jungle of Venezuela. It is hot and humid and sparsely populated by about 134,000 people. Amazonas contains about 70 per cent of the indigenous population of Venezuela, who live in protected areas. The Piaroa Indians live in thatched *churuatas* (conical huts) and practise *conuco* (subsistence) agriculture. Traditional dress is loincloths, beads, feathers and body paint. This is now mixed and matched with jeans and T-shirts. The Yanomami live on the border with Brazil and are semi-nomadic hunter-gatherers using curare-tipped blowpipes.

Puerto Ayacucho

Puerto Ayacucho is a hot, humid outpost with a languid approach to life. The capital is the only city in the state and it was created by the dictator Juan Vicente Gómez. It is the main entry point for tourists into the Amazonas. It is a port and border town where soldiers and Indian market traders rub shoulders. You can pick up Indian handicrafts or try deep-fried ants (*hormigas culonas*), which are also eaten coated in chocolate—a romantic gift for a loved one?

To look at the incredible fertility of Venezuela and its impressive resources, especially oil, you would be hard pressed to explain the obvious poverty of a significant slice of the population. The creole elite has, in the past, been quick to blame the people. A joke goes, "Why was God so generous to Venezuela? He gave it everything, a perfect climate, bountiful natural resources, everything." "Ah but he also gave Venezuela the Venezuelans." This is an unfair and shallow assessment. If you want answers to many of the questions that will spring to mind, you must understand Venezuela's rich and fascinating history.

As you will see in this chapter, colonialism left permanent scars on the country and forced it to wander down the road it still treads today. Venezuela has played its part in the development of the capitalist economic system that dominates the world, but the political issues it faces today are those that have faced governments for hundreds of years. This chapter will also hopefully give you a clear picture of the reasons behind the differences between rural and city life in Venezuela.

Venezuela is a proud country and its history is a source of enormous national pride. It is, of course, the birthplace of the great Liberator of South America, Simón Bolívar, whose statue stands in virtually every main square in every town. The names of many of his fellow heroes of the Liberation adorn statues and monuments, the names of states, streets,

You will find statues of Bolívar, father of the nation, all over the country.

universities and many other places. Naturally you cannot visit the country without at least a basic knowledge of this legendary time and the people who made it.

History, economics and politics have been combined in this chapter because they influence each other. Moreover, colonial policies have directly affected the politics and economics of Venezuela and Latin America today. As many aspects of history and culture are held in common by all Spanish-speaking countries in the region, this chapter will also give an outline of the region's early history.

EARLY MIGRANTS

When Columbus arrived in 1498, he found a land rich in cultural diversity, the result of migrations into the country of various ethnic groups. The first wave of migrants wore little clothing, fished and grew root vegetables. The second wave, the people Columbus saw, hunted and fished and lived in huts on stilts (*palafitos*). The Arawaks formed the next group. They created pathways and grew corn, cassava, tobacco, beans and yam using slash-and-burn agriculture: cutting down and burning the vegetation in an area, then digging with sticks to plant their crops. This is the *conuco* method of agriculture, still in practice today. They bartered goods and spun clothes from home-grown cotton. Hard work was valued and malingerers were expelled from the tribe. Ceramics and hammocks made from palm leaves were among their crafts. They played a form of football as an initiation into war for the young, and even used a form of slavery.

The fourth group was the Caribes, a warlike people who were boat builders and navigators. They were polygamous but matriarchal, classless but with a strong military organisation. The chiefs were distinguished by their haircuts and the plumes they wore. The military vigour of the Caribes pushed the Arawaks into the west and south-west of the country. Among the tribes of the Caribes were the Caracas, who gave the capital city its name. The Timoto-Cuicas, a peaceful group who settled along the Andes, made up the final wave of migrants.

Each ethnic group had a number of tribes whose members spoke the same dialect. Once settled in the country, some tribes from different groups mixed and began to share cultural characteristics. At the end of the 15th century, there were approximately 350,000 Indians in Venezuela. This had diminished to 50,000 by the end of the 16th century. Current estimates are that there are around 100,000 Indians. Indians in Venezuela either retreated into remote areas to protect their identity or became absorbed into the majority *pardo* (mixed) population. There is now a Day of the Indian on 19 April and there is bilingual education in those states with Indian communities.

THE CONQUISTADORS

In the mid-13th century, the Christian kings of northern Spain had almost completed the Reconquest, expelling the Moors and leaving only Granada under Muslim control; Granada was conquered in 1492. Spain was unified when Ferdinand of Aragón married Isabella of Castile. They became known as the Catholic Sovereigns and they instituted a hierarchical system with all government ultimately controlled by themselves. This system was imposed on the colonies.

With Spain now unified, the potential of exploiting Columbus' discovery of America presented itself. Spain found itself economically underdeveloped compared to its European neighbours (a vital factor in the future of the colonies) and with its wealth concentrated in the hands of a very small number of royals and nobility. Most of the nobles (*hidalgos*) were not rich and many had just fought in the Reconquest. There was little opportunity for anyone to carve out a good life in Spain, but from very humble backgrounds they could make heroes of themselves in the New World.

The conquistadors were drawn from all levels of Spanish society and even from other countries. The legendary ability of a handful of conquistadors to defeat vast numbers of Indian warriors was due not only to their advanced weaponry and equipment but also to centuries of battlefield strategy. Their relative poverty, the climate of violence in Spain at the time, and greed for riches formed hard individuals.

The Indians of Latin America found themselves subjected to the rules that colonial governments forced upon them. In many cases, these rules followed a pattern of exploitation set by the original rulers of the land who extracted tributes from the Indians in their area in return for protection. The Indians were kept poor, and the Spaniards enriched by a system that forced the Indians to work on land no longer their own and pay tributes for that privilege. The Spaniards also paid what they desired for any Indian products not assigned as tributes/

tithes or debt payments, thus making the Indians' bondage complete. Those Indians who owned land could exist only at the level of subsistence, until gradually, through the colonial period and the early stages of independence, even that land was confiscated.

EARLY EXPLORATION OF VENEZUELA

On Columbus' third voyage, he encountered 'the most beautiful lands in the world, well populated'. He landed at Macuro (in modern-day Sucre, on the Paria Peninsula) on 1 August 1498.

After 1498, Venezuela was subjected to further exploration. Alonso de Ojeda and Amerigo Vespucci headed an expedition to the Paria Peninsula and Margarita Island. They also explored the island of Curaçao before moving on to the area of Coro and journeying over Lake Maracaibo. In this and later voyages, they sacked towns and enslaved Indians. Pearls and gold gathered in raids were brought back to Spain. Further expeditions were conducted by Vicente Yáñez Pinzón, who explored the Orinoco Delta from the coast of Brazil.

From the earliest of times, the legend of El Dorado had gripped the mercenary conquistadors. One of the first to search for this elusive domain was Lope de Aguirre, alias El Tirano—the tyrant—by his troops for his lethal rebellion against his superiors. Lope de Aguirre wished to set up his own kingdom. He landed all along the Venezuelan coast, from Margarita in the east to Barquisimeto in the west, where he was captured and sentenced to death in 1561 as a traitor. He killed his own daughter to save her from the Spanish authorities.

The 16th century was a period of settlement during which the conquistadors came into regular conflict with the Indians. Missionaries sent to convert the natives were slaughtered and a punitive military force was sent that led to the establishment of Cumaná, which quickly became a centre for expeditions to the surrounding regions. Bartolomé de Las Casas conquered the coastal lands from the Paria Peninsula in the east to the Cape of La Vela near Coro in the west. He extracted tithes from the natives and became a powerful landowner. This man later became a friar and was the strongest voice in Latin

The oldest Spanish castle in South America, in Cumaná.

America against the exploitation of Indians. He attempted to establish a model society near Cumaná but this failed.

The Caribes fought so successfully in their defence that the conquistadors were forced to move west. Santa Ana de Coro became the western centre for exploration.

The west, being populated by peaceful tribes, presented few problems for the Spanish. Manaure, an influential *cacique*, helped them settle the area. In return, he was allowed to rule his territory undisturbed and exempted from paying tributes. Barquisimeto was founded in 1557.

The jungle and difficult terrain initially favoured the Indians of central Venezuela. Diego de Lozada founded Santiago de León de Caracas in 1567, and used it as a base to launch attacks in the interior. He burned the *cacique* Guaicapuro as he slept and executed 26 other *caciques*. These brutal acts ended resistance and created a legendary martyr in Guaicapuro, who had battled successfully until his murder. Caracas became the centre of power in the region due to its numerous advantages—the surrounding fertile land, its protected position, the port at La Guaira and the gold discovered at Los Teques, just south of Caracas, by Francisco Fajardo.

The conquest of the eastern region was begun by Antonio de Berrío, who founded Santo Tomás de Guayana (now called

Ciudad Guayana) where the Orinoco and the Caroní meet. Angostura (Ciudad Bolívar), founded by Moreno de Mendoza, became a powerful base for exploration.

The vast llanos were settled by Capuchin missionaries under the leadership of Lorenzo de Magallón. They founded Araure (1664), San Juan Bautista de El Palo and Todos Los Santos de Calabozo (1762), place names that bear testimony to the religious fervour of their founders. This area stretched from the Orinoco, Apure, Meta and Arauca rivers to the southern jungle. San Fernando del Paso Real de Apure (now more manageably San Fernando de Apure), the region's capital, was the last major town to appear, in 1788. The llanos provided abundant fish and livestock for Spanish Venezuela and so held early importance for the growth of the country.

Maracaibo was founded as Ciudad Rodrigo by Alonso Pacheco in 1562. The ferocity of the natives was such that the city had to be abandoned. In 1574, Pedro Maldonado founded Nueva Zamora on the same site. It grew into the country's second city, Maracaibo.

TIME OF THE HAPSBURGS

When Ferdinand died in 1516, his grandson, Charles I, inherited the wealth of the two houses of Burgundy and Hapsburg (through his grandparents Marie of Burgundy and the Holy Roman Emperor Maximilian). His succession to the throne spelt disaster for Venezuela and almost for Spain. Charles I spent vast sums to conquer new territories and also to have himself elected Holy Roman Emperor, which he was (as Charles V) in 1519. This involved a massive amount of debt to Italian and German bankers. The German bankers, the Welsers, were granted the right to control and exploit Venezuela as they wished. They did so with almost a scorched earth policy, committing terrible atrocities against the Indians for short-term gains.

Charles was succeeded by his son Philip II in 1556. Philip III and then Philip IV continued the Hapsburg dynasty, proving to be even more ineffective rulers than Charles. Spain was hit hard under the Hapsburgs. It struggled under the yoke of enormous inflation and a flight of gold and silver out of the country. The population dropped by two million due to emigration, expulsions (of the Moriscos, converted Moors) and diseases caused by poverty.

ENCOMIENDA AND REPARTIMIENTO

The *encomienda* system forced Indians to work on the land to benefit the *encomendero*, the conquistador given the right to make use of the land in return for a tribute paid to the Spanish king. The *encomendero* was given tribute or labour by the Indians, and in return provided safety, shelter, clothing, food and medicine. The *encomendero* also acted as legal guardian for the Indians, providing civil and legal justice. The Indians were converted to Christianity and taught Spanish and the skills for whatever tasks they were assigned, be it construction of buildings and roads or military service. In spirit, *encomienda* was meant to protect and guide Indians; in reality a Spanish belief in natural and divine law meant that the Indians were perceived as subhumans designed to be slaves. *Encomienda* imposed a work system that was alien to them, and non-cooperation meant that labour was often forced. For the Spanish, it was not a recipe for wealth, except where mines could be opened on the land.

Another form of land ownership was the *hacienda*, a large landed estate for commercial agriculture whose owners are called *hacendados*. A *hacienda* for livestock raising is a *hato*. *Haciendas* and *hatos* are found all across Venezuela today. They were first established by Spaniards who took land from the Indians. There were three ways to gain this land: *congragación* whereby Indians were forced into new communities; *composición* whereby a Spaniard took Indian land and legalised this by making a small payment to the king; or by extending the *encomienda*. The Indians became day labourers on someone else's land rather than working their own.

Repartimiento has multiple meanings. In the early period of the Conquest, Indians and land were given out to conquistadors and other settlers. This was a *repartimiento*. If a landowner needed a temporary workforce, he was allowed to press a number of Indians into service, but the *repartimientos* in Venezuela gave no control over local Indian populations, and consequently no obligations towards them. Another method of controlling the capital owned by Indians was to buy their goods at the official shop, or from royal officials; this process was also known as *repartimiento*.

Repartimientos were set up in Venezuela with royal stipulations that generally went unheeded, especially in regard to the Indians, who were supposed to be protected and over whom the receiver of the *repartimiento* had no legal power. In practice, *repartimientos* were seen as *encomiendas* and the Indians were forced to live on the land and cultivate it. All levels of colonial administration were given the power to *repartir* land. *Repartimientos* formed the basis for the agrarian development of Venezuela. They represented the first private property and allowed a creole landed elite to develop.

Most of the land workers lived on small plots that they used for subsistence farming, producing corn , beans, rice, cassava and plantain. This is the *conuco* method of agriculture. Their homes had one or two rooms. They slept in hammocks and cooked outdoors. They wore *liqui-liqui*—cotton shirt and drill pants, hats and sandals. The *hacienda* or *hato* owners, despite their social status, lived similarly, with just a few possessions more.

While other European countries streaked ahead in developing capitalist economies, selling, marketing and manufacturing products, Spain merely served as a large marketplace for the Latin American goods. It may have been a country of merchants, but it did not have much industry for the production of finished products or the capital to invest in businesses to sell these products.

THE CHURCH IN VENEZUELA

The Pope gave the right to conquer the lands discovered by Columbus, provided the Indians were converted to Christianity. The first mission to establish itself in Venezuela (in 1513–1516) was not quite the success that had been hoped for. Franciscan and Dominican friars were sent to Cumaná, where they were slaughtered by the *cacique* Maraguey, in revenge for the depredations of Alonso de Ojeda.

It was not until 1650 that the first successful missionary settlements were made. In present-day Anzoátegui, the missionaries found themselves welcomed by the Píritu Indians. The friars established a large number of *pueblos de indios* (Indian towns) in the region. They were formed either by inviting families of Indians to set up home together, often with gifts, or by capturing the Indians and forcing them to found a new *pueblo*. Each missionary had the responsibility of founding one of these towns, also known as *pueblos de Misión*. Once the missionaries had given the Indians knowledge of the immortality of their souls and other salutary lessons, the town was granted the name of *pueblo de Doctrina*.

The missionaries did not own land but were allowed to gain some benefit from it. The Indians worked the land and provided domestic service. Profit from their labour was divided: half to the Indians; two-thirds of the rest to the friars and the remaining third to the king.

Friars from Aragón settled in the east, Catalonian friars went to the Orinoco delta, those from Andalucia stayed in the Caracas region, and Valencians established themselves

A simple, homely, small-town church.

in Maracaibo. The Franciscan missions were located in the region of Anzoátegui, the Jesuits in the Amazonas and the Dominicans in Los Llanos.

The missionaries founded varying numbers of *pueblos* in each region, more than a hundred around Caracas. These greatly helped develop Venezuelan society in terms of organisation and administration, and also possibly agriculture. The cultural benefits, on the other hand, are debatable, and it is even an issue whether these towns were of more benefit to the Indians than the *encomiendas* and *repartimientos*. They did at least form the basis of Venezuelan Catholic society and help transmit the Spanish language.

THE COLONIAL ECONOMY

Over time, separate, isolated communities of colonists established trade links with each other. To develop roadways, exploit difficult terrain, put down Indian resistance, increase population growth and form larger cities, some form of administration was necessary. From the outset, Venezuela found itself organised into individual autonomous provinces. Barinas, Mérida and Maracaibo formed an agricultural unit stretching from the Andean highlands to the Maracaibo basin. Cumaná and Barcelona were market centres for the livestock rearing so suited to the vast open expanses of the llanos. Ranching is still the major commercial activity there today.

Caracas itself was a province, the wealthiest, most vibrant trading centre stretching from Lake Maracaibo to the Unare River in the east. It thrived from the exploitation of Indian workers on cacao plantations. (The Indians also grew cacao in the Andean regions.) The *encomenderos* found that African farmers readily adapted their knowledge to cacao production, so great numbers of slaves were imported. Venezuelan cacao was the driving force behind the national economy from the 17th to the 19th centuries.

EARLY AGRICULTURE

When mines and pearls were exhausted as a source of revenue, agriculture became the basis of the economy until the exploitation of oil in the 1920s. The *encomiendas* and *repartimientos* grew a number of crops besides cacao. The Andean regions provide a favourable climate for wheat. Tobacco, originally smoked by the Indians, soon became a roaring success. It was grown all along the Caribbean coast and in the llanos and became the favoured loot of European smugglers who frequented the coastline. Tobacco was banned in 1606, but when its damage to the economy became evident, the ban was repealed in 1621. Indigo was introduced as an export crop in the 18th century and enjoyed great success. Venezuela became the main exporter of indigo from the Spanish colonies.

Coffee succeeded cacao as the main export crop. In the 18th century, it was produced only around Caracas but by the 19th century, it had reached the Andes. Coffee was more resistant to fluctuations in climate than cacao, which aided its development in the Andes. Cotton was another native product found abundantly in the western regions. Spain sent experts to aid in its cultivation as demand grew in Europe. Sugarcane also became important.

Livestock first became significant with the founding of El Tocuyo in 1545. The success of this town presented a fount of prospective wealth for impoverished Venezuela in the 16th century. From El Tocuyo, livestock ranching spread to the llanos and eastward to Valencia and Caracas. Cattle, horses, sheep and pigs were raised. Cattle are still overwhelmingly important in the llanos. In the 17th century, Venezuela began to export hides and by independence there were over a million cattle in the country.

COLONIAL ADMINISTRATION

The Council of the Indies was the legislative, judicial and executive body. It formulated laws and nominated all colonial officials. Viceroys held large swathes of Spanish territory. Captains general commanded subdivisions of this land. Viceroys and captains general had the same powers over collecting dues and forming defence. Other subdivisions were governed by audiencias. Governors ruled the provinces which were centred on areas rich in exploitable resources. Many officials bought their positions from the king. The town council represented the only political power the creoles had. Its responsibilities included guaranteeing the safety of citizens and their property, administering justice and determining prices in the marketplace.

THE BOURBONS AND CAPITALISM

In 1700, Charles II died, leaving his possessions to the French Bourbon, Philip V. The Spain inherited by the Bourbons was an economic mess. The expulsion of Moors damaged industry and agriculture, while the expulsion of Jews damaged the financial sector and industry. War had exhausted the economy and Spain had only a small share of the European market. The Bourbons reformed Spain, developing agriculture and manufacturing and encouraging trade.

In the 1720s, the Royal Guipuzcoan Company of Caracas, also known as the Caracas Company, was founded to protect the Venezuelan coast from smugglers. In return for this service, it had monopoly of trade in Venezuela. Venezuelan merchants were angered by the company's low prices for cacao, high prices for imports from Spain and reluctance to take other Venezuelan products. This situation created resentment and led to two rebellions that were put down. In 1785, the company was abolished, four years after its monopoly had ceased and the market had been thrown open.

PRE-INDEPENDENCE

You will find the name of Francisco de Miranda, the greatest of the pre-revolutionaries, used all over Venezuela. His vision for Venezuela included the unification of all the Spanish colonies under a confederation called Colombia. His government would be led by an Inca and a cabinet of *caciques*. He shared this dream with the English prime minister, William Pitt the Elder. Moving to New York, Miranda also gained the support of the United States. In 1806, he set sail for Venezuela in the Leandro with a multinational crew of mercenaries and two schooners. Unfortunately the Venezuelan government had been alerted, and Miranda was defeated at Ocumare.

The indefatigable Miranda returned to Venezuela the same year, this time with eight boats and 400 men. He took Coro, a popular site for insurrections. His downfall this time was due to the lack of support among Venezuelans, who had been encouraged to see him as an enemy of the Church and England's puppet. Miranda again left Venezuela, this time to return to England.

THE RISE OF THE CREOLES

The creoles, also known as *mantuanos*, used to be pure blood descendants of the Spanish ruling classes. In contemporary Venezuela, saying "*Soy criollo*" (I am *criollo*) is a way of saying you are Venezuelan through and through. Venezuelan Spanish is *criollo* and products from the countryside are called *criollo* as a sign of authenticity. The creoles formed Venezuela's upper classes and were the only Venezuelans to receive university education. In 1793, the Real Consulado was set up in Caracas to placate the creoles by giving them some administrative power but they were still denied high positions in the church or government.

On 19 April 1810, the First Republic was formed when the creoles of Caracas formed a junta to overthrow the Spanish rulers. In 1811, the first congress was elected and Felipe Fermín Paúl became its first president. The vote was restricted to the creole elite. The country was named Confederación de Estados de Venezuela and its capital was Valencia. Its watchwords were liberty, equality, prosperity and security, and its official religion was Catholicism.

The First Republic had internal divisions. Missionaries instigated uprisings in Cumaná and Maturín, and Miranda himself put down a revolt in Valencia. Coro and Barquisimeto were taken by royalists under Domingo de Monteverde. Miranda was made Dictator with extraordinary powers, in an effort to save the fledgling Republic. Simón Bolívar, a creole prominent in the independence movement, was responsible for the defence of Puerto Cabello.

The royalists were joined by some creoles, free blacks and *pardos*, who felt ostracised by the new constitution. The country descended into chaos, with townsfolk fleeing as troops approached and slaves revolting against their masters. Into this chaos terror struck when an earthquake hit Caracas and the surrounding region in 1812, causing widespread death and destruction. Miranda surrendered and was imprisoned. He died in exile in 1816.

BOLÍVAR AND THE SECOND REPUBLIC

Bolívar escaped unharmed to Nueva Granada (present-day Colombia). The patriots there saw his potential in his Manifesto to the Citizens of Nueva Granada, a call for unity and the need to liberate Venezuela to ensure the security of the region. Bolívar pronounced a *guerra a la muerte* (war to the death) against the Spaniards in a consciousness-raising speech calculated to instill in Venezuelans an appreciation that the war was between Venezuela and Spain, and that Bólivar himself was an instrument of vengeance against the invaders, the protector of his 'Americans'. With little resistance, the royalists abandoned Caracas, enabling the people to bestow the title of El Libertador on their hero. The restored congress gave him dictatorial powers to continue to prosecute his War of Unification.

The Second Republic proved to be as short-lived as the first. The terrifying José Tomás Boves, an able leader, threw in his lot with the Spanish and led his llaneros—a mix of *pardos*, blacks and Indians—against Bólivar's creole-commanded forces, including Bólivar's second-in-command Rafael Urdaneta. Boves captured Caracas in 1814, ending the Second Republic.

GRAN COLOMBIA

Bólivar left for Nueva Granada and after further military adventures sailed to Jamaica to reformulate his plans. Here he composed revolutionary propaganda including his famous 'Letter from Jamaica', in which he made an insightful analysis of the state of the colonies and made bold predictions for the future. His conclusion was, somewhat unsurprisingly, that only a Republic would meet the needs of Latin America. The present, however, was grim. The Spanish had landed a considerable force under General Pablo Morillo, whose mandate was to pressgang the necessary militia. His force mopped up all resistance.

Bolívar found support in Haiti from the mulatto president Alexandre Pétion, who requested that Bolívar free all slaves in the region. His spirit undiminished, Bolívar led yet another assault on Venezuela. After some minor victories, he regrouped in Haiti. Unlike Miranda, Bólivar had carefully sown the seeds of grassroots support with his pronouncements and writings. The republicans in the country banded around his leadership and the leaders of two revolutionary groups of llaneros, José Antonio Páez and Francisco de Paula Santander, threw in their lot with El Libertador. Finally, a number of veterans from the Napoleonic wars came in the name of liberty and formed an invaluable British Legion. English help came with loans from merchants, enabling Bolívar to equip his men.

The war continued, throwing up heroes such as Soublette, Santander and Anzoátegui. In 1820, Bolívar and Morillo signed an armistice that ended when republican forces freed Maracaibo. Caracas, Coro and Barquisimeto were liberated by republicans, and Bolívar and Páez defeated the last royalist force at the Battle of Carabobo in June 1821. Venezuela was once again a free republic.

In 1821 Bolívar formed the state of Gran Colombia, uniting contemporary Venezuela, Colombia, Ecuador and Panama. The vice president, Santander, carried out a number of reforms, including the abolition of slavery and the transfer of Indian communal land into private hands. In this fashion, wealthy creole supporters of the revolution gained vast areas of land, which they built into great estates known as *latifundios*. It was progress on the one hand, but greater disenfranchisement for the Indians on the other.

Gran Colombia quickly proved an almighty task to hold together. Rivalries sprang up between the capitals and between the commanders. In Venezuela, Páez showed resistance to the unity of Gran Colombia. Venezuela was a country damaged by 20 years of war, with exhausted mineral supplies and agriculture that could not support the population. Dissent and discord were rife. Bolívar was faced with choosing between giving himself emergency powers as a dictator, allowing Gran Colombia to collapse, or reforming the constitution of 1921. Santander and his Santanderistas opposed this last recourse and they and the Bolívaristas could not reach an agreement. In 1829, Venezuela separated from Gran Colombia.

Antonio José de Sucre, whom Bolívar had seen as his natural successor, was ambushed and murdered in Colombia in 1830. With his death the hopes of Bolívarianism died. General Rafael Urdaneta took provisional control of the government, while calls went out to Bolívar to return to power. But his health was failing, and Bolívar decided to seek medical treatment in Europe. He died on his way there, at the age of 47. Bolívar's almost superhuman efforts to liberate the continent from Spanish rule had taken a terrible personal toll. The finest military leader of his era, a powerful orator and insightful thinker whose words still influence the thinking of Venezuelans today, he died seeing his dream falling to pieces. But the successful integration of Gran Colombia could not have been achieved within his lifetime. The distance between the capitals and the pressing needs of the people of each country made integration impossible at that time. Inequalities of wealth and dependent economies of the countries of Gran Colombia are unresolved problems even today.

Former slaves continued to work on their masters' land as tenant farmers or labourers bonded by debts. Slavery still existed, as did labour under the *repartimiento* system in which wages were paid in tokens that could be used only at the expensive estate store. The majority of Venezuelans had seen the quality of their lives diminish during the independence revolution. In times of hardship, nationalism increases as people become concerned with their own welfare and use foreigners as targets for their frustrations. Gran Colombia was too big a leap for Bolívar, whose desire for liberty and brotherhood throughout South America eventually turned his own country against him.

In 1830, Venezuela unveiled its third constitution. The vote was given to literate people over 21 with a high income. This did nothing to change the social structure of the country, whereby the creole elite dominated in commerce, agriculture, government and the military. Naturally, the elite had close ties through marriage and the defence of their mutual interests.

Bolívar's revolution also created a new breed, the *caudillos*, whose power evolved through military prowess and the favours granted to them by the new republic. The *caudillos* were a force from which would spring some of Venezuela's charismatic leaders, capable of commanding large followings.

POST-INDEPENDENCE LEADERS

Páez inherited a country troubled by rivalry between the military and civil government, widespread corruption, the breakdown of law and order, the lack of higher and technical education and unrest caused by a stagnant economy. Poverty and disease were endemic. The *caudillos* were autocratic and corrupt and oppressed their workers. The spirit of patriotism Bolívar had worked hard to generate had died with him.

Páez attempted to improve lenders' rights, encouraging a situation where loans became a highly lucrative business throughout the country. By the end of his term in government, Páez had brought peace and the beginnings of capitalist agricultural development. He had also gained some rapport with the clergy, who had supported Spain during the independence struggle.

The conditions were now right for Venezuela's first civilian government, which came into being under Dr José María Vargas in 1835. Vargas was the candidate of business, academia and the hacendados. His administration was honest and tried to liberalise the economy. The military, under Anzoátegui, attempted a coup in the same year, and Páez came out of retirement to defeat the rebels. Vargas returned to power but when he became embroiled in conflict with Congress, he resigned in favour of Andrés Narvarte.

Venezuela was only too happy to serve the world market under neocolonialism. The developing capitalist markets of Europe—Britain in particular—encouraged production of one or two products. In Venezuela's case, the switch was made from cacao to coffee as the main product for export. The economic boom of the 1830s saw a rise in coffee prices, and planters borrowed heavily to increase production. Depression hit Venezuela in the 1840s as prices of Venezuela's main exports (coffee, fruit, cacao and livestock) fell dramatically and debts went unpaid. This was an early warning of the perils of neocolonialism.

New political parties emerged in this time of discord. Páez led the Conservatives to victory for his second presidential term against the Liberals under Antonio Guzmán. Páez was succeeded by Carlos Soublette, who sentenced Guzmán to death for his involvement in the revolts of 1846–1847. Soublette's successor, the first Liberal president, the *caudillo* General José Tadeo Monagas, merely exiled Guzmán, who soon returned to become vice president. Tensions between the Liberals and Conservatives escalated, and Monagas kept the upper hand by intimidating Congress leaders. When Páez once again took up arms, he was imprisoned and eventually exiled from the country.

This marked the beginning of a dictatorial and nepotistic dynasty. José Tadeo Monagas was succeeded by his brother José Gregorio Monagas, who finally abolished slavery. Many coffee planters were in such trouble that freeing slaves was more attractive than paying for their food and shelter; it was cheaper to employ peons at minimal rates. Most slaves stayed on the plantations as salaried workers.

Venezuela's economic woes continued under the Monagas regime, which did nothing to counter government abuses. When Monagas attempted to change the constitution to extend his presidential term, the Liberals and Conservatives joined forces under General Julián Castro and overthrew the government in the May Revolution. A new constitution was established in 1858, which was more federal in nature than any of its predecessors as powers were granted to municipal governments. In 1858, Julián Castro was elected president with a more liberal cabinet.

There began a period of civil unrest. In the region of Coro, General Juan Crisóstomo Falcón had begun a military uprising, assisted by Ezequiel Zamora, a *caudillo* who had the support of the workers. Castro was forced to resign and his vice president, Manuel Felipe de Tovar, took over the presidency. The rebels formed a junta and proposed a federal programme that included many populist measures, such as the right to social security and freedom of speech. They went on a march, forming federal states as land was taken. It was easy to sway the people; while the economy had progressed in some areas, increase in wealth was restricted to a tiny slice of the population. Antagonism towards the ruling classes was easy to exploit when the agricultural system of *haciendas* and *hatos* employed few people and the ravages of war had ground the wheels of productivity to a halt.

In response, the government made the now ageing Páez minister of war. Tovar stepped down in favour of Pedro Gual. Páez attempted to reach an agreement with the rebels, and Gual demanded his resignation. Instead Gual was imprisoned and, at 71, Páez, or El Centauro (the Centaur) as he was known, was made the civil and military leader.

The rebels fought a guerrilla war that denied the government outright victory. The strategy of General Antonio Guzmán Blanco, the ex-president's son, forced Páez to reach an agreement highly favourable to the rebels. As before, a new government called for a new constitution. In the 1864 constitution, all men were entitled to the vote and the 20 states became independent federal bodies, most of which are in existence today. The Federal District was created and centred on Caracas. To prevent abuses of power such as those under the Monagas brothers, re-election was disallowed. Falcón was confirmed as president and the country, true to the federalist nature of the government, was renamed the United States of Venezuela (Estados Unidos de Venezuela).

Caudillismo soon reared its ugly head again. José Tadeo Monagas once more swept to power in the Blue Revolution. General Antonio Guzmán Blanco and his supporters began uprisings around the country and entered Caracas in triumph in 1870. Guzmán Blanco's first period of rule lasted seven years and so was called the *Septenio*. He had been the minister for foreign affairs (El Exterior) and the treasury (Hacienda). Much of the 1864 constitution was his work and at the time of the Blue Revolution he had been in London negotiating a massive loan. He wanted a 'practical republic', which meant a developed capitalist power. He stabilised politics by uniting the quarrelling *caudillos* under him and improved the country's infrastructure. In education, he made primary school free and compulsory and built schools for children and adults. He built the institute of Bellos Artes, a Museum of Natural History, and the Academia Venezolana de Literatura. The foreign loan also served to finance road and bridge construction and aquaduct repairs and the improvement of ports. Today Venezuela does not have a single working railway line, but Guzmán Blanco built 11 with the help of British capital. Coffee production was increased as its value picked up again. He set up a Compañia de Crédito to regulate finance and the Junta de Agricultura to stimulate agricultural development. Other workings of the government were modernised. Venezuela's mountain of foreign debt grew to dangerous proportions.

Guzmán Blanco had his chosen successor, Linares Alcántara, elected as president. Unfortunately he died a year later, in 1878. The Assembly made José Gregorio Valera president, much to the anger of the Guzmancistas, who called for Guzmán Blanco to return to power. In his second term, Guzmán formed the Compañia Petrolia del Táchira in 1878, the first serious attempt at oil exploitation in the country. His other achievements in this period were the introduction of the bolívar as the national currency and the national anthem (*Himno Nacional*). The Capitolio was built in Caracas, as well as the Panteón Nacional. Many of the statues and grand buildings in Caracas were built during his term. There was also a contretemps with England over disputed territory in Guyana. England eventually won, but to this day the region is shown as the Zona en Reclamacion on Venezuelan maps, indicating that Venezuela still believes in its sovereignty over this marshy and nearly impenetrable land.

Joaquín Crespo became president in 1884. He did little to improve the economy or deal with the growing international debt. Guzmán Blanco was elected yet again in 1886, but with less success and more public discord. In this climate he failed to complete his term and went to Europe, leaving a still agricultural and even more dependent Venezuela in his wake. Guzmán Blanco suppressed militarism and modernised the political and economic structure of the country, but left a national debt that has grown to crisis proportions in today's Venezuela.

Juan Pablo Rojas Paúl was the first university professor to be made president but achieved little in his brief time in power. He was threatened by an uprising led by Joaquín Crespo, but with the support of the Guzmancistas, democracy carried the day. Raimundo Andueza Palacios, who became president in 1890, wished to extend the period of government from two to four years, arguing that two years were insufficient to make a difference to the country. Joaquín Crespo saw this violation of the constitution as the perfect pretext to seize power and his followers took the capital. Once again installed in power (in 1892), Crespo immediately lengthened the period of office to four years, thus showing his defence of the constitution for the sham it was.

At the end of the 19th century, Venezuela was locked into a political pattern inherited from independence. The use of force to gain control of the country resulted in a fragile democracy almost continually threatened by autocratic leaders with little respect for the sanctity of the constitution. A powerless, impoverished rural population threw in its lot with whichever *caudillo* promised a revolution 'for the people'. Presidents surrounded themselves with powerful followers, encouraging *compadrazgo* (helping your friends) and other forms of corruption. However well meaning and progressive the policies of the presidents, there was neither the time nor finances to put them into practice. The exception was Antonio Guzmán Blanco, at the cost of incurring loans that the country could never hope to pay off. Civil wars trampled productivity, taxes were difficult to collect, investment was not systematic and government debts were a constant burden. Education and culture were generally left to stagnate.

ENTER THE WESTERN CAUDILLOS

In this era of political uncertainty, it took strong *caudillos* to unite the country and battle the worsening economic situation. Cipriano Castro came from Táchira, aided by wealthy rancher and coffee grower General Juan Vicente Gómez, to unite the warring factions. In 1901, yet another constitution was formed, allowing the president to rule for six rather than four years. Castro was the first of the Andeans to enter the political arena. The Andean states of Mérida and Táchira had been largely isolated from the rest of the country due to their inaccessibility, and their customs and lifestyles had more in common with the Colombians. These states had been untouched by guerrilla warfare and had been enriched by its abundance of coffee plantations.

Castro faced numerous difficulties including *caudillo* revolts and falling coffee prices. His policies were nationalist and he gave no incentives for foreign investment, thus alienating the United States and European powers. Desperate for loans, he looked to Manuel Antonio Matos, the richest Venezuelan and Guzmán Blanco's brother-in-law, and other financiers, whom he imprisoned amid a public display. Castro had his money—at a price. Matos rebelled, gathering support from financiers, *caudillos* and foreign investors, but was defeated by Castro's vice president Juan Vicente Gómez in 1902. Gómez suppressed other small revolts, decimating the opposition.

Castro also suspended the payment of all government debt—another Pyrrhic victory as the British and German governments sent warships to occupy some Venezuelan ports and blockade others. Castro's response, jailing the German and English representatives, caused Puerto Cabello to be bombarded. United States mediation led to re-establishment of diplomatic relations and a Venezuelan promise to contribute 30 per cent of La Guaira and Puerto Cabello's customs duties toward debt repayment. Castro also moved aggressively to defend the border with Colombia, and there were military incursions by both countries into each other's territory. The border dispute has gone on ever since, although the battles are now between Colombian guerrillas and Venezuelan soldiers. Castro amended the constitution to give himself more powers. The dictator (said to be a sex addict) found his health failing in 1908.

Juan Vicente Gómez manoeuvred to oust Castro with the backing of the United States and France. While Castro was in Europe for medical treatment, Gómez staged a coup. Castro was prevented from landing in Venezuela by US ships, and on Martinique the French exiled him to Europe. He never returned to Venezuela. Meanwhile, Gómez jailed or exiled the *caudillos* who had supported Castro, freed politicians jailed by Castro, and allowed other exiles to return. He built up the army, investing heavily in modern equipment. As today, military service was made compulsory and the *recluta* was put into force, whereby people were drafted if they had no documents proving exemption from service. The airforce and a new military school were established, and foreign specialists were recruited to train the army.

Gómez reorganised the states early in his term. New laws prohibited carrying of arms, banned gambling and established or reorganised bodies administering public health, immigration and colonisation. Another innovation was the systematic organisation of taxes and other government income. Small advances were made in health, education and social security.

Under Gómez landowners lost land, not only to the dictator's depredations, but also to the new oilfields. Gómez's dictatorship rode the back of the oil boom. He gave concessions to his backers, including the United States, Britain and Holland. The oil companies that left Mexico after the fall of the dictator Porfirio Díaz were invited to Venezuela. With foreign investment, oil income increased rapidly, but Venezuela saw only a tiny proportion of the profit. Moreover, the new class of oil workers saw no benefits—there were no social security payments, holidays or job security. Gómez had reversed Castro's policy of making Venezuelan law binding on non-nationals.

Despite this, the agrarian population left in droves for the new riches of the oilfields, contributing further to the decline of agricultural productivity. Venezuela lost its position as world leader in coffee and cacao production, and from being exporters of cane sugar, cotton and tobacco, it now became an importer. The predominance of oil caused agriculture to become a weakness in the economy, incredible in such a fertile and environmentally diverse country.

During his term, Gómez put down a number of armed revolts. Less violent protests included an oil strike and student protests. Rómulo Betancourt and Raúl Leoni were among the leaders. After promising free elections, Gómez backtracked and began a period of unprecedented repression. His son was made vice president and army commander, his brother second vice president, and other members of the Gómez clan state presidents. The army and Gómez's secret police (Sagrada) were instruments of repression. Torture became common and many people disappeared in castles such as La Rotunda in Caracas, Las Tres Torres in Barquisimeto and Libertador in Puerto Cabello. Freedom of speech was repressed and the only newspaper available was the official *El Nuevo Diario*. Politicians fled the country and set up political groups in exile: the Revolutionary Party in Mexico, the Venezuelan Workmen's Union in New York, the Venezuelan Civic Union in Costa Rica and the Revolutionary Alliance in Colombia. Raúl Leoni and Rafael Caldera belonged to the last group.

Before entering politics, Gómez was a powerful landowner. While in office, he confiscated enormous tracts of land for his cronies but mostly for himself. He owned most of the cultivated land in the country as well as many houses and factories. He was also the major shareholder in several companies, such as the Compañía Aeropostal Venezolana. He installed himself in Maracay, which he modernised with government funds. Government funds were also used to renovate and build public buildings such as the Arco de Carabobo, the museum and house of Símon Bolívar and the Panteón Nacional.

When Gómez died in 1935, there was chaos. An attack by Gómez's cousin on the presidential palace in an attempt to win power was repulsed. The cabinet elected Eleazar López Contreras as provisional president. Yet another Andean, López had served as the minister of war and the navy and was also a noted author of historical and military texts. He immediately reinstalled civil rights and allowed the exiled politicians back into the country.

After Congress made López president, the nation was paralysed by a strike to protest a new law giving López near dictatorial powers. The political situation was extremely volatile and López suspended the right of free association. A huge demonstration led by Jóvito Villalba of the FEV (the students' political party) at the Central University in Caracas saw clashes with the police. Demonstrators were shot and killed. López responded by banning press freedom and ousting the *gomecistas* who remained in the government. He then set about restoring to the nation the property expropriated by Gómez and dismantling the instruments of torture and repression. López allowed the formation of a large number of new political parties.

López's rule was beneficial to the country. He decreased the power of the army and set up the Banco Central de Venezuela to issue currency. He also established institutes to combat diseases such as malaria and created schools and a ministry of education. Museums were built in Caracas. When freedom of the press returned, newspapers such as *El Universal* (still published today) emerged.

His chosen successor was the *tachirense*, Colonel Isaías Medina Angarita, the minister of war and the navy. Medina was progressive and introduced some democratic reforms such as improved social security, income tax and trade union development. He extended the reforms of López by legalising the Communist Party. World War II, in which Venezuela supported the Allies, created a massive demand for Venezuelan oil. Medina introduced the identity card (*cédula de identidad*), the vote for women and obligatory social security. He would have passed state land to landless peasants but revolt once again stopped the course of democracy.

Medina chose another *tachirense*, Angel Biaggi, the minister of agriculture and livestock, to succeed him. The president of Democratic Action (Acción Democratica—AD), Rómulo Gallegos, proposed a plan to have the president freely elected. The government refused, and in 1945 AD led a coup known as the October Revolution.

DEMOCRATIC ACTION INTERLUDE

Rómulo Betancourt, one of Venezuela's great statesmen, came to power in a coalition with the military under Marcos Pérez Jiménez. The military had young, ambitious officers hoping to introduce progressive politics. Despite the well-intentioned policies of the previous two administrations, disagreement over the speed of reform was reason enough for democracy to be trampled on yet again. Members of the previous administration were jailed for alleged embezzlement, and the last two presidents were exiled.

Unlike past presidents, Betancourt came from the bourgeoisie. His party manifesto included diversifying the economy away from its dependence on oil, increasing industrialisation and revolutionising agriculture. AD governed for three years (1945–48)—the *Trienio*.

Betancourt allowed political freedom. New parties were formed including the Social Christian Party (COPEI), the Democratic Republican Union (URD) and the Communist Party. In 1947, the Constituent Assembly created a new constitution in which secret ballots, direct elections for president and both houses of Congress and civil and social rights were all enshrined. Trade unions expanded under AD and some state land was given to peasants. Unemployment benefits, paid holidays and regular pay rises were given for the first time. The business sector gained a champion in the Federation of Chambers of Commerce and Production. AD imposed a 26 per cent tax on large companies, which were primarily the oil companies. This revenue bolstered government income and industrialisation. The Corporación Venezolana de Fomentos gave loans to both private and government businesses. Malaria was nearly wiped out in the *Trienio* and health and education were given more revenue. The first serious levels of immigration occurred as Europeans entered this newly wealthy country in the wake of World War II.

Rómulo Gallegos was voted president in 1948, but just as AD began its series of reforms, there was a coup.

MILITARY JUNTA

The three leaders of this *Junta Militar de Gobierno* were Luis Felipe Llovera Páez, Marcos Pérez Jiménez and Carlos Delgado Chalbaud. Delgado Chalbaud had served in the ministry of defence under the two previous administrations.

The junta wasted no time in dismantling the policies of the AD administration, attacking the unions and imposing censorship. Leaders of the previous regime found themselves in the now familiar position of being jailed and then exiled, with the exception of Rómulo Betancourt, who had sought refuge in the Colombian embassy. AD was outlawed, as were the trade union organisation Confederación de Trabajadores and the Communist Party. The junta faced its first crisis in 1950 when there was a massive oil strike and over 40,000 men took part in demonstrations. Delgado Chalbaud promised free elections and the prompt return to a civilian constitutional government. This message was not welcomed in all quarters, however. He was assassinated, and the military had an excuse to intensify repression.

Under the junta's new leader, Germán Suárez Flamerich, elections were held for a constituent assembly. Pérez Jiménez, a *táchirense*, then took the drastic step of taking office as 'provisional president' and ordered a recount. Imagine the nation's surprise when it transpired that the government party had in fact won a great victory. A grateful constituent assembly named Pérez Jiménez president.

A NEW DICTATOR

Pérez Jiménez was in power from 1952 to 1958. He filled his government with his supporters and created a virtual police state. His secret police, deceptively called Seguridad Nacional, removed opposition figures and student activists to concentration camps.

The government began mining iron ore in partnership with international companies. At the InterAmerican Conference of Chancellors, the US Secretary of State, John Foster Dulles, praised Pérez Jiménez as a statesman of great stature for his fight against communism. At the same conference, COPEI demanded press freedom, reinstatement of civil rights, reopening of universities and political freedom.

Pérez Jiménez gave Venezuela a New National Ideal (*Nuevo Ideal Nacional*) to create improvement in the general living standard. To this end, Corporación Venezolana de Fomento was entrusted with import substitution. Industries were set up to make Venezuela self-sufficient in textiles, paper, beer, cement and other products, while national monopolies were created in other areas such as investment, finance, the media and utilities.

This enormous investment was helped by oil revenue, which had escalated after the closure of the Suez Canal restricted transportation of Persian Gulf oil. Another recipient of investment was the military, which bought modern fighter planes, navy destroyers and new military installations. On the other hand, education suffered, with a 43 per cent absenteeism rate in primary schools. In Caracas, though, Pérez Jiménez intensified his campaign of public works and improved infrastructure.

The oil boom ended in the late 1950s and dissatisfaction with Pérez Jiménez's regime was running high in all sectors. AD, URD, COPEI and the Communist Party united underground in the Junta Patriótica. AD published Noticias de Venezuela, and COPEI had its own paper in Spain, where its leaders lived in exile. In Venezuela, two possible successors to Pérez Jiménez emerged—for the civilians, Dr Rafael Caldera, and for the military, Tamayo Suarez. Pérez Jiménez imprisoned Caldera, fired Suarez, and was duly re-elected.

Despite this victory, his support was diminishing rapidly and his administration was being attacked by students, workers, the middle classes and even the clergy. A widespread general strike called by the Junta Patriótica and a threatened military rebellion finally brought the government to its knees. After five years of power, Pérez Jiménez fled to Santo Domingo.

GOVERNMENTS AFTER 1958

A military junta restored democracy and freed political prisoners. To quell demonstrations, it initiated the Emergency Plan to provide jobs. In 1958, the junta set general elections. AD, COPEI and the URD joined forces in the Pact of Punto Fijo to form a coalition government. General elections were held to determine a president and Rómulo Betancourt of AD was proclaimed the winner.

By then there were several political parties and students had become more politically active. The number of parties in the political spectrum after the Pérez Jiménez era continues today. Due to their large number, a Venezuelan voting card is a lengthy and many-splendoured thing. Each party has its own colour for ease of identification and the card is a riot of colours and party symbols. The 1998 elections used electronic voting cards, increasing efficiency but also enabling machines to be blamed for the failure of thousands of votes to be registered.

Betancourt returned to power in a highly politicised climate, with fear of communism growing worldwide. When Fidel Castro's revolution occurred in 1959, many URD and AD members looked to Cuba as a role model. Betancourt, however, supported the United States' anti-Castro stance and ended diplomatic relations with Cuba. The most left-leaning of AD's members formed a new Marxist-Leninist party, the Movement of the Revolutionary Left (MIR).

Betancourt was determined to disengage the army from party politics and also banned the Communist Party, despite its work to topple the previous regime. This decision would return to haunt the government. Other troubles included a series of strikes that developed into a takeover of land and property. The Emergency Plan instituted by the junta was assessed as being too expensive. The proposal to scrap it met fierce protest in Caracas, resulting in a number of deaths, and the government suspended personal freedoms and the right of assembly. AD's radical student wing separated from the government line by organising strikes and demonstrations while leftwingers from various parties demonstrated and planned strikes to protest against the government's stance on Cuba. As violence spread through cities and their *barrios*, classes in schools and universities were suspended. Military uprisings had to be put down in Caracas (the Carupanazo) and Barcelona (the Barcelonazo). The Porteñazo, which began in the naval base of Puerto Cabello, was also put down. The government also faced guerrilla activity for the first time. All across mountain ranges, groups of inexperienced and poorly armed men, mainly students, worked to destabilise the government. They were unsuccessful in this aim, merely managing to destroy a train carrying tourists. What little public support they had had before now vanished.

It was in the field of foreign affairs that Betancourt's government distinguished itself. A small success was in extraditing Pérez Jiménez from the United States. Joining OPEC (or OPEP in Spanish—Organización de Países Exportadores de Petróleo) had more lasting importance. An accord with the Vatican, the Modus Vivendi, was signed, supplanting the Law of Ecclesiastic Patronage that had been in force since 1824, permitting the Catholic Church to spread Catholicism and build in Venezuela. The government also gained the right to refuse candidates from the clergy in elections to high posts. Foreign oil companies were denied future concessions. Instead, there were contracts regulated by the Venezuelan Petroleum Corporation (Corporación Venezolana del Petróleo). The CVP was formed in the face of the cancellation of exploration by multinationals in favour of new fields, and the consequent heavy loss of jobs within the industry. It would be responsible for the exploration and exploitation of future oilfields and would pass half of its profits to the government.

The unstable political situation had decreased foreign investment and government funds and forced a devaluation of the bolívar. As the construction industry began to falter and banks refused to give credit, Betancourt reduced public sector wages. Despite the difficulties, his administration made some improvements to infrastructure, built more schools, expanded public education and made advances in health, particularly in the area of infant mortality. Many factories were built, usually in partnership with foreign companies, and consequently much profit still left the country. A minimum level of import substitution was achieved.

Another government target was to halt rural depopulation. In Betancourt's term, ten cities had populations of over 100,000. Besides improving living standards through better provision of electricity, roadworks and sanitation, the government also distributed land evenly and gave technical support to farmers.

In February 1961, the latest in a long line of constitutions was formed. The 1961 constitution provided for proportional representation of parties in Congress and disallowed the president from succeeding himself. However, the president gained emergency powers to suspend personal and civil liberties. Rafael Caldera would have recourse to these laws over 30 years later.

Raúl Leoni won the 1963 election with the intention of forming a government with a broad political base. However, COPEI refused to cooperate with the AD government and his base narrowed further when Dr Arturo Uslar Pietri's Frente Internacional Democrático withdrew from the coalition. The Communist Party was accepted back into the political fold when it renounced guerrilla warfare. Meanwhile, Pérez Jiménez was released after serving only four years in jail.

Under Leoni's presidency, multinational companies gained an even stronger foothold in Venezuela, which had become industrialised but was still dependent on foreign capital. Leoni established the Universities of Simón Bolívar and Lisandro Alvarado. He continued agrarian reform, and sought the exploitation of iron and aluminium.

In 1968, COPEI's Rafael Caldera was elected president. He began an extensive nationalisation process that suspended oil and natural gas concessions. He also barred foreign companies from holding any investments in Venezuelan electricity, radio and television concerns. He offered a total amnesty to the guerrillas and legalised the Communist Party, which became the Union for Advancement (Unión para Avanzar). Many guerrilla groups used the Church to mediate between them and the government.

Caldera made legislation in education a priority. The National Council of Universities was formed to oversee universities. When the Central University rebelled over their loss of power, Caldera cleverly passed jurisdiction for the university grounds and property to the National Guard and the Metropolitan Police.

Under Caldera, the metro of Caracas was begun as well as the airports at Maracaibo (La Chinita) and Maiquetía (Aeropuerto Nacional Simón Bolívar). The gas industry was privatised and the petroleum industry prepared for privatisation. A treaty was signed with Guyana whereby neither country would lay claim to disputed territory. The Andean Subregional Pact was signed with Ecuador, Chile and Peru while other agreements with countries in the region strengthened ties in that part of Latin America and delineated the bounds of national sovereignty. This done, Caldera created laws to stimulate exports.

The Venezuela that the now infamous Carlos Andrés Pérez Rodriguez of AD inherited as president in 1973 had seen 30 years of democracy but little improvement for the poor. Thousands of peasants were still landless. The agricultural system was also inefficient, and almost half of all foodstuffs had to be imported. Malnutrition was rife among the poor and the overall division of wealth was more markedly unequal than ever. Pérez exploited this situation by promising to attack the twin evils of privilege and poverty.

BOOM AND BUST

Venezuela's prosperity increased suddenly in 1973 when the Arab oil embargo pushed up oil prices. Pérez nationalised the oil industry and formed a state company, Petroven. He compensated the foreign oil companies and maintained links via shipping, equipment and technology. Pérez used oil revenue to expand heavy industries, including the petrochemical, shipbuilding and steel industries. He also oversaw the building of railways and the French-designed Caracas metro, modernised ports and established a national fisheries industry. Unfortunately Pérez was forced to borrow heavily from foreign banks to support this ambitious programme. The oil-fuelled boom covered the faults in the economy. In this time of great prosperity, city dwellers aspired to the high life and wealthier Venezuelans spent their weekends shopping in Miami. The population, especially in the cities, continued to grow rapidly, but so did food imports.

After the boom comes the bust, and Venezuela had to suffer falling oil prices and large debt repayments under the next two presidents, Luis Herrera Campins (COPEI), elected in 1978, and Jaime Lusinchi (AD), elected in 1983. Lusinchi took the extreme measure of announcing a moratorium on all debts taken up with foreign banks before his term began in 1983.

Pérez returned to power in 1988 for a far rougher ride as president. He found himself forced to accept an austerity package from the International Monetary Fund, whose bitter pill included neoliberalising the economy to make it more attractive to foreign investors and other capitalist measures that hit the average citizen hard: currency devaluations, subsidy cuts and interest rate increase. As the largest oil provider outside the Middle East, Venezuela had always massively subsidised the petrol price for its domestic market. One consequence of cutting the petrol subsidy was a rise in bus fares. The people rioted, first in Caracas and then in towns and cities throughout the country. Brutal suppression of the riots caused up to a thousand deaths. This action possibly prompted the US Treasury Secretary Nicolas Brady to set up the Brady Plan to reduce Latin American debt. Despite a loan from the US government, inflation increased dramatically. Pérez continued to toe the IMF line, privatising industries he himself had nationalised. He sold 40 per cent of the phone company CANTV to the American GTE, the national airline VIASA to the Spanish Iberian Airlines, and hotels to other foreign companies.

The economic medicine Venezuelans were being fed by Pérez and the IMF did not go down well. Poverty and inflation had increased greatly, as had government corruption, particularly where privatisation was concerned. The embattled working classes went on strike. They found a working class hero in Lieutenant Colonel Hugo Chávez Frías. He led an unsuccessful coup, demanding immediate aid for the poor, corruption trials and other measures. A second coup in November 1992 was also defeated.

In the face of a storm of public protest, however, the Supreme Court indicted Pérez on corruption charges and lifted his presidential immunity. Pérez was suspended on charges of embezzling $17 million and Ramón Velásquez was made acting president. In the December 1992 elections for governors, mayors and city councils, Pérez's AD predictably suffered at the hands of embittered voters. The December elections also brought the leftwing Causa Radical (Causa R) into being as a political force. Rafael Caldera was returned to power at the head of the coalition party Convergencia, which formed the ruling bloc in Congress with MAS (Movimiento al Socialismo). Causa R became influential and COPEI and AD banded together to form a majority to continue their domination of Congress.

Caldera presided over extremely turbulent economic times. Pérez had pumped government funds into Banco Latino, making it the second largest bank in Venezuela, in deals that made his personal fortune and those of his friends and associates. Banco Latino suffered government intervention under the cloud of corruption. Eighty-three bank executives were accused of embezzling millions of dollars and laundering drug money. The government suspended the bank's operations and unfortunate investors queued for hours to recover a part of their investments. The government later intervened in eight other banks to save them from collapse and liquidated their assets. Since then it has sold Banco Latino's insurance branch (Latino de Seguros) to a Colombian group. Banco Republica has also been sold to Colombians and Banco Provincial is managed by Banco Bilbao de Vizcaya. Inflation increased so much that prices in stores changed almost daily. The government was forced into currency devaluations.

Under IMF pressure, the government continued with privatisation but it also undertook other measures to control the economy. The exchange rate for the bolívar was set at 100 per dollar (at its height it converted at nearly 300). Price controls were set; this meant that many products were unavailable in supermarkets. Only those who could prove a business necessity or were travelling could buy dollars.

Constitutional guarantees were suspended to fight corruption and also possibly the attempted coups. People could be stopped, searched and arrested. Police routinely stopped public transport and deported those who could not provide identification.

Caldera began his term of office promising measures that would relieve the suffering of the poor but ended with Venezuela more closely tied to the neoliberal economic policies of the IMF than ever before. Caldera, who in his last administration had nationalised industries, was forced to accept an austerity programme that included mass privatisation. The country was opened up even further for foreign investment, especially in the oil industry. Caldera's government, with the Agenda Venezuela, sought foreign investment in oil, gas, electricity, aluminium, gold, nickel, coal and tourism, among others. The United States was the biggest investor followed by Japan, the United Kingdom, France and Spain.

In conjunction with multinationals, Venezuela exploited previously untapped sources of oil and a new fuel source, bituminous tar, in the largely untouched Orinoco basin. The tar was sold as a liquid fuel, Orimulsion, to China, Taiwan, Japan, Canada and Denmark. As Venezuela was self-sufficient in electricity, thanks to hydroelectric power and natural gas, all the Orimulsion was exported, and there was nearly two billion tons of it. Caldera also streamlined the oil industry, eliminating the three subsidiaries and shedding 10,000 workers. Seventeen oilfields were auctioned in 1997.

In 1998, the optimism of 1997 dissipated in the cold wind of reality. Petrol prices rose, the fiscal deficit grew, investment in the petrol industry froze, the steel industry and the textile industry hit recession and unemployment increased.

Venezuela's Economy Today

Venezuela has the world's largest refinery and is the largest oil exporter to the United States. Also targeted for privatisation are the electricity supplier Cadafe and Sidor, the state steel company, and four aluminium companies.

Tourism is the second largest source of income and foreign companies are being lured with a package of incentives. Venezuela has diverse attractions for tourists, not least the national parks containing a variety of environments and wide expanses of beaches and tropical islands. Venezuela is trying to organise a free trade zone for the Andean Community, which includes Colombia, Ecuador and Bolivia. It is also looking to join Mercosur, also known as the South American Common Market, which includes Brazil, Argentina, Paraguay and Uruguay.

Chávez Against the Devil

Colonel Hugo Chávez Frías came into power in February 1999 on the back of a tidal wave of public support. The populist ex-coup leader promised radical measures to combat Venezuela's difficult situation. He swept away what he saw as a political system that favoured the established parties. This happened through the creation of a National Assembly, whose 167 deputies are elected from representatives of all strata of social groups across Venezuela, three of these must be drawn from indigenous people. Aims of the assembly are to reduce corruption and bureaucracy and make the judicial system more answerable. The Supreme Tribunal of Justice (Tribunal Supremo de Justicia) is elected by the National Assembly for a single twelve-year term. Chávez also had a new Constitution passed by the National Assembly in 1999, which went through with 71.78 per cent of the vote. The Constitution has 350 articles and enshrines facets of human rights such as the right to: free education, free quality health care, access to a clean environment, for indigenous peoples to maintain their languages, cultures and religions.

He has decreed a 20 per cent wage increase for state workers and brought in a 15.5 per cent VAT and a 0.5 per cent bank handling charge to balance this. Chávez undertook another populist measure by allowing over 10,000 families to occupy unused land or buildings, as he refused to send the National Guard to expel them. Chávez has set up community councils to encourage grassroots political participation, although they are obliged to sign up with the president's office to access funds and it is alleged that they have to demonstrate absolute political loyalty to be registered. Chávez has aimed for 50,000 community councils by the end of 2007.

Another tool in supporting the poor are Chávez's Missions. These focus public money on areas of need to provide significant targeted improvement where government agencies have proved to be ineffective. The Bario Adentro Mission is discussed elsewhere. Some of the other missions include: the Robinson Missions to eradicate illiteracy via an audio-visual teaching programme, the Ribas Mission assists people to complete High School, the Milagro Mission that provides free eye surgery for the poor, the Guiacapuro Mission that promotes the needs of indigenous communities and provides them, with a sustainable agricultural base.

In April 2002, an attempted coup, backed by big business and allegedly involving the US, brought Chávez down for a mere two days. The coup took place at a time of great political instability, when chaotic demonstrations were focused on the Presidential Palace (Miraflores Palace) and senior military figures rebelled. Eighteen people died in shooting as Chávez was forced to resign in favour of the President of Fedecámeras, Pedro Carmona Garcia. A spontaneous demonstration, this time in favour of Chávez, again headed to Miraflores Palace. The Vice President, Diosdado Cabello, took the opportunity to exert his authority under the constitution and take power until Chávez could re-assume control.

There was also a general strike in 2002, called by business organisations and workers' groups. The strike, which lasted 63 days, was highly effective in halting the wheels of industry as the country lost 7.6 per cent of its GDP. Again Chávez survived and claimed a popular victory. In the 2005 General Election, the major opposition parties withdrew, alleging electoral fraud. Chávez's MVR (Fith Republic Movement Movimiento Quinto Republica) and allies consequently won all 167 seats. Chávez has twice been granted the power to rule by decree for limited periods (in 2000 and 2007), although the first limitation the Venezuelan people have put on his rule occurred in 2007, when a referendum voted not to allow Chávez to stand for re-election an unlimited number of times (other proposed measures included making Venezuela a socialist state, bring the Central Bank under full state control). Chávez accepted the voice of the people, but claimed he had only suffered a setback '*por ahora*' (for now). His many followers see him as a genuine man of the people, his opponents as a dangerous dictator, an echo of Venezuela's *caudillo*-dominated past.

In May 2007, President Chávez severed all ties with the World Bank and IMF. Chávez has further attempted to bolster

Venezuelan sovereignty by passing a law (January 2007) that decrees that the state-owned oil company PDVSA (Petroleos de Venezuela SA) must hold a minimum 51 per cent stake in all joint-venture projects involving exploration, exploitation and transportation. BP, Statoil, Chevron and Total have accepted the terms, but ExxonMobil and ConocoPhillips have refused, entailing massive losses as they have pulled out on projects in the Orinoco region.

CHAVISMO AND BOLIVARIANISMO

The phenomenon of the rise to power of Hugo Chávez has wrought enormous change in the political and social life of Venezuela. Chavez has changed the symbols and language that represent Venezuela to itself and to the outside world. He identifies his Venezuelan republic with Simon Bolivar, thus attempting to allay himself and his regime with Venezuela's greatest national hero and also put his own indelible stamp on the history of the nation. Venezuelans have a strong sense of pride in their country and Chávez has attempted to use the symbols that embody this pride to translate the pride to his administration. The colours of the national flag have their own meaning. Red stands for the blood spilled in the liberation of the country, yellow for the gold or wealth of the country and blue for the water over which the Spanish journeyed to reach the new land. Chavez changed the Venezuelan flag by changing the seven stars to eight. The old seven-star flag can now only be found on the black market as a representation of the time before Chávez.

The 'rebranding' tag of Bolivariano also marks something out as part of Chavez's new Venezuela and distinct from the rest of Venezuela's modern history. Many aspects of Venezuela now have the bolivariano adjective. These range from the country, the '*Republica Bolivariana de Venezuela*', to the army '*ejercito bolivariano*' to a new car '*carro bolivariano*' and so on. This labelling will also provoke a strong positive reaction of acceptance from the Chavistas or rejection from the *escaulidos*. In Chávez's vision, Bolivarianism stands for anti-imperialism, popular participatory democracy via universal (post 18) suffrage and grassroots involvement, economic self-sufficiency, equitable distribution of oil income, anti-corruption and a populace that has an ethos of national pride and belief in the tenets of Bolivarianism.

THE INFLUENCE OF CUBA

In Havana, Cuba, in 2001 in the Jose Marti museum, I saw an ornate jewel-laden ceremonial sword that Hugo Chavez had presented to Fidel Castro. Since Chavez's accession to power, the themes this scene brought together, of revolution, communism and socialism, history and power, have been far more than symbolic. The ties between the two nations have had tangible results. Many Cuban doctors have been brought in to work in Venezuela and spread the benefits of Communism/ Revolutionary Socialism alongside their healing work. Important contracts have been signed between both countries.

Chávez clearly sees Cuba as a natural 'sister' country to Venezuela, but relationships with other countries have been less successful. Chávez was famously told to shut up by King Juan Carlos of Spain on a visit in 2007. He has called the then Mexican President Vicente Fox a 'puppy dog' of the USA. Chávez has also accused Colombia of 'spitting in the face of Venezuela' during a hostage crisis in Colombia which the Venezuelan president eventually helped to resolve, although relationships between the sister nations are still fraught. Chávez has also called George Bush 'the Devil' and he has a provocative relationship with the USA, attacking the government as oppressive whilst engaging in projects to help the poor, such as the provision of low-cost heating oil to the poor in New York (Venezuela is the USA's fourth largest supplier of oil). In 2006, 25 million gallons of oil were provided at 40 per cent of the normal cost. This has brought political good will from many in the USA, especially Chávez's natural constituency, the poor. In Venezuela, it has angered those who feel oil profits would be better re-invested in boosting Venezuela's economy. Chávez has also aligned with other left-wing leaders in the region, such as Evo Morales in Bolivia, which adds further to the Bolívarian claims for his government, as echoes of Bolívar's dream of a united Gran Colombia are re-awakened. Chávez has also offered to extend his oil subsidy plans to Uruguay, Argentina and Bolivia.

CHAPTER 3

'I, on my horse, above me my hat,
above my hat, God.'
—Llanero motto

THIS CHAPTER WILL LOOK AT WHO the Venezuelans are, what their own perceptions of themselves are and how they view and react to people of other nationalities. Although some of the information may appear to be contradictory, there are profound contradictions in all people and all societies. If you find yourself asking "Why is someone who went out of his way to help me when I met him in the street being so awkward when he is being paid to help me?" this chapter will help. It has been necessary to generalise to a certain degree, but it is hoped that the drawing of broad stereotypes has been avoided. You may have little idea what the average Venezuelan is like, and at first contact it is easy to put them into the Latino pigeonhole. While the Latin stereotype holds true in some ways, in others it can blind you to reality and encourage unfair prejudices to grow.

PERSONALITY

It would of course be a crass generalisation to say that there is a personality type applicable to all Venezuelans. However, it would be true to say that some characteristics fairly common in the Venezuelan population could create a general impression different from that given by the people of another country.

Venezuelans are often open and talkative. They speak directly and nearly always speak their mind. This can mean that you have to develop a thick skin to survive in Venezuela with your pride intact. A friend of mine showed his neighbour a photo of his girlfriend in the United States. She commented, "Oh, she's ugly, but don't worry, you'll find a much more attractive girl here."

The fiery Latin image does not apply here. This misconception is based on a false interpretation of body language. Venezuelans may seem to be angry because they use expressive gestures and raised voices, but within minutes they will be laughing and smiling. Venezuelans are generally laid-back, but this does not mean they are lazy or lack ambition. They are generous with both their time and money. They take pride in their country, appearance, possessions and achievements. Venezuelans are usually friendly, fun-loving and warm. This means they are in many ways the ideal people to learn a new language with, as they are talkative and will be delighted to hear a foreigner speaking in Spanish. You will make friends easily and soon have a number of people willing to help you settle in and adapt to their culture. You will not feel lonely while you are in Venezuela.

On the other hand, Venezuelans can seem tactless and insincere. This is a question of different values. Venezuelans even seem to not believe in keeping their word. Do not be upset when you are invited out to see the town and to parties, and these promises come to nothing.

The same applies for the perception that Venezuelans have little regard for punctuality and do not like to be bound by time constraints. When someone is late, be prepared to wait for up to and possibly beyond an hour after the given time. This flexible approach to time also means that even when something gets started, events take a long while to warm up. Those who have been some time in the country learn to be relaxed about time and let things happen when they happen. Be prepared to linger awhile in casual conversation before whatever you are waiting for takes place.

This is easy enough to adapt to in your free time but can be enormously frustrating when you are at work or have an urgent matter to attend to. In this situation, it is best to stress that the issue is a really important one for you. Things will be speeded up as long as you stay polite and

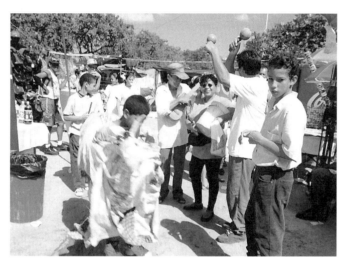

Venezuelans are not slow to enjoy themselves at Carnival time.

do not let your frustration turn into rudeness. This is all part of the Venezuelan outlook. Being friendly is the most important thing; time spent just chatting is valuable. It is better to make plans and then drop them than cause any unnecessary aggravation.

THE NATIONAL SELF-IMAGE

It is interesting to look at Venezuelans' self-image, although this is not necessarily a true reflection of reality. There is a great deal of national pride, based on the great days of the independence revolution, the country's elevated position from oil revenue, pride in Latin culture generally and a firm belief in the Venezuelan people. Venezuelans rally behind the flag (*la bandera*), the shield (*el Escudo*) and the national anthem (*el Himno Nacional*) as symbols of their national identity, and Simón Bolívar and the other great figures associated with the revolution (*los proceres*) constantly remind them of their great forebears. However, being a country with a young population, most Venezuelans would rather live in the present and look to the future than to the past.

Venezuelans can be unfairly critical of themselves despite their great national pride. Seduced by the ideal of becoming a wealthy non-racial democracy, they have set themselves very high standards for a country with a fairly small population. Maybe it is asking too much for this young country to live up to promises inherent in a constitution written with one eye on those of France and the United States. The more cerebral Venezuelans honestly, if unfairly, blame themselves for this failing, and at times see themselves in a generally less than heroic light.

In his book *Crisis de Identidad en Venezuela* (Identity Crisis in Venezuela), the Venezuelan author Pedro Mirabal Level gives the following negative characteristics of Venezuelans. They see themselves as being ill-mannered, disrespectful, offensive and aggressive. They are jokers who do not respect laws or social norms and actively enjoy transgressing laws, even at the expense of others. They are lazy in consideration of their duties and arrangements. They are impatient, inconsistent and lack perseverance. The men are macho, selfish womanisers, who like to drink and gamble. They are optimistic and believe that everything will turn out fine without them needing to put in the hard work required for a secure future. They are also wasters (*echón*) who love to spend and do not bother to save. They believe that they are seen as a corrupt and lawless society.

While some of the above has a ring of truth, much of it will seem curious to outsiders. Venezuelans are not an aggressive people and do not look for trouble or get drunk and get into fights. You may see crime-related violence, but you won't have to put up with the sorts of thuggishness that you could encounter in some European cities. Venezuelans like to have a joke and can be rude, but this is never an invitation for a punch-up. As far as being ill-mannered is concerned, this is a combination of a number of peculiarities of Venezuelans. They are open and will talk to you as if they have known you for a long time, which may seem too informal for your liking. They will quickly take you into their confidence and possibly tease you with a joke or two. This rapid decrease in the social distance between people may take getting used to, but it must not be interpreted as rudeness. Venezuelans will be deliberately rude when they feel that their rights have been infringed, such as if you take their parking space or question their authority. Although Venezuelans are generally disrespectful towards authority figures (because the general sense is that they are corrupt and corruptible), once in authority they will demand respect and be very rude if you do not let them conduct matters as they see fit. Venezuelan men do like to spend time with their friends, drinking, playing dominoes and talking about women, sports or cars—but then, who does not?

On the other hand, Mirabal mentions some positive aspects of Venezuelans, including a great capacity for knowledge and a profound respect for self-improvement, especially through education. He points to achievements in sport, medicine, music, the arts, writing and engineering to highlight the ability to achieve on a world stage. As Venezuelans will tell you, they know how to enjoy themselves. They are religious and have a profound belief in great ideals, as their reverence for the words of Simón Bolívar clearly demonstrates, although as Chávez has so closely tied his words and philosophy to that of El Liberator, Bolívar now cannot be viewed separately to the contemporary political climate. Venezuelans also have a deep belief in the importance of family life.

My experience bears out all of the above. For every *echón*, you will find someone who starts work at seven in the morning, finishes at the same time in the evening and goes to night school for postgraduate study. The idea of Venezuelan laziness is really just a matter of a different approach to life. In the Venezuelan set of values, all aspects of life involve a good deal of small talk and the chance to establish and maintain friendships. This does not preclude hard work. These values also mean that they are extremely hospitable to friends and visitors alike, although under the current political climate, politicized areas of the big cities may manifest some anti-Western sentiment.

They are inclined to be liberal in a political sense, but they have become sceptical about the promises of democracy, having watched its struggle over more than 40 years, with revolutions a consistent shadow in the background. They generally feel disgust towards political figures, whom they

Despite importing a large amount of their modern culture from the United States, the government has attempted to redress the balance by using laws and regulations to encourage a more *criollo* flavour to television and radio programming, for example by regulating the quantity of programming that can be brought in from abroad and setting minimum quotas for Venezuelan cultural programming.

see as self-serving, corrupt and unable to deal with the problems that face the country. As history reveals, they can show a yearning for a political strongman, a dictator unafraid to rule by decree. Hugo Chávez has proved himself to be strongman worthy of the *caudillos* who have marched through Venezuela's history. He has polarised opinion with convinced Chavistas almost in reverence of him while Escuálidos see him with loathing.

Venezuelans are fiercely proud of their independent status and position as a modern and youthful country. On the other hand, they have taken in many aspects of US culture with great avidity, but this does not mean that they see it as being in any way superior to Venezuelan culture. The favourite motif for any item of clothing, from caps through sportswear to babies' clothes is a Disney or Warner Brothers character. In some markets, it can be quite difficult to actually find clothing without these distinctive symbols. Venezuelans are extremely proud of how well their players do in US major league baseball. They obviously see baseball as a world game, much as football is.

GLAMOUR

Venezuelan culture glorifies glamour. The people are very proud of their reputation for a steady stream of Miss Worlds. They will ask you, if you are male, what you think of Venezuelan women. They already know what the answer will be. In this society, appearance is of enormous importance. This becomes less true as you head out of the cities and larger towns—country folk are ridiculed by their city cousins for their supposedly unsophisticated ways. In general, wherever you are, it is vital to have new clothes and shoes, not just for important occasions but for every event you attend.

It can seem that Venezuela's demand for beauty sets a standard that all Venezolanas must struggle to live up to.

Make-up is expertly applied and clothes are usually skin-tight and always fashionable. Even girls not blessed with perfect figures (which in Venezuela means large-bottomed and not necessarily big-breasted) wear revealing clothing. Styles are flexible; if it is fashionable, it is in. A friend of mine once ridiculed a student for an outlandish pinstriped jacket and non-matching trousers, only to see the same ensemble in that month's edition of *GQ*. The fashion-conscious are impervious to the heat, and leather jackets with fur collars may be worn in 96 degree weather, although more usually the taste is for the scanty and summery, all year round. In general, thick clothing is not necessary except in the Andes, and clothes made of thin cloth are highly effective in protecting you from the worst of the heat. Umbrellas are required for the rainy season and waders would be very helpful to combat the potentially knee-deep water, yet neither waders nor rubber boots are worn here.

Traditional Attire in Venezuela

The traditional Venezuelan male's attire, or *liqui-liqui*, is a suit of two parts, a close-fitting jacket and stiff trousers made of the thin sort of cotton that the climate demands. It is usually cream-coloured and worn with a narrow-brimmed hat that resembles a Panama hat. It is worn occasionally, even in the cities. Traditional women's dresses, colourful and voluminous, can be seen in traditional dances but are not otherwise worn.

All shopping malls, and even the work of Venezuelan designers, reflect the fashions of the United States and, to a lesser extent, Europe. Designer labels are easy to find. Smart is always in. Weekend clothes can be more relaxed, to the extent that many pairs of shorts seen around town bear an uncanny and possibly comical resemblance to boxer shorts. But do not wear shorts to work! Work demands a tie for men and nothing frivolous for women. Work clothes are always smart, never casual. Casual clothes must be clean and not dirty or ripped. Punks are not unknown but are rarely seen although a slightly beatnik style is adopted by 'alternative' young people.

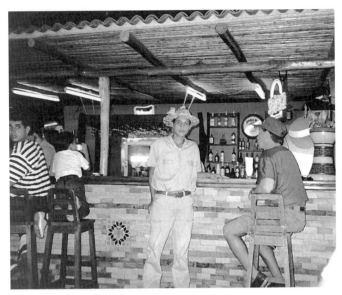

Traditional and casual styles mingle at a restaurant bar.

The pressure to dress up is obvious wherever you go. It is also equally obvious that, in a country which still retains a strong flavour of machismo, there is one set of rules for women and another for men. In public parks at the weekend, you will see women who have obviously spent hours getting ready arm in arm with guys in jeans and T-shirt. This male lack of pomp is more than skin-deep. Many Venezuelan males exercise rigorously to stay in shape, but many others do not, nor do they feel the need to dress to impress.

In one area, however, men are every bit as meticulous as women—personal hygiene. Any hint of body odour is a social catastrophe, so make sure you are always well protected. Venezuelans shower at least twice daily and make repeated applications of deodorant and perfume, as this is vital in the unremitting heat. They have at least one change of clothes, from day to evening. Talcum powder is a common, effective way of avoiding sweat. This aspect of Venezuelan social mores may well both please and annoy you. You are guaranteed a sweet-smelling journey on buses and other public transport. On the other hand, you will find you cannot work up a good sweat in the gym and on the sports field. Venezuelans will not hesitate to tell you that you smell. In this country, even soldiers smell as sweet as a rose and it is not unknown for men to paint their nails with clear varnish.

Miss Venezuela

Venezuela is rightly renowned for its beauty queens. Venezuela has won more international titles than any other country, with an impressive roll of honour that includes five Miss World winners, four Miss Universe winners, five Miss International winners and one Miss Earth winner. The power behind the tiara is Osmel Sousa, who, as president, exercises control over all aspects of the Miss Venezuela pageant. He even selects the contestants for the prestigious event, even at times not selecting a regional winner to go forward to the national contest, instead choosing a girl who finished as a runner-up in another state, making her the official regional 'winner'. The show is a four-hour extravaganza that is broadcast live across Latin America, with edited versions shown in the USA and Mexico. The finalists are put through an intensive programne that includes modelling, make-up, elocution, English and a rigorous fitness regime. Many contestants augment this with plastic surgery and cosmetic dentistry. An international title, or even merely a Miss Venezuela crown, is a stepping stone to fame and fortune and many former title winners have become household names in various fields, not just modelling.

Maria Conchita Alonso is one of Venezuela's most familiar faces. She was born in Cuba but grew up in Venezuela. She was crowned Miss Teenage World and the first runner-up in the Miss Venezuela pageant of 1975. Although she is most famous for her acting career, she started out as a singer with the group Ámbar in 1979, then became a solo artist in 1982. Her major success was the Gorgio Moroder-produced *Vamos a Bailar* that was on the soundtrack of *Scarface*. Her first Hollywood film was in *Moscow on the Hudson* with Robin Williams, which was followed by numerous Hollywood roles in movies such as *The Running Man*, *Predator 2*, *Vampire's Kiss*, *The House of the Spirits* and *Colors*. She was also the first Latin American actress to star in a Broadway musical, playing Aurora in *Kiss of the Spiderwoman* in 1995.

Irene Sáez won Miss Venezuela and Miss Universe in 1981 and eventually found her way into politics, She won acclaim as the Mayor of Chacao (a municipality of Caracas) in the 1990s, keeping the commercial district clean and relatively crime-free. In 1997, she launched her own party with the awful acronym of IRENE and briefly led in the polls for the 1998 elections, before reality hit and she finished fourth with a dismal 2.8 per cent of the vote. She spent the next two years as governor of the state of Nueva Esparta, but then gave up her political career to have a family.

Ruddy Rodríguez was the first runner-up in the Miss Venezuela contest of 1985 and followed that by becoming third runner-up in the Miss World contest of 1985. She has hosted the TV shows *De Moda* on Televen and *El café de Ruddy* on RCTV. She has starred in numerous telenovelas in Colombia and Venezuela in the 1980s and 1990s and 2000s, including the Latin American Desperate Housewives *Amas de casas desesperadas* as Eugenia (Bree).She has appeared in a number of feature films produced in Venezuela, Spain and France. She made a very brief appearance in the 1987 James Bond film *The Living Daylights*.

Barbara Palacios won Miss Venezuela, Miss South America and Miss Universe in 1986. She hosted Miss Universe, Miss USA, Miss Hispanidad and Miss Venezuela pageants in the 1990s, as well as television work that included talk shows and documentaries. She continues to have a stellar modelling career and her own line of jewellery and her own chain of stores in Latin America and the USA.

Still a Winner

Patrica Velasquez failed to win Miss Venezuela in 1989, but she has become an international model and an actress who has had several film roles. Most notably, she has starred in *The Mummy* and *The Mummy Returns* as Meela Nais/Anck Su Namun.

Dominika van Santen came nowhere in the Miss Venezuela contest of 2005, but then won the Top Model of the World contest in the same year. Alexandra Braun Waldeck won Miss Earth in 2005 and the two have since become rising stars in the modelling world, both securing modeling contracts for major international companies and working worldwide.

LOVE AND MORE

What about that Latin lover image? Venezuelan men are proud of their virility and can be macho in the way they express it. Women can expect to be followed down the street by catcalls and craning necks, eyes fixed firmly on their behind. However, looks that travel down and then fixate on the bottom accompanied by cries of *mamacita linda* (pretty little mother!) are the worst that happen in public places. These comments occur even when you are out as a couple. Men should not take any offence as nothing nasty or aggressive is meant by this behaviour; an aggressive reaction would come as a surprise. Happily, most Venezuelan men will try to talk themselves out of a violent situation. Incidentally, the macho image is confined to looking and commenting—this is not a nation of bottom-pinchers.

No Venezuelan wants to be humiliated in front of his friends, and the admiring words and glances are often half-hearted attempts for peer approval. It may seem surprising but the men actually show disappointment when their unsophisticated advances are totally ignored. This is often explained by the excessive mother-love they receive, boosting their self-esteem and their value to women to unmerited levels. Another reason is that Venezuelan women are often guilty of being overprotective and subservient to unworthy males. Some women say they appreciate the attention, as long as it is polite, a sincere form of flattery. Others find it offensive. All of them know that the best response is to ignore it completely.

The male dominance in Venezuelan culture means that it is perfectly acceptable, and encouraged, to have more than one girlfriend. It creates a climate in which just about anyone is seen as being available as a potential partner, even if married. This applies to women too, and many of them are not afraid to make advances. Some women will actually try to exploit this situation by offering themselves as a second girlfriend, in the hope that they will then oust their rival. There is an expression, *amigos con derechos* (friends with rights), to explain that casual friends may have a sexual relationship. Men are actively encouraged to take opportunities when they arise, encouraged by comments like, "She's a woman, you're a man, you are attracted to each other, go on, why not?"—a simple philosophy that leaves many Venezuelan women looking for that needle in a haystack, a loyal man. It is not surprising to find that Venezuelan women are particularly jealous and possessive. There is a word for a possessive woman *cuaima*, taken from the species of snake called the *cuaima-piña* because these snakes are said to fight each other over the males. The expression *mi esposa (novia) es u a cuaima* is very common. Low-class, pay-by-the-hour hotels proliferate to cater for spur-of-the-moment casual sex.

Venezuelan women can be very traditional and at the same time want to be independent and have careers of their own. They do enjoy being courted and it is normal for the man to pay on dates. If someone invites you out, that person will pay, otherwise assume that the man will pay. Romantic touches are especially welcome. Venezuelan women appreciate gentlemanly conduct as much as other women. The old notion that a man provides for his woman is still true here, and even if a woman has a career, her ideal man should have a salary that will provide for both of them.

Venezuelans are unfortunately fed a media diet of blonde and blue-eyed beauty that does not match the *mestizo* reality, as there are few natural blondes in the country. As this particular brand of beauty is especially favoured, if you fit the type, you will be stared at with open admiration. Height is also a novelty factor, so the tall and blonde might feel like film stars. There is a high female-to-male ratio which means that single men are hard to find, especially in Caracas.

Girls are often carefully guarded by their parents and have their free time strictly regulated. Despite this, Venezuelan hospitality will mean that you will not feel uncomfortable at your first 'meet the parents' dinner invitation. One of the most striking features of Venezuelan dating life is that age is no barrier to relationships. Nobody will frown upon a man in his thirties having a girlfriend in her late teens and vice versa.

The friendliness of Venezuelans may mean that it is fairly easy to form relationships but what you get within that relationship is as much open to possibilities as anywhere else. Venezuelans may kiss on a first date, or they may go all the way. Your date may be looking for a lifetime partner or a one-night stand—or will take it as it comes.

FAMILIES

Venezuelans are very family-centred. Despite being a nation dominated by the young, children are still very close to their parents. Unless someone has moved to the city to find work, the family group usually lives close together. Quite often they will live in one building, not just the grandparents but also cousins and aunts and uncles. They believe strongly in looking after the members of their family. Parents are expected to look after their children whenever they can and offer them all the assistance they need, even long after they have left home. Family members should be helped when they need it in whatever way possible. This might involve using contacts to get a family member a job. Venezuelans also assume the responsibility of taking care of aged parents. The practice of leaving one's parents in an old people's home rather than taking them in and caring for them is a dereliction of duty in Venezuelan eyes. The old folks are an integral part

Keeping in Touch

It is always important that close family contacts are kept, and a level of social closeness maintained, either by phone or letter and e-mail. Many families are dispersed, to the United States or Spain (especially the Canary Islands), so visits, letters and phone calls are treasured.

of family life and still have an important role to play not only in childminding but also in contributing to family life. The family—and, to a lesser extent, the community—functions as a support network.

Children also stay at home longer. This is partly due to the high costs involved in renting or buying property. It is not unusual to find men still at home up to their late twenties and sometimes thirties, only leaving home when they get married. Girls tend to leave home earlier because it is common for young women to marry earlier than men, often from 18 to 25. This fact means that young men can often still live under the rule of mother and run the risk of being seen as 'mummy's boys' by Westerners because of their relative lack of freedom and the fact that mother always takes precedence and can still have a large say in how her son chooses to spend his time. The call of mother is one that is impossible to ignore.

HUMOUR

The Venezuelan sense of humour, especially among the young, often revolves around poking fun at people, whether present or not. One way of making you feel part of the group is to have a little light-hearted fun at your expense. A capacity for laughing at yourself and not taking these jokes personally is important.

Unfortunately for those who do not have a good grasp of Spanish, jokes hardly ever translate well. Someone tells one and everyone laughs except you. The joke is explained and finally you can understand it, but by then it just is not funny any more. Many jokes rely on word play or cultural references so they can help you with the language, but they probably will not be funny unless they are instantly translated. Many of the national expressions display this *pantalleria* (joking around). TV humour is slapstick and heavily satirical.

ATTITUDES TO RACE

Venezuela has been called a pardocracy, meaning it is governed by its mixed ancestry masses. Most family albums contain shots of very dark-skinned family members, an aunt here or a grandfather there. Venezuelans say they do not discriminate in terms of race but only of social colour. This means there is no bar to social integration. Wealth, status and possessions make one considerably 'whiter', that is, success can change someone's social colour. But there is a certain amount of racism among some people, so even an extremely well-integrated country like Venezuela is not free from this malaise. People who might easily be considered black may say that they do not like black people. You will still find that the wealthiest people are white and that the poorest are black, so if a Venezuelan expresses a dislike for black people, this can be synonymous with a dislike for the poor.

So, Who are the Venezuelans?

Modern-day Venezuelans are a rich mix of many nationalities and cultures. The people are 67 per cent *mestizo*, 21 per cent of European descent, 10 per cent of African descent and 2 per cent Indian. Such is the degree of integration that it is hard to say what the defining physical characteristics of the people are. As Simón Bolívar himself said, "It is impossible to determine with any degree of accuracy where we are in the human family. The greater portions of the native Indians have been annihilated; Spaniards have mixed with Americans and Africans, and Africans with Indians and Spaniards." Consequently it is impossible to describe Venezuelan physical characteristics.

Other Nationalities

Venezuelans are as much prey to forming national stereotypes as anyone else. Some nationalities are seen as dominating some professions. There is the stereotype of the Portuguese *abastos* (general store) owner with a pencil for writing down orders tucked behind his ear. As a teacher I used to put a marker behind my ear and it took a long time before I found out why my students said, "You look Portuguese." The Portuguese

There is a small Chinese presence in the cities, mainly due to the proliferation of Chinese restaurants and 'bazaar' stores.

are also seen as dominating supermarkets, *panaderías* (bakeries), restaurants and bars.

The Italians predominate in construction, butcher's shops, shoe-making, sewing and, of course, restaurants. The Spanish are sellers of fish and other seafood, and they also own restaurants, travel agencies, bookshops and private schools. The majority of priests in Venezuela are from Spain.

The modern wave of immigration occurred in the 1970s, when Venezuela's oil industry made it one of the top players in OPEC. The neighbouring countries that did not share this natural wealth provided many immigrants who came with little money but in the hope of a better standard of living and a means of assisting their families back home. From Panama, Perú, Ecuador, Trinidad, Haití, the Dominican Republic, Argentina, Uruguay and Chile because of their totalitarian regimes during the 1970s, Ecuador and Bolivia due to poverty and most of all Colombia, they came and settled into their previous professions or took what work they could find. Those who had developed skills in their own countries could readily find work in the same fields in Venezuela. Those without training or experience found that as immigrants from poorer countries, the only work they were offered was both casual and menial. Some even had to find their own sources of gainful employment. You can be sure that the man selling oranges or balloons or toys in the middle of a choking, polluted highway is an immigrant. Others work as cooks, chauffeurs, security guards, painters and decorators, electricians, plumbers and in manual and blue-collar jobs. Immigrant women worked usually as domestic help; now there are mainly Venezuelan women doing this work.

As many of these people have entered the country illegally, in the modern age of (relative) economic hardship for Venezuela, crackdowns by the authorities are common. The police can stop traffic and inspect everyone's documents (specifically the *cédula* or identity card) It is illegal in Venezuela to be out of the house without a valid picture ID. You may find yourself on the bus to work and the next minute in a detention centre awaiting deportation. This is one of the reasons why you must carry your passport with you at all times. With the worsening economic situation since the mid-1990s, many immigrants have returned to their countries as there is far less work available in Venezuela and the exchange rates no longer give comparatively better pay for the same type of work.

However, there is a thriving black market economy across the border since other currencies than the Bolivar can be bought and sold. The Colombian peso is in demand at the border since you can change it into dollars or euros.

The original Venezuelans have largely either been assimilated into the mainstream of society or if they want to retain their culture, pushed out into the interior, where there are still some tribes who live in that curious halfway point between their traditional culture and modern society. You will find villages in remote regions such as the Orinoco Delta where the buildings are much as they have been for hundreds of years and the people may wear a blend of traditional dress and Disney T-shirts. They make a living by combining traditional methods, such as catching fish from canoes, and from tourism, for example renting out sparse concrete buildings strung with hammocks, as well as selling handicraft.

As the Indians have become isolated, so they have largely disappeared from the national consciousness. They have been left alone and ignored by both society and government. Some Indian families have even been forced to resort to begging in city centres.

GENDER ISSUES

Women in Venezuela have achieved a level of independence that is impressive for Latin America. There are significant numbers of professional women in senior positions across all types of companies and the government. Despite this, Venezuela is still traditional in some ways, such as the good manners shown to women in term of opening doors and so on. Men are generally expected to pay for women when going out to dinner and when sharing taxis. Women receive open sexual attention, flirtation with comments known as *piropos* are the norm and the pressure to always look your best is intense.

RELIGIOM

The national religion is Roman Catholicism and many fine churches in the country attest to this. Around 90 per cent of Venezuelans are baptised as Roman Catholic. As Venezuela has become more materialistic, it has also become more secular, although Sunday mass is always well attended and most people still retain the tradition of wearing their Sunday best. Appearance is as important in church as it is elsewhere. Those attending mass are usually single people who are middle-aged or older, or families. Attendance at church has improved over the Chávez era as people seek succor and solace for their changing fortunes. People have an emotional attachment to the church as its provides a sense of stability.

There is a strong missionary aspect to Venezuela's Catholic Church and an important part of church work is carried out abroad. Joining the priesthood is not seen as a good career move so the *padres* who serve mass and hear confession are often from overseas. Mass is given in Spanish and you will hear a variety of interesting accents. In the countryside and throughout the Andean region, religion is stronger.

Other religions are represented in Venezuela, most in very small numbers. Over 5 per cent of the population are Protestant, and this figure is growing thanks to evangelical work done mainly in the *barrios*. Several thousand Jews are concentrated in Caracas and Maracaibo and represented by an Asociación Israelita de Venezuela and a Unión Israelita de Caracas. They have synagogues and run their own schools. A shining mosque, the largest in South America and one of the central attractions in Caracas, is the focus of Muslims. A tiny number of Indians (less than 2 per cent of the population) practise traditional religions, but most have been converted to Roman Catholicism.

The worship of the Catholic Saints has taken on a unique flavour in Venezuela, as it has been infused with pagan and

African belief and ritual. The Virgin Mary and the saints can be beseeched for succour, and each has their individual powers. They may or may not decide to intercede in the fate of the believer, but may utilise their god-given powers.

Madre María is the closest Venezuelan to becoming a saint. She was granted beatification by Pope John Paul II in 1995. She first became a nun in 1901 in Maracay and became Mother Superior of a newly-founded Augustine order. She founded over 30 charitable institutions, mainly schools and hospitals. In her work with the sick and poor, she was seen to perform miracles. The miracles extended to her tomb. A nun, who had been lame for many years, prayed at her tomb and was able to walk again and be fully healthy. As part of the process of beatification, her body was exhumed and found to be in a state of perfect preservation. Her body is now housed in a basilica opposite the convent in Maracay and hundreds of people make a pilgrimage there every year.

Doctor of the Poor

José Gregorio Hernández graduated as a doctor in 1888. He came from Isnotú in the Andes and practiced in Caracas, tending to the poor, thus gaining the nickname of 'Doctor of the Poor'. Ill health prevented him from entering the priesthood and he was killed in 1919 by a car. He is venerated all over Venezuela and beyond, and has a singular image, dressed in a black suit, hat and tie with the trademark doctor's bag. He is seen as being able to protect ones health and his birthplace and tomb in La Candelaria in Caracas are sites of pilgrimage. There is widespread support for his beaitification and many miracles attributed to him.

Some religions in Venezuela are only afforded the lowly status of a cult, but these are fascinating nonetheless. Possibly the strangest of these is the cult of Maria Lionza. The home of this cult is Sorte, a hill near the small town of Chivacoa, east of Barquisimeto, in Yaracuy state. Maria Lionza is a mythical Venezuelan witch born from the union of an Indian and a wealthy Spanish creole woman. She is accompanied by her henchmen, El Negro Felipe and the Indian cacique Guaicapuro. Together the three are known as the *tres poderosos* (the three powers).

Maria Lionza worship is at its most fervent on the Día de la Raza when altars and shrines are erected and offerings made in her honour. She is popular among all social groups and has been venerated as a goddess of nature and protector of the environment. There are CDs and DVDs of powerful, hypnotic music written to evoke the mood of a worshipping session. Her priests paint themselves with charcoal, drink rum and fall into trances in an attempt to divine the secrets of supplicants' psyches. Gatherings are held high on the hillside. Maria Lionza's influence extends as far as thoroughly modern Caracas—a statue (by Alejandro Colina) of her riding naked on the back of a tapir is a bizarre sight that greets travellers on the Francisco Fajardo freeway near the city centre.

Traffic fills Avenida Bolivar with the twin towers of 'El Silencio' at rear in downtown Caracas.

Tourism is growing fast throughout Venezuela and one of the draws for the increasing number of visitors is the country's stunning beaches.

Baseball is the Venezuelan national sport and attracts a huge following. Tickets for crucial games are often sold out way in advance and well-known players are revered by many.
Opposite page: The La Asunción City Cathedral. The capital of Margarita, La Asunción is the seat of government for the islands. It is also the town of residence of a great number of artists and intellectuals.

Rows of apartments on a busy street in Caracas. Accommodation in the city ranges from the luxurious *quintas* of the wealthy to the ramshackle *barrios* of the poor.

A cable car ascends El Ávila National Park. Many Venezuelans hike, camp or visit the recreational areas and on clear days, El Ávila Peak offers breathtaking views of Caracas and the Caribbean.

FITTING IN WITH THE VENEZUELANS

CHAPTER 4

'Only the unity of the people and the solidarity of their
leaders guarantees the greatness of nations.'
—Andrés Bello

BIRTH

About 96 per cent of Venezuelans are baptised Catholics and baptism is another significant event in Venezuelan life that brings families and friends closer together, while providing another opportunity to buy new clothes and to dress up baby in beautiful white or cream garments. The *padrinos* (godparents) play a central role in the baptism (*bautizo*), anointing their godchild with holy water and reading passages that affirm their role in the child's life. This *compadrazgo* brings the family and godparents together, as the godparents become the *compadre* and *commadre* of the parents and will be involved in the child's life, not just by promising to take care of the child if something happens to the parents, but also by providing some form of support during the child's life. Some godparents are chosen due to their status and the reflected glory this brings.

FIRST COMMUNION

When a child can tell the difference between good and evil, from the age of seven to 11, they attend their First Communion. The age is probably chosen more for the parents' ability to pay for the white dress or suit for the child, new clothes for themselves, photographer or videographer and perhaps a lavish party. At the ceremony, family, close friends and a new godparent chosen by the child will be present.

BIRTHDAY PARTIES

In the many parks of Venezuela, there are mystifying structures that resemble bandstands, being circular and roofed. Whatever the original purpose, their main use seems to be as venues for children's birthday parties. As children arrive, they hand presents to the *cumpleañero/a* (birthday boy/girl) and then play familiar party games such as musical chairs, dance, eat (anything sweet, especially ice cream) and await the most exciting moment, the breaking of the *piñata*.

A *piñata* is a large model, usually made of papier-mâché in the form of a favourite figure—Disney characters are popular. This delightful and carefully crafted toy is attacked by the birthday boy or girl wielding a baseball bat. To attempt to even up the contest, the child is blindfolded and often spun around. If the child misses, another child can have a go. The joy in breaking the *piñata* lies in the fact that it is filled with small toys, sweets and confetti-like paper, which rain down on the children when it bursts.

Adult birthday parties revolve around the lavish banquet featuring buffet food and the hot *pasapalos*. Presents should be given and dress is usually formal. Besides food, whisky and small talk, there will be dancing, possibly to a live band. The evening may end with the appearance of a mariachi band, whose members surprisingly do not seem to mind some inebriated accompaniment.

QUINCEAÑERA

In many Latin American countries, a girl is seen to come of age at 15, and a special celebration is given. This used to be a way to introduce a girl to society and announce her as a *señorita*, but now it is an excuse for an extravagant bash. The girl's parents may decide to push the boat out and hire an expensive venue for hundreds of guests with full catering and outfits and a tiered cake to

Recordatorios are souvenirs of any of the above special events and will have the name, date and details of the event printed on them. They are often made in the ceramic form of an angel, the child's favourite Disney character, or other image representative of the celebration.

rival any wedding. The party usually lasts from 9:00 pm to the small hours, with a live band. The girl is allowed a sip of champagne from her father's glass and takes the first dance (traditionally a waltz) with her father, before being allowed to dance with her male peers. An extended trip to the USA or Europe may also be part of the celebration in wealthier families.

GIFT GIVING

Generally speaking, you have to give gifts for birthdays, Christmas, weddings and *bautizos*. Always bring a card with a few words from you; they will appreciate it. You should always use wrapping paper, and most stores wrap presents as a common service. If you want to give a gift and do not know what to give, buy a recent CD as music is always welcome.

WEDDINGS

Weddings in Venezuela are typically lavish events centred around the church ceremony. The civil ceremony is a much smaller affair, unless, of course, there is no church ceremony. The organisation of the event will be familiar to anyone who has attended a Christian wedding worldwide.

Despite the feasting and dancing, formal dress is the only rule for a typical Venezuelan wedding. Most guests will be wearing new dresses, suits and shoes as this is generally the rule for any big celebration in Venezuela. Champagne will be flowing once the guests have returned from the church and alcohol in various forms, principally champagne and whisky, will be available into the night, so pace yourself! At the meal, people are usually sat in a pre-arranged order at round tables, hopefully your companions will have been chosen to provide you with stimulating conversation in English or Spanish, depending on your language skills. If you can show some grasp of meringue (just a couple of steps to learn!) or salsa, your fellow guests will be delighted and impressed in equal measure. It won't matter if you are less than perfect, as they will expect all *gringos* to be terrible.

The wedding gift is often some money in an envelope with a card and a few words inside. This can be given to the bride or the groom and it is delivered by hand at any moment during the night. They will remember you forever, because they keep the cards as a souvenir.

FUNERALS

Venezuelan funerals are solemn affairs and the wake afterwards serves as a chance for the guests to console the family members. It is poles apart from the English version where family members often catch up with each other and chat merrily, while eating and drinking as at any party. Black clothes are worn, formal or semi-formal. You may pass by the coffin to pay your respects and you have to say some words of condolence to the close family, but you are under no obligation to stay for the whole wake. Particularly religious widows will wear black for the whole period of mourning, but black may not be worn at all. Widowers may wear dark clothes for a week or up to a month.

BEING NEIGHBOURLY

Even in the city, Venezuelans like to keep in touch with their neighbours and maintain a close relationship with them. Neighbours will not hesitate to help each other out or ask for help with any problem. They usually group together to combat varied problems such as robberies, water supply, power cuts, lack of basic products or medicines, taking care of each other's children and so on. You will not see women struggling in the street with bags of shopping and raucous children. When mothers go out, they leave the children at home with relatives or with neighbours. (You are unlikely to see men on their own and out-of-doors with children, as this is a fairly macho country.)

In fact, wherever you live in Venezuela, it will seem like living in a small village. You can say "hello" and receive a friendly reply rather than being looked at as if you were crazy. You can easily start conversations with strangers on public transport or they may easily start one spontaneously. On the other hand, in cities, if you do not talk to your neighbours they will not bother you, so you can find anonymity, if that is what you want.

GREETINGS

As you have probably already noticed, Venezuelans are warm and find physical closeness and intimacy (without being sexual) easy and natural. You may feel your personal space is being invaded as they will stand close to you, look you intently in the eyes while speaking to you and kiss and embrace you warmly as a greeting. Women kiss both women and men but men only kiss women. Once on either cheek is standard practice for acquaintances, although two between friends is common. You may make actual contact or give an 'air kiss', as long as you don't go too far in either direction!

Greetings may extend to a hug (*abrazo*) between male friends, perhaps with an arm squeeze or two, especially if you have not seen that person for a while. Men also often touch each other on the arms or jacket while talking. Posture is important, slouching comes across poorly and feet must be kept off furniture. Pointing with the index finger is rude, and the whole hand is used or a pursed mouth and head move towards the object/person in question.

NAMES

Venezuelan forms of address are often quite informal and make use of nicknames. It is amusing to hear a wife call her husband *gordo* (fatty) while in the company of strangers. If people do not know your name, they will give you a nickname. Do not be offended if someone insists on referring to you as *catire* (light-haired) even when they know your real name. Hopefully the nickname will be watered down by the diminutive *ito* or *ita*. Somehow *gordito* does not sound nearly as bad as *gordo*. This is probably because the diminutive also signals affection.

A bit more contentious is the reference to black people as simply negro, often to their face, which for English speakers has obvious unpleasant undertones. There is no racist message here. Although you may not feel comfortable referring to people by their colour, it is very common in Venezuela. In fact, people will also be named for their nationality. In this way you get *chino* for Chinese people, *portu* for Portuguese origin and so on... *moreno* or *morena* for brown-skinned people and so on for every colour and nationality.

Venezuelan names are always surprisingly long and it is not easy to figure out what parts are important—or even which is the first name and which the surname. Many names are composed of four parts. The first two are first names, the first of which is nearly always the one in use, while the second can be a middle name in true Western style. However, the person in question may prefer the second name and use it more frequently than the first name.

These things have to be checked; it is not unknown for someone to call you on the telephone and announce themselves as someone you are sure you have never heard of. When you next meet and they refer to that mysterious conversation, the penny will drop and they will say, "Oh, that's my other name." You think, "Yes, but you didn't tell me that, did you?"

The third and fourth names are the paternal and maternal surnames. The third name, the paternal surname, is the more important of the two. The final name, the maternal surname, can be omitted. If you see a name that is written as Miguel Angel Rojas Cruz, you can think of it as the equivalent of Miguel Rojas. However, always bear in mind how the person likes to be called, as some people use both of their first names. The confusion can work both ways. On my passport my name is Kitt Stephen Marcus Baguley. Any official reading my passport would then address me as Señor Marcus, not realising that this was one of my middle names known to only my closest friends.

Venezuelan Names

Names are colourful and imaginative and are often taken from two equally fancied names put together, such as Mariluz (Maria and Luz). They can also be Spanish spellings of English names with the original pronunciation, such as Yaneth for Janet, or Spanish corruptions of English, such as Yefrei for Geoffrey. There are those filled with meaning (Esperanza, or hope), the simply strange (America) or the very popular Mercedes, a name whose root (*merced*) has a multitude of meanings, including 'favour'.

Marriage changes the structure of the name. If a woman marries and takes her husband's name, this will replace the maternal name and be prefixed by *de*. Thus Sofia Cecilia Olmos Valdes becomes Sofia Cecilia Olmos de Baguley.

SMALL TALK

Good topics to bring up in a casual conversation can be more or less anything, as long as it is not too serious or too personal. There are no set openings, such as talking about the weather. Most Venezuelans would be comfortable discussing any topic you might care to bring up, although they do enjoy a good gossip. Public figures from the world of entertainment or politics, friends and relatives are all grist to the mill of gossip, which naturally entails a good seasoning of criticism. Politics is such a burning issue that there is no way of avoiding it in almost any conversation. In any case, people need to know if you are pro or anti Chávez before they know if they want a conversation with you or not.

Latin Americans in general love to talk up their country and their people. If you are male, the first question you will be asked is what you think of the women. As mentioned earlier, Venezuelans are well aware of the fact that they are best known worldwide for winning Miss World competitions, and are immensely proud of this. They will tell you in glowing terms about how wonderful, warm, open and friendly the people are. If they contrast this with the coldness of 'your' people, try not to be offended, because by being in the country you are presumed to be on their side. You might be inclined to play devil's advocate and give the other side to the story to add balance, or simply to defend your country. Restrain these urges, unless you enjoy provoking an argument and the risk of giving offence. By agreeing, you are giving your seal of approval to the country, which your proud hosts will appreciate. Feel free, however, to complain about the things that Venezuelans complain about—corrupt politicians, awkward bureaucrats and the lifestyles of the rich and famous.

Venezuelan speech is often peppered with adjectives that might seem overstated in translation. If praise appears fulsome, this is just a manner of speech and not indicative of a superficial nature, as some Westerners have suggested. You didn't just sleep well; your sleep was *sabroso* (delicious). Dinner was not delicious; it was *exquisito* (exquisite), and so on. Compliments can readily be taken at face value.

Venezuelans are also direct in their speech. The imperative is used frequently, for example, *damelo* (give it to me) may seem unnecessarily abrupt, but the meaning behind it is just as polite as "could you give it to me". Westerners' speech is governed by the same conventions. If a Westerner says "I think this is true", the Venezuelan would interpret this as meaning "I don't actually know if this is true", whereas the Westerner's meaning is "I'm sure it's true".

Venezuelans are also proud of their status as Americans. They belong to the continent of America—note, not *South* America. Any attempt to deny there is only one American continent is merely a snobbish ruse by Northerners trying to disown its more impoverished neighbour and raise its own profile. If you are looking for a fierce argument, just suggest that there are seven continents and not six.

Venezuelans have taken on board the culture of the United States more than any other Latin American country but despite this still fiercely cling to their own culture, which is seen as embedded in the music and the nature of the people, especially their outlook on life, as much as the country's unique history. This has been much emphasised under Chavez, to point of demonising the USA and Europeans as imperialist aggressors and viewing the colonial period as a time of invasion and cultural destruction.

The United States has given Hollywood, baseball, basketball, fashion and many types of food to Venezuela. The only sticky point between the countries is a sense that the United States looks down on other countries in the region. Some Venezuelans are indignant at what they see as the United States' disregard of other cultures and are of the opinion that their northern neighbour has exactly the same social problems as Venezuela. In conversation with Venezuelans, the best approach any American, or indeed European, could possibly take is to show an interest in Venezuelan culture and the willingness to learn more about it.

GOING OUT
Movies and Theatre

Wear jeans and a T-shirt, also bring a sweater since some theatres can be very cold. It is an experience for those from colder climes to emerge from a cold building to the far hotter open air! Any kind of shoes but sandals, and most definitely not sandals with socks; this is the social suicide it deserves to be. Try to get there early since there are long lines for the movies in Venezuela and bring some money for the candy corner. Sometimes you don't have to pay for the tickets when you have been invited, but you may need to, so bring your own money.

Restaurants

Wearing shirts with a collar or polo shirts is acceptable, and always wear long pants or jeans. Never wear shorts or sandals. As a general rule, you are not expected to pay if you have been invited, but a polite act of helping with the bill will be fine. You can at least propose it, but leave it if your friends insist that you don't have to pay, never insist twice. (Only when invited to the beach can you wear whatever you want).

GAY AND LESBIAN LIFESTYLES

In Venezuela, there is a resistance to accepting gays and lesbians due to the influence of machismo, so most gay and lesbian culture is very much underground. Caracas is the best place to make contacts and there are some gay clubs and bars. The code phrase in advertising is 'en *ambiente*'. For more information look at the websites http://www.vengay.com and http://www.rumbacaracas.com, although both are in Spanish only.

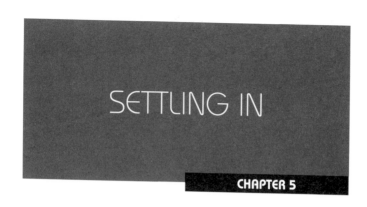

SETTLING IN

CHAPTER 5

'Compatriots. Arms will give you independence,
laws will give you liberty.'
—Símon Bolívar

CLASS WAS NOT AN ISSUE that overly preoccupied Venezuelans, who would not describe themselves in terms of class. However, the gulf between rich and poor is immediately apparent. But there are new social descriptions that Venezuelans use to describe each other. There are the 'Chavistas' who are the followers of president Hugo Chávez. This term used to stand for those in poverty but within the last five years with a meaning of popular-power but still in apparent poverty. On the other side are the 'Escuálidos', who are those who oppose the Chávez government. But they don't call themselves Escuálidos as the meaning is still 'people-with-money', so they generally say they are 'not Chavistas'. Money still matters, but politics define social class in Venezuela nowadays because some previously rich people are poor now and vice versa, some poor people in the recent past are now newly rich. *Escuálidos* was a word with negative connotation (meaning something weak) but the Escuálidos changed it and empowered it. So people now ask "*Tú cómo qué eres (o no) Chavista*" ("Are you for or against Chávez?") when meeting for the first time instead of "where are you from!"

The fact that the *barrios* are occasionally situated near the most luxurious of houses in Caracas is the clearest demonstration of the enormous social inequalities in the country. This situation occurs as the exclusive *colinas* are built on high ground and the *barrios* exist on high ground that was thought to be too difficult to build on. You will most likely drive past (but not through) the *barrios* as you enter the city. You will see all that you need to on this one trip.

The *barrios* exist in the form of tumbling hillside corrugated iron-roofed shanties piled on top of each other. Each house is often no bigger than one room. An entire family has to live here and share whatever facilities are available with their neighbours. The neighbourhood may well be deprived of water, electricity and waste disposal, not to mention telephone lines. There is often a rubbish tip nearby, which presents a considerable health hazard. These areas have extremely high death rates, and they are infiltrated by drug dealing (although glue-sniffing is the only common form of drug taking in the *barrios*) and semi-organised crime, run by gangs called *bandas*. In older areas of cities, the existence of some community organisations makes a difference in the level of degeneration of the area.

Despite their surroundings, *barrio* dwellers maintain their dignity through work and family and by not letting their appearance slip below the impeccable. The most noticeable feature of this is the washing-powder advertisement brightness of their clothing: 'You may be poor, but that is no excuse for dirtiness' sums up this attitude.

The *barrios* are dangerous places. There are unsubstantiated tales of people being taken into them by unscrupulous taxi drivers and then dumped, but you are unlikely to wander into one by accident. The people who live in the *barrios* come from both Venezuela's interior. Many have given up a rural paradise where no work is available to look for casual work in the city. The youth of the *barrios* are called *malandros* if they engage in petty crime. Nike shoes and branded shorts and T-shirts (this is often basketball and baseball wear) is the uniform of these gang members.

The majority do not enjoy a comfortable lifestyle. According to the newspaper *El Nacional*, the minimum monthly salary of 614.790 bolivares (May 2007) can buy only 26 per cent of a

The least fortunate of the Venezuelans are those you will see begging on the streets. Beggars here are nearly always physically incapacitated and obviously live in terrible conditions. Those without obvious handicaps often grow a mass of dreadlocks and dress in rags. Many are mentally handicapped.

family's basic requirements. This helps to explain why many families stay together and children leave home in their late twenties or even thirties. Venezuelans of all social levels see education as the means to personal progression.

Food for the Poor

In the last five years, some popular markets called *Merkal* have been created to help poor people. It has become difficult to find most basic foods in supermarkets, due to conflict between the government and producers. Chávez has imposed prices below the cost of production for basic foods like milk, sugar, flour, meat and chicken, so producers prefer to sell on the black market in order to make a profit. Under the name of *Merkal*, any in poverty can have rationed basic products such as milk and sugar. There are long lines to get the basics since demand is high. In the *Merkal* lines, you are marked with an indelible marker on your hand with your turn number and after purchase you are marked on your finger again so that you can't buy twice that day as goods are rationed (*racionamiento*) to one piece or kilo per day per person.

Most Venezuelans live in rented flats, which are often sub-let. City zones (84 per cent of Venezuelans are city dwellers) are clearly divided in terms of how desirable they are to live in. Venezuelans are not shy about their social status and it is only the young who might not dress to reflect wealth. In contemporary Venezuela, cars are a ready guide to status and wealth as more and more poor people are buying brand new cars, even the expensive ones, since they revalorise instead of depreciate. This is a relatively secure way to save money as it is only possible to have savings in Bolivares, although currencies less liable to fluctuation would be preferable. In Venezuela, cars are often all sold the very first day they arrive at dealerships, so people are put on a waiting list for their latest model luxury car. Hummer dealerships have opened up across Venezuela to meet the demand.

The Venezuelan middle class—composed of proprietors of small businesses, industrialists, government workers, professionals, technicians, managers and teachers—has contracted rapidly in the time of Chavez. Many professionals, technicians, managers and teachers have emigrated to find work or can be found working as taxi drivers. Middle-class Venezuelans are almost all city-dwellers.

The richest Venezuelans live in areas physically separated from the rest of the population and their superior resources are clearly visible. They own luxury houses built in European or North American styles hidden behind security posts with armed guards, high walls or fences and European evergreen trees. Guard dogs that leap out at passers-by patrol the gates.

All cities have areas that are largely the exclusive parade of the wealthy and the well off, as well as tourists, dominated by restaurants and entertainment. Venezuela is still a consumer society despite recent economic decline, and the government's attempts to foster a new consciousness and the many shopping centres of the cities reflect this. In these areas you could easily conclude that Venezuela is a wealthy country, but walk through the street markets and you will reach the opposite conclusion.

THE ENVIRONMENT

One of the features of Venezuelan cities is the lack of planning and control. In the centre of Caracas, modern developments next to Plaza Bólivar overshadow this most important of historical areas. Pollution pours into the rivers in many-hued threads and the air quality in some areas is abysmal. Pollution and congestion are the main reasons why it is always such a relief to get out of the cities. Occasionally clouds of pollution are seen hovering over the coastal cities, causing some respiratory problems. In general though, there is little that you can do to combat pollution except to avoid the most congested areas and drink bottled water.

On the streets, much eating goes on and everyone discards their rubbish onto the streets. Wrappers, cans, even half-eaten burgers are simply tossed aside or hurled out of windows. There are public waste bins, but they always seem to be full. It is quite common to see some people (men, usually) indulging in the art of spitting, although most Venezuelans would regard this as disgusting.

PROPERTY

Housing in Venezuela comes in many forms, from the huts on stilts (*palafitos*) that gave the country its name to the high-rise buildings that predominate in cities. Virtually all types are available to rent or buy at the right price. Mortgages can be arranged: payment generally consists of an upfront down payment followed by monthly sums. The government has moved to control mortgage rates so it is relatively easy to obtain a mortgage with low installments, however demand outstrips supply.

Any country that considers itself to be modern and progressive must have city skylines dominated by skyscrapers and Venezuela is no exception. In Caracas, the majority of people live in high-rise buildings, the condition of which depend on location. In most areas, they are nearly always excellent. Lower-rise buildings are invariably located in poorer districts and have much smaller flats concentrated together in much greater numbers. An apartment building is usually set back from the street in its own grounds, with the first floor often reserved for parking. Concierges or janitors (*conserjes*) are usually present and many buildings have their own security (a man or two with an old rifle).

Most flats are spacious and have balconies (often with marvellous views) and *lavaderos* (rooms with sinks for washing and hanging clothes). Larger flats have a room for a live-in servant. The most luxurious houses are *quintas* that are located on the outskirts of the city, in their own grounds, kept separate by security gates guarded by men who will ask who you are visiting. They are often built on a grand scale with impressive gardens and possibly a swimming pool.

Renting

As the lessee, you will be asked to provide references from your employer and your bank. You will also need a guarantor, which typically is a parent or a near relative, as few employers would take the risk.

The landlord will require a deposit. Six months' or even a year's deposit may be demanded; two months is more common. Contracts are all drawn up for a year's duration, renewable every year. Landlords want to avoid a situation where the lessee leaves without paying or where the lessee refuses to pay and a lengthy court case to evict the lessee ensues. It is common not to get all of your deposit (or any of it!) back. The reprehensible individual who was one of my landlords kept our deposit and got away with it as he also kept the only copy of the rental contract! It is important to write into the contract how the deposit is to be paid and returned.

Finding a Home

Newspapers carry large numbers of property advertisements, especially in Sunday editions. There are American real state offices all around the country such as Century21, Brokers, etc. Naturally location is the fundamental selection criterion and anyone from the town you are in can tell you what the desirable areas are. A quick glance at the ads, divided by area, will tell you as much. The ads will give you an idea of what you will get for your money. Details such as any parking spaces with the property will be included.

Most renting is done through agencies. Talk to a few of them and have a good look at the types of places available in different areas. Agents charge something less than 10 per cent of the total rent and sometimes ask for the equivalent of the first month's rent. For sales of apartments/ houses, they charge 4 per cent.

Rent is high, especially in Caracas, and all agreements are in Bolivares. For a two-bedroom apartment in a decent zone in Caracas, you may have to pay as much as 1,500 to 2,000 bolívares more or less a month. For apartments, the cost of security, water, the *conserje*, garbage collection, etc. come under the *caja chica*, which may be paid by the owner or the renter. The contract terms are variable and could be any combination of service payments, but they are regulated to protect the renter, so there is considerable security built in. You are under no obligation to pay bills in the

Flats/houses may come furnished or unfurnished. Furnished flats will usually have all that you need in them, although some things such as washing machines and televisions might be negotiable.

previous tenant's name. Electricity and gas are payable monthly but phone bills come monthly, so make sure you are paying only for your own calls. Bills are paid at the respective offices, which can entail some queuing. Apartments can come fully furnished or without furniture, but there is enough selection and freedom in negotiation to find whatever suits you best. As in any Western country, there are stores with affordable furniture and appliances in any major shopping district.

Moving In

If you have a local friend, ask for help. People usually move with the help of friends and/or family; companies are for rich people, very heavy things and foreigners. Removal companies are easy to find via newspapers and the Internet. It is wisest to go for the largest and most reputable companies as there are many ways for the removal men to attempt to extract some extra cash. For example, there may be charges outside your written contract according to the number of floors in your building, the elevator size, the number of heavy items and so on. It would be wise to inform the removal men at the time they arrive that there is a tip for them as this will smooth the whole process.

HOME HELP

It is less common in the 21st century than in the 20th century to hire someone to clean your house or apartment two or three times a week and possibly cook for you, but it is still possible. The wealthiest families have a multi-purpose servant, who acts as a bodyguard, chauffeur, gardener and also does other domestic duties. Although it might seem exploitative to hire people to do your cleaning, you would be providing badly needed jobs, and you can always pay them well if you get good service. Most domestic help are paid according to their duties. The only way to ensure that you have someone reliable is by recommendation from other people who have help who are looking for more work. Reliable help can be left alone in the house or allowed to pick up and return keys from neighbours.

PETS

The pampered pets of Western society are not so common in Venezuela. Dogs can be pets, but just as often serve as guards, roam the streets in packs, or lie dead on the highways, forming a bloated barrier to traffic. You will only see cats sniffing around rubbish. They will be greeted with a volley of abuse rather than cuddles and gourmet treats. They are thin, mistrustful and ill-tempered beasts.

Parrots in cages are a common feature of poorer districts. Alongside tropical plants, they festoon the balconies of blocks of flats. You will find very little evidence of animal companions in the home, although pets are not unknown. The idea of allowing your animals to walk all over the furniture would be repulsive to the average fastidious Venezuelan. Due to their extended families, most Venezuelans have all the company that they require. Venezuelans think that Westerners shower their love and affection on pets because they are unable to express their feelings for other people. They may be right.

TELECOMMUNICATIONS

Getting a Phone Line and Internet Access

A mobile (cellular) is a must in Venezuela as public phones are very rare and always broken. All you need to purchase a mobile is your passport and any service receipt (phone, electricity, etc). It is also quite common to buy a SIM card that will access local providers for your phone. There is also Internet access easily available though the phone line.

Mobile Phone Etiquette

In Venezuela, status is shown by having the latest and best models of mobile phone so people carry them in their belts. Venezuelans talk loudly in public places whether on the phone or not, so etiquette is comparatively relaxed.

EDUCATION

The Venezuelan national system of education is to some extent now analogous to the Cuban system. The government has implemented a new set of schools and universities called 'Misiones', naming them after Revolutionary heroes. Here

Even in a school playground, a sense of nationality is encouraged.

anyone can study for free. Critics claim that these schools are not regulated and that these centres accept only Chavez followers (they look for you in the politic party lists to get in). Christopher Columbus (Cristobal Colón) and the Spanish conquistadores are no longer seen as discoverers and founding fathers but as despoiling bandits. Into the pantheon of national heroes have been inducted the Cuban revolutionary giants José Martí, Che Guevara, of course Fidel Castro.

The ages of up to six are *preescolar*. Beyond that students study at *colegios* or *liceos* where there is a grade system up to the level of *bachillerato* at the age of 18. At each grade, a number of subjects are studied, all of which must be passed in order for the student to progress to the next grade. There are opportunities to re-sit failed examinations. Primary school has nine grades, followed by secondary/high school with two grades. At the end of the 9th grade, the student chooses between science and humanities subjects.

The vast majority of good *colegios* and *liceos* are private, although there is a law that is likely to be passed to ban private schools so they will all be public in the near future, in order for Chavez to be sure that they teach a socialist education. Fees must be paid, although the large number of Roman Catholic schools and colleges are moving towards either accepting more scholarship students or becoming free.

To gain entrance to schools or colleges in Venezuela, you must meet the entrance requirements, which vary from school to school. These may be copies of previous school records (transcribed into Spanish), medical records, a psychiatric test, birth certificate, proof of vaccinations, a letter of good conduct, photocopies of identity card (*cédula*) or passport and also possibly photos of the parents. Except for international schools, lessons are conducted in Spanish.

Education is seen as vital in Venezuela and the standard of private schools and colleges is generally high. Most expatriate families send their children to an international school, where there are clubs and activities for the children as well as parents' groups. These use the American K–12 system, and fees are among the most expensive.

School Holidays

School holidays are the Christmas break, from 17 December to 7 January, and the summer break, and 15 July until 6 October.

University degrees are known as *carreras* (careers). Each university offers a restricted range of subjects and its name may reflect the nature of the courses offered. Most *carreras* last four or five years divided by year or semester. Graduates are known as *licenciados*. For professional degrees, students continue into postgraduate education. Two years of unpaid work in the interior is part of the qualifying process for doctors.

Most universities are private, but the fees are not prohibitive. The best universities are public, but the entrance requirements are extremely stringent and only the cream of the candidates is accepted. The Universidad Central de Venezuela in Caracas is the best of this kind.

International Schools

There are a number of good private schools in the major cities for international students, with classes in English that generally follow the American educational programme. They often teach from pre-nursery to Grade 12, preparing students for university entrance, but with a wider remit. For

A group of young schoolgirls wait for the day's lessons to start. Education is valued in Venezuela and the standard of private schools and colleges is generally high.

example, the CIC school in Caracas claims to be a 'training camp for world citizenship'. The facilities are normally of a very high standard and include excellent sports facilities as well as programmes in fine arts, music, ICT, Latin American and Venezuelan history, sports and also community services with links with local charities. Most international schools have websites in Spanish and English.

MEDICAL SERVICES
Health and Hospitals

Once settled, look for the nearest *clínica* (private hospital). Those who can afford it go private by paying monthly for healthcare via companies such as Rescarven and Sanitas, where treatment and emergency care is provided in private centres in all major cities. Foreign insurance policies are a good idea, but may take longer to be accepted once in the *clínica* and you may need to pay upfront in cash or by credit card. The public hospitals are often short of basic equipment and have an unreliable ambulance service. It may also be difficult to find certain prescription drugs and it would be wise to bring as much as possible when coming to Venezuela. Medicines obtained through private services will be expensive.

Life expectancy for men and women is over 70 and the death rate is only four in one thousand. Persistent diseases such as malaria, yaws, the plague and Chagas' disease are all but eliminated. Venezuela now suffers from familiar medical woes of developed countries—heart disease, accidents and cancer. AIDS and other ailments of industrialised countries are the major causes of death.

Queues are terrible and resources are never sufficient. On the other hand, you can have any standard of healthcare that you care to pay for. Health insurance is essential and you may not be treated without either cash payment or proof of insurance. Check with your current medical insurance provider to see what coverage you will have in Venezuela, especially emergency expenses such as medical evacuation.

There are mixed public and private hospitals and private *clínicas*. It pays to know where to go, as you will be charged for both attention and medicine. Before learning this, I went to the nearest *clínica* in Caracas, discovering later that it was the most expensive one in the city. If your workplace does not have its own doctor, take the time to visit *clínicas* and have a check-up at your favourite one. Bear in mind that there are specialists in different areas in different *clínicas*, but services such as Rescarven or Sanitas will cover different treatments.

As always in Venezuela, it pays to have a second (and third) opinion. A friend developed a growth on his neck and went around half a dozen *clínicas*. The most extreme diagnosis was that an operation was needed at once. My friend accepted the medicine proffered by one doctor and the swelling went down in days.

This is also one time where you will need excellent Spanish (yours or someone else's) or a doctor with a good command of English, which is possible in most *clínicas*. During his treatment, the same friend had a CAT scan. Inside the machine, he admired in wonder the laser running over him until he noticed a small sign in English, "Do not under any circumstances look at the laser." The details of the procedure had not been explained to him or they had passed him by.

Misión Barrio Adentro

The cities are well provided with doctors and hospitals but the countryside has insufficient medical cover. This is ameliorated by a service called *barrio adentro* which provides medical services for *barrio* dwellers who cannot afford to go to a private clinic. Venezuela now has a large number of doctors from Cuba. *Barrio adentro* has provided new medical centres inside the *barrios* which are well-equipped. Many of the doctors and nurses are from Cuba and there have been claims that Cuban doctors provide socialist indoctrination along with medical care

Traditional medicine is practised by a very small number of healers (*curanderos*). This can involve all manner of superstitions, including the evil eye, in which a surprisingly large proportion of Latin Americans believe. A believer puts a child ill due to the evil eye to bed, taps the child on the stomach with a sprig of basil, makes a sign of the cross three times over the child and utters a magical incantation between the teeth. The spell is believed to be broken when the child urinates and the basil has shrivelled. Common ailments and accidents can be alleviated through incantations. For example, if someone is choking, hit them on the back and recite *La Oración de San Blas*:

> San Blas, San Blas,
> Mártir de Cristo,
> Que suba o que baje,
> Espina o huesito.

To have someone under your power, all you need to do is to go to their sleeping body at midnight on Saturday when the moon is right. Call their name three times and then capture their breath in a jar. Seal the jar with wax and bury it in an uninhabited spot.

Another method used by women to get their man is *El Cordón Hechizado*. The woman must first make the man tread with his bare left foot on an area she has spread with ash. She measures the foot from heel to big toe with a length of cord, which she keeps close to her breast for eight days. On the eighth day, she visits the *hechicera* (witch) who will make seven knots in the cord while muttering an incantation. If the woman then ties the cord to her left sleeve, she will have power over her victim unless he suspects he is under a spell, in which case its power is gone.

THE POLICE

The police in Venezuela. are rather frightening for a number of reasons. Not only do they not have a carefully crafted relationship with the community, they also appear to be a particularly crack division of the army. They are stern protectors of *La Patria* (the fatherland). They are not public servants and no one would dream of asking a policeman the time. They are not openly corrupt and do not stand at street corners taking bribes. Instead they stand at street corners and look menacing in the body armour and weaponry they sport. Tear-gas canisters, sub-machine guns, rifles, swords—they have the lot, and not just for show.

Policemen in Action

I once saw and followed a military helicopter to the centre of Caracas. A stream of policemen on motorbikes (armed, of course) followed it and gathered outside a building. Over a hundred fearsomely armed policemen lay in wait for the two armed robbers inside. Eventually the robbers ran out and were chased by the police without a shot being fired. This was a real life Keystone Cops chase that was at once hilarious and very frightening. On another occasion, I was walking down the street laden with shopping bags and listening to my Walkman, (although this is now an open invitation to being robbed). Three policemen on bikes drew up and pointed guns in my direction, somewhat interrupting my reverie. They approached a man who had been walking behind me and made him spread against the wall in classic fashion. I carried on with a heart rate possibly quicker than normal. If, like me, you have had little contact with guns, such experiences can be unnerving.

There are many allegations against the Venezuelan police of corruption and involvement in organised crime. They may also do little to prevent petty crimes such as theft, as the president has publicly downplayed the seriousness of minor criminal acts. For insurance claims, thefts need to be notified to the police who will write a report and give you a copy.

CRIME

Crime in Venezuela varies enormously depending on where you are. In the countryside, petty thefts and petty fraud is the bulk of what the visitor has to contend with. In the *barrios*, life is dreadfully cheap and people die over arguments concerning girlfriends or small business deals and can be murdered for a low price. This is a side of life that never needs to be seen by those settled in the country. Do avoid the *barrios*, those on the hills around Caracas are especially dangerous and contribute to Venezuela having one of the highest murder rates per capita in the world.

Outside the major cities, the other area of serious crime is the border area with Colombia, where drug trafficking, terrorism and kidnapping are more prevalent. In the cities, robbery and assaults can take place everywhere there are crowds and when you are standing still. To avoid robbery, keep on the move and avoid standing still in street traffic, elevators, on corners waiting for traffic lights, in the metro and so on. Gangs may surround a victim and use a choke hold to knock them unconscious. Randomly being held up at knife (or even gun) point is a hazard of city life in Venezuela and naturally you should give whatever is asked for. There may even be fake police checkpoints, where documents, money and valuables could be stolen. Serious crime takes place more frequently in holiday periods when drinking increases, and on public holidays when people leave their homes for the countryside, and also during public demonstrations.

In the cities, there are sporadic outbreaks of armed violence. Most people who have lived in a city have witnessed a shooting and possibly murder.

Despite government efforts, corruption is something you will have to contend with sooner or later. The greasing of palms occurs frequently and is usually optional but sometimes essential if you do not wish to wait an eternity. Once again, public servants see no difference between themselves and

Carjacking has been a problem in recent years and this explains why some motorists will not stop to help accident victims, in case it is a trap. Stolen cars are never traced and the crime is a relatively safe one for perpetrators unless the police catch them in the act, which will result in a shootout.

the post they occupy. They are authority, and what they say goes. In effect, their word is law. In my time in Venezuela, the highest officials of the DIEX (immigration department) were changed several times to eliminate the problem, without great success.

A crime that captures the imagination of the gossipmongers is kidnapping. Obviously it is the wealthy who are targeted and there is a lot of intrigue and whispers of conspiracies in these situations. 'Express kidnapping' is becoming more prevalent, where people are taken to ATMs to withdraw cash or forced to make purchases in shops.

MONEY MATTERS
Changing Money
It is best to change as much money as is feasible before entering Venezuela. Maiquetía Airport is an area of frequent

crime and even those who appear to be uniformed officials are involved in robberies, so attempting to change money at the airport is fraught with risk. Money can be exchanged at bureaus de change (*casa de cambio*), which are located near major hotels. Some banks also exchange money, although this has to be approved by the Commission for Administration of Foreign Currencies (CADIVI). There are fines and imprisonment in place for those who exchange money on the black market, and there is also the likelihood of being conned by being given fake notes, incorrect amounts and so on. Money can be withdrawn from some cash machines using Visa or Mastercard credit cards, but some do not and some may have no money to dispense. Some are rigged to copy card details, so check all credit cards transactions, especially if you have used a cash machine.

How to Open an Account
All you need is your passport and an address to open an account. Credit cards, debit cards and checks are available automatically. To open a bank account, go to the nearest office with your passport and any service receipt (phone, electricity) as proof of address (original and a photocopy) and some money of course.

SHOPPING
Upmarket Shopping
There are a number of ways to do your shopping in Venezuela. The most popular method in the cities is to visit one of the shopping malls that cater for all your shopping needs, from food to high fashion. Shops range from very stylish clothes shops full of local, American and European fashions to large supermarkets. There are food courts known as *ferias*, restaurants and cinemas. Caracas is particularly well represented, with South America's largest mall, El Centro Sambil, and other large malls dotted around the city. Smaller towns have commercial zones along their main streets or near public areas such as bus stations. Venezuela does not have a culture of haggling, but you can always try and ask for a discount (¡¡*Un decuentico por favor!!*).

Street Shopping

The street stalls (*buhoneros*) tend to sell poor quality products and are mainly located in dangerous areas and are also the major source of black market, and therefore illegal, goods.

Shopping from Home

While you can't have the supermarket deliver to your door, a number of things are normally delivered. When at home, you will find people buzzing your apartment and shouting, "*Zapatero! Zapatero!*" Do not be alarmed. Among the door-to-door services is the *zapatero* or cobbler. You can also get crates of beer or soft drinks delivered to your flat. It is essential that you have your bottled water delivered. The huge bottles, which you simply put on top of your frame-and-tap device, are very cheap. If you place a regular order, your empty bottles will be replaced by full ones automatically, although you do have to pay on the day.

What to Bring From Home

Clothing: Jeans, bermudas, shorts, baseball caps, beach clothing, towels, T-shirts (not Hawaiian please), short sleeve shirts, one sweater, sunglasses, sneakers, formal shoes and semi formal shoes and sandals (for home or beach only). Sometimes citizens have no water supply for days in a row so bring extra underwear and socks!

TRANSPORT
Buses

The small buses known as *carritos* used to be the easiest way to travel around, but are now quite risky as robberies are common. People take the metro or a line taxi instead, even going by foot is safer during the day. *Carritos* come in a variety of shapes and sizes, are colourful and highly decorated according to the driver's taste or lack of it, and are always full of salsa sounds. A bus fare will cost you between 1 and 1.5 bolívares.

Storefronts and cafes along a street in Caracas. Venezuelans place emphasis on their appearance and fashionable boutiques and large shopping malls will cater to all your shopping needs.

Coaches

Coaches come in two varieties. Basic coaches are just like larger *carritos* and you can expect a squeeze and to occasionally share your seat with a couple of chickens. Alternatively you can pay more for a luxury coach with air conditioning and curtains you cannot draw. Entertainment is provided by a TV screen probably showing a straight-to-video US film. For me, part of the fun of coach travel is to see the world rushing by.

To travel from city to city, you need to go to the *terminal de autobus*—anyone can direct you to this. In Caracas, the depot at Nuevo Circo should be avoided. Instead of Nuevo Circo, there are two new lines located near metro stations: Aeroexpresos and Rodavias de Venezuela. These services are comfortable, inexpensive, organised, fast and incredibly run on schedule most of the time. The terminals work like airports and also look somewhat like them. The downside is that the curtains are drawn, you are shown a movie and the bus remains in darkness for the whole trip. There are a couple of stops to allow passengers to get out and stretch their legs, buy something to eat or use public services.

There is only one train running in Venezuela, the line between Puerto Cabello and Barquisimeto. The trip is cheap but less than luxurious. On the Caracas Metro, you can buy tickets from the machines. Fares cost 250 bolívares for a maximum four-stop journey. The best bet is a *multiabono* ticket that will give you up to ten rides. If you are a student, you can get special *multiabono* tickets at a fraction of the normal cost. *Multiabono* tickets are also valid for use on the Metrobuses, which do have signposted stops. Service is regular although the buses get crowded at peak times and queues can become very long. Fare evasion is punished by on-the-spot fines.

Travel Etiquette

On public transport, people do not apologise when they tread on someone, but they do say "*disculpe*" before pushing past you and "*Ay! Perdón!*" whenever they bump into you.

It is the custom to squeeze on and queuing is not practised, requiring a fairly physical approach to be taken. There is usually a crush to get on, seats may be given up for women and the elderly. On the Underground, there are now exclusive carriages reserved for them; these are usually the first and last carriages coaches.

One of the more curious customs is that people who are seated will offer to put on their laps anything that is being carried by other passengers, including strangers. This is as much due to the Venezuelan fear of putting things on the floor, where they might get dirty and become unhygienic, as helping to relieve weight.

Taxis

Taxis from the airport should be booked in advance from a reputable hotel or arrange for a radio-dispatched taxi. There are frequent armed robberies in taxis, and many of these have official licensed taxi plates. Most respectable lines have some table of fares inside the cars, but it is still common to discuss the fare in advance. It is wise to agree on the fare before you get in and even wiser to get a Venezuelan to negotiate a fare for you. Tip if you want to.

DRIVING

Venezuelans like their driving fast and loose. Their style of driving is something you can get used to fairly quickly. Cars cut in and out of lanes endlessly and drivers don't wait for pedestrians or stop for anybody. This is not as dangerous as it sounds although whenever it rains, there are many accidents, as much due to old tyres as to the sudden inability to go bumper to bumper at high speeds. On coastal roads, even buses go fast and furiously, while on the narrow and winding hill roads there are many close calls. There are no pedestrian crossings so pedestrians have to rely on traffic lights or their own sense of judgement.

Many people actually buy their driving licence without taking the test, naughty but true. Your international licence is valid in Venezuela. Be careful in traffic lights when crossing since drivers may not stop since they are afraid to be robbed;

this is worse during the night. Night-time driving is also hazardous as road damage and repairs are not marked, except by a pile of rocks or an upright stick. There may also be cars driving without lights on. Child car seats and seatbelts are not required by law and, as a rule, aren't used. There are few inhibitions about driving after drinking alcohol, so some drivers are even more erratic!

Hiring a car and driver is the safest option if you can afford it. Drivers will also use their knowledge to avoid any potentially hazardous situations. Owning a car is the best option since renting is very expensive. Cars revalorise instead of depreciate, so you will always have more money at the end when selling it, as demands far outweighs supply.

Getting Around

The basic method of finding your way in Venezuela is by asking. The same principle works on buses, where you ask the driver if he is going to a certain place. Buses have the final destination marked on the front. Catching a bus can be confusing at spots where there are various groups of people waiting. Again, asking is the key. The trial-and-error approach requires patience and an ability to memorise details is important.

In cities, most people live in large buildings that have their names marked on them and the flats are, of course, clearly numbered. In smaller towns, once you are in the right area, you will easily find people who can help you.

VISAS

To enter Venezuela, a valid passport and a visa or tourist card are required. Tourist cards are given out on flights to Venezuela for anyone staying less than 90 days. Your visa needs to have at least six months validity and be in good condition, or you risk being sent back or delayed. Venezuelan citizens are required to travel with Venezuelan passports, so anyone holding dual nationality should take both passports.

To obtain a visa, you need your passport (conditions given above), two recent colour photograhs (2" x 2"), a visa application form and a money order payable to The Embassy of Venezuela ($30 for tourist and transit visas and $60 for other visas).

A Tourist Visa can be used to make contact with Venezuelan businesses and businesspeople, but not for remunerative activities. You must provide a document to prove you have an address in a country outside Venezuelan (to show you are not an immigrant), a letter of reference from your bank (stating your solvency and date of opening your account), a letter of reference from your employer (stating your current position and date of employment) and an SAE.

A Business Visitor Visa requires a company letter on headed paper that stipulates your position, the purpose of your trip, the name and address of the person you will contact in Venezuela, the length of stay in Venezuela and the name of the company who will pay for expenses. Also required is a photocopy of the round trip or itinerary and documents that prove that you own your company (if applicable). This visa is valid for one year with multiple entries. On each entry, the stay in the country may last up to 180 days.

For an Investor Visitor Visa, you will need to show a document that proves that you have had an investment accepted by the appropriate official agencies in Venezuela. The visa is valid for three years and permits an unlimited stay in the country. The visa may be extended for two years and residency applied for after that.

An Entrepreneur/Industrialist Visa is for those who have established branch offices in Venezuela and who enter the country on associated business matters. You need a visa application addressed to the Consular Section of the Venezuelan Embassy stating the purpose of travel and the contacts to be made in the country. A letter from the Chamber of Commerce is also required, or the relevant mercantile registry number. The visa is valid for two years and allows multiple entries and stays of up to four months.

The Venezuelan Family Relation Visa is for the spouse of a Venezuelan citizen (if the marriage was overseas and registered with the Venezuelan Consulate), dependents under 18 and parents or parents-in-law. The marriage certificate certified by the Venezuelan Consulate must be produced. The visa allows unlimited stay of up to one year and multiple entries. An extension can be applied for.

A Student Visitor Visa is valid for professional or technical courses and undergraduate or graduate courses at any college or university. An application by the institution supporting the student is required (detailing the funds available to the student), along with an admission letter from the educational institution in Venezuela. Academic degree certificates or attestations also need to be shown. The visa allows unlimited stay of up to one year and multiple entries. An extension can be applied for. Extensions are available if the course continues beyond a year.

For a Religious Visitor Visa, a written request from the head of the religious order is required, as it must be approved by the Ministry of the Interior and Justice. The religion, ritual or any other religious activity to be carried out must be detailed, along with the length of stay, address in Venezuela, date of entry, all the applicant's names, place and date of birth and a passport photocopy. The visa allows unlimited stay of up to one year and multiple entries. An extension of one more year can be applied for.

A Work Permit must also be approved by the Ministry of the Interior and Justice, with the consent of the Ministry of Labour. The company employing the individual must apply to the aforementioned ministries. The applicant must prove suitability for the post by presenting academic degrees and evidence of relevant work experience. The Consular Section of the Venezuelan Embassy must receive prior authorisation from the National Office of Identification and Foreign Population Affairs (Oficina Nacional de Identificación y Extranjería ONI -DEX). The visa allows unlimited stay of up to one year and multiple entries.

MAKING A MEAL OF IT

CHAPTER 6

'Love is as important as food, but it does not nourish.'
—Gabriel Garcia Marquez

YOU MAY WELL FIND YOURSELF faced with a major change in your eating habits. On entering the country, leave any notion of healthy eating at customs. Repeat to yourself, "There is nothing wrong with fried food," until you believe it. Venezuelan cuisine reflects wider Venezuelan society in that its defining characteristic is a tendency towards exaggeration. Venezuelans love to eat and to eat plenty. Their food is a varied cuisine with many influences, but retains a flavour all its own. As the geography of the country is highly diverse, there is an abundance of regional specialities.

If there is an overall tendency, it is to high cholesterol food cooked with plenty of oil. Meat plays a central and vital role in Venezuelan cuisine and provides the centrepiece of any meal, surrounded by a tempting array of carefully prepared vegetables, beans figuring prominently. Venezuelan desserts are similarly self-indulgent. They are always sweet, always tempting and usually irresistible, with obvious French influences. In Venezuela, you will eat purely for enjoyment— count those calories and be doomed!

Venezuelans subscribe to a traditional system of a hearty breakfast, a large cooked lunch and a slightly smaller dinner. However, they have also embraced the North American taste for snacks and many kiosks (*kioskos*) and stores stock potato chips, chocolates and biscuits. Coffee is also consumed frequently as in the United States. Venezuelan hospitality is renowned and extends to offering guests something to eat and drink.

The country's weather makes outdoor eating possible almost all year round. The magnificent climate also yields bumper harvests of exotic fruits, seasonal vegetables and livestock. The Caribbean provides the seafood, the llanos produces fine beef, and from tropical Amazonas come fried ants and piranha for the brave!

AREPAS: VENEZUELA'S STAPLE

Arepas are thick discs made from *harina pan* (pre-cooked cornmeal), fried in a pan or cooked on a hot plate. These unappetising-looking objects are Venezuela's staple food. They are eaten at all times of the day and even accompany main meals in a diminutive form. You either love or hate—usually hate—them at first bite but they will grow on you. At first the thick dough, although well cooked, is heavy on the stomach and you may feel incapable of tucking into them with anything other than barely concealed loathing. However, it is well worth the initial acclimatising period as they are so fundamental to Venezuelans: enjoying them represents an easy way of gaining the respect of the locals.

The good news about *arepas* is that they can have a variety of fillings, from plain cheese to weird and wonderful combinations. This range includes: white cheese (*queso de mano*)—soft and squeaky but tasty—grated yellow cheese (*queso amarillo*), tuna salad (*ensalada de atún*), devilled ham (*diabolitos*), chicken and avocado (*reina pepiada*), octopus (*pulpo*), baby shark (*cazón*), scrambled egg with onions and tomato (*perico*), shredded beef (*carne mechada*) and ham and cheese (*jamón y queso*). In fact, ham and cheese is the favourite Venezuelan combination, from *arepas* to *empanadas* (deep-fried elongated pasties or turnovers), sandwiches (hot and cold) and the semi-sweet *cachapas*, which resemble pancakes.

THE NATIONAL DISH: PABELLON CRIOLLO

This makes a hearty meal and features some of Venezuela's most typical foods. Black beans (*caraotas negras*) are served with two strips of fried ripe plantain (*plátanos fritos*), a fried egg and rice, all topped with grated white cheese and *carne mechada*, which is carefully prepared. The meat is boiled and then fried with a variety of vegetables and condiments, including capsicum peppers, tomatoes, onion, garlic, Worcestershire sauce (a Venezuelan favourite), cumin, salt and pepper, and possibly soy sauce and tomato ketchup!

MEALS

One of the mysteries of this country is that you will find yourself eating much larger quantities of food than before but losing weight. The only explanation that comes to mind is that your body has to expend more energy than normal to keep itself cool, although a friend from Florida suggested that the climate was the same as he was used to, and the difference was in the quality of the food. Perhaps visiting Venezuela should be marketed as the world's most pleasant way to lose weight!

Breakfast is cooked and features *arepas* with *perico* (eggs, tomato and onion, fried together) or cheese and ham. Venezuelans drink milky coffee as well as fruit juice. Hot chocolate is another breakfast favourite. Slices of cake are commonly served. Cereals or slices of toast are regarded as unsubstantial, although American brands are readily obtained.

Lunch, the main meal of the day, is satisfyingly filling. Sandwiches are a modern alternative, although Venezuelans are generally loath to break with proud tradition and believe deeply in the necessity of large and indulgent lunches. Office workers will either step out for lunch or bring something they can microwave. Everything stops for lunch and offices are often filled with the rich odours of food that workers eat at their desks.

Dinner is another cooked meal similar in complexity to lunch although usually smaller. If you are not very hungry, an *arepa* or two will suffice!

Meal Times

Meal times are familiar to Westerners. Breakfast is eaten at any time between 5:00 and 8:00 am. A 7:00 am start to the working day isn't unusual. Lunch is at noon. Dinner is eaten at about 6:00 pm.

DAILY FARE

Some of the most popular, and most Venezuelan, dishes are given below. Normal accompaniments to a meal are beans (red kidney beans, black beans) or lentils, carefully prepared with a wide variety of typical Venezuelan ingredients. A popular sauce in Venezuelan homes is *salsa rosada*, a blend of ketchup and mayonnaise. It sounds strange but quickly grows on you.

Pernil de Cochino

Pernil de cochino is ham hock, a popular lunch or dinner food for Venezuelans. It is marinated overnight in lemon and *adobo*, a seasoning that can be bought ready-mixed. It is cooked for all of five hours and served with a hot sauce that features orange juice, cloves, Worcestershire sauce and soy sauce, among other ingredients. It is eaten with rice or mashed potato (*puré de papa*).

Asado

Asado is a whole round of beef, fried and then boiled until it is tender. It is stuffed with raisins, capers, ham and olives and boiled with other ingredients, including lime juice. The result is a tender and tasty meat dish, which is cut into slices before being served. This is a typical *caraqueño* (from Caracas) dish.

Bifstek a Caballo

Steak served with fried eggs! The steak is fried with onion, garlic, black pepper and Worcestershire sauce. A delightful way to head for an early grave!

Cachapas

A heavy corn pancake, folded and served with a variety of fillings, including white cheese (*queso de mano*), ham and bacon. *Cachapas* are a pleasing combination of both savoury and sweet flavours.

Chuletas Ahumadas

Smoked pork chops can readily be bought at any supermarket and are usually fried with onions. Depending on whether

Cachapas, a Venezuelan pancake. *Sabroso!*

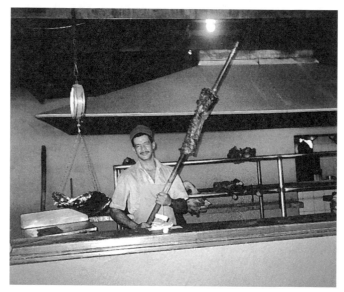

Venezuela's answer to the kebab, *carne en vara* (meat roasted on a pole).

it is served with beer or orange juice, this meal assumes a different and distinctive slant.

Steak
Venezuelans are justly proud of the quality of their steak, which rivals the more renowned Argentinean beef in quality. As it comes from the vast plains, it is plentiful and sold at a price that must be taken advantage of. You might easily eat enough to last you the rest of your life! Steak always occupies pride of place on any restaurant menu.

And the Vegetables?
The large amounts of meat consumed do not preclude vegetarianism, although this would be a bit like being a teetotaller at Jack Daniel's distillery. Beans, salads and fruit juices are the main way in which Venezuelans give a nod to foods that don't walk or fly. Salads are varied and do not stint on the calories.

The most basic Venezuelan salad is lettuce, cucumber, tomato and onion, with a sharp vinaigrette. Tuna salad (*ensalada de atún*) is the same but with the addition of chunks of tuna, lime juice and salt. Other salads are made with carrots and potatoes with mayonnaise and American mustard, or potato and cabbage with mayonnaise, which is similar to coleslaw. Caesar salad is a restaurant staple.

LA PARILLA

Barbecues perform just as vital a social function here as elsewhere and are just as delicious. The centrepiece of the barbecue is—you guessed it—steak. It is served on a wooden slab furnished with a businesslike meat knife, with at least two types of sausage: the more familiar *chorizo* and *morcilla*, the heavy but near irresistible blood sausage. You will find the ubiquitous tomato, lettuce and onion salad. Add to this that subtle root vegetable, cassava (*yuca*), and you could ignore the steak and still leave full.

SEAFOOD

Seafood is essential to Venezuelans, fried fish being particularly cherished. Fish is usually eaten with rice, *yuca* and salad. All parts are eaten (except bones)—head and the

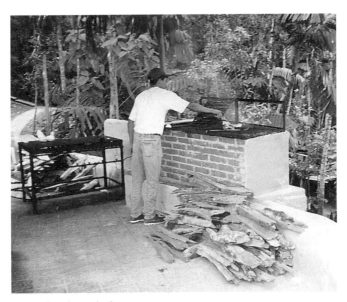

Venezuelans love a barbecue.

eyes too, if they take your fancy. Popular varieties are *bacalao* (cod), *pargo* (red snapper), *mero* (grouper) and *merluza* (hake). Unless you live in the interior of the country, take advantage of the wide range of *mariscos* (seafood). Happily, *pulpo* (octopus), *calamare* (squid) and *camarones* (shrimps) can all be found in one dish, *tierra y mar*, so named as it combines the best of land and sea. *Consomé de chipi-chipi* (small clams) is a delightful broth flavoured with garlic and lime.

PASAPALOS

No Venezuelan party would be worth its name without a mouth-watering range of *pasapalos*. These are similar to hors d'oeuvres and can be eaten as snacks or as an accompaniment to drinks, their single identifying feature being that they can be eaten without a plate, either in the hand or on a stick.

Tequeños, a Venezuelan favourite, is named after the city of Los Teques, outside Caracas. They are long rolls of pastry filled with hot cheese. Alternatively they can be filled with chocolate and consumed with a cup of hot chocolate. When eaten at parties, they are usually served upright in a dish and taken by the guest with a pair of tongs and then placed in a serviette. Be careful not to take one too quickly or they may all fall out, creating amusement and embarrassment in equal shares.

Plantains can be sliced thinly, fried and salted and sold as *tostones*. They can also be cut more thickly, pressed flat and fried. *Bolitas de carne* are small round nibbles of fried pork or beef. They are formed by mixing the meat with the usual Venezuelan ingredients (peppers, onion, garlic, Worcestershire sauce, soy sauce, etc) and are irresistible. Thin strips of nearly raw meat are also served; they are absolutely exquisite but be careful—it is easy to eat too many.

VENEZUELAN DESSERTS

A good dessert is the essential complement to a good meal; dinner guests often bring it with them. All sorts of sugary delights are concocted and amazing cakes baked, from the familiar carrot cake and cheesecake to *torta de guanábana* (soursop cake) and *torta de plátano* (plantain cake). Some of Venezuela's specialities are given below.

- *Bienmesabe*: Venezuela's speciality, an exquisite soft, sweet cake made from egg yolk, coconut, salt, sugar and cognac. With your first bite you will understand why it is called 'tastes good to me'.
- *Suspiros* (breaths): Sweets light enough to deserve the name made from egg whites, sugar, lime juice and grated rind, vanilla and cream.
- *Rosquitas*: Fried rings of *harina pan* sprinkled with sugar and spices.

DRINKS

In a country as hot as Venezuela, liquid refreshments need to be taken in quantity and often. Luckily Venezuelans are more than aware of this and a cold glass of something (with ice, even in beer!) is no more than a street corner or jingling cart away. Whatever your taste, you will find something to slake your thirst, for a minute or two at least!

Casual drinking in Venezuela happens at parties, barbecues and at friends' houses. If you go into a bar, you may not be allowed to drink beer at the counter but asked to take a table. This often involves buying a bottle of whisky, unnecessary if you want a few quiet drinks with friends. Going into a Venezuelan restaurant and merely ordering beer can redress this untenable situation. The waiters, indifferent at the best of times, won't mind.

Soft drinks are readily available in all the flavours you could hope for, and more! Cola is the exception. Years ago, Pepsi was the first large company to break into the market and until very recently, it was quite difficult to find Coca-Cola, especially in supermarkets. Within the last year or so, the situation has been reversed and Coca-Cola is now plentiful, at the expense of its competitor. Cherry Coke remains sadly unavailable though.

Venezuela has its own brand of soft drinks which are, of course, sweet, but not too much so for most tastes. Flavours worth trying are pineapple and grape.

Water should always be drunk from the bottle, whether in a restaurant or from the giant bottles delivered weekly to your home. When asking for mineral water, be sure to specify if you want it fizzy (*con gas*) or still (*sin gas*).

When it comes to beer, the giant corporation Polar has no equal in the country. They produce the light and excellent pils Polar, the stronger lager Solera and the stout Bock. Nacional, Regional and Cardenal provide some competition, all much less popular than the Polar brews. Polar even has its own shop where you can buy Polar beach towels, mugs, pencils, sportswear and other essentials, all featuring the distinctive cute bear logo.

A POLAR BEER PLEASE

Supermarkets also stock a range of American beers, which Venezuelans will not be best pleased to see you drinking as they are fiercely proud of the quality of Polar. Polar also makes Maltín Polar, a very popular strongly malted soft drink.

Whisky is the drink of choice at parties and all festive occasions, as the large number of billboards advertising the best scotch testify. It is drunk with ice and often with Coca-Cola, irrespective of the quality of the scotch. It is also the reason why the best parties are only over when the guests have lost consciousness. Rum is also popular, particularly the brand Pampero, but is not perceived as classy (unlike whisky). Wine is rarely drunk, except with meals.

As in any country that values the quality of its coffee, it is usually served in cups that appear to have been designed to quench the thirst of a sparrow. It is often drunk black, but you can get it with steamed milk.

You may find some coffee vocabulary handy. You can have it *pequeño* (small) or *grande* (big). You can drink it *marron* (with a little milk), *marroncito* (with even less milk), *con leche* (with milk) or *negro* (black). For most Westerners, *con leche grande* is the norm. Capuccinos are in the irresistibly rich Venezuelan style, covered in a sea of real whipped cream and sprinkled liberally with cinnamon.

Coffee is drunk throughout the day, whenever the opportunity presents itself. If you want tea, it is readily available, although kept low profile. Iced tea is popular, drunk with plenty of sugar.

Hot chocolate is drunk often, especially in the morning, when coffee in the form of *con leche* is also popular. Drinking chocolate can be bought in powdered form or in potent slabs, which must be melted and blended with milk. Hot chocolate with cinnamon is a common variety.

Oat-based drinks are also popular. They are bought in tubs and mixed with ice and milk in a blender. Flavours are limited to vanilla, strawberry and chocolate.

Refreshing drinks include *papelón con limón* (cane sugar with lime) served in small plastic cups from small metal carts, announced with the cry, *"papelón con limón, papelón con limón"*—music to the ears! *Limonada frappe* is a lemon drink sunk deep in crushed ice, very cold, very refreshing.

Fruit Juices

Fruit juices are the very best feature of Venezuelan drinks, although opinion is divided on whether they are more refreshing than an ice-cold beer. There are even small shops that serve nothing but fruit juices.

You have three basic varieties—*jugos*, *batidos* and *merengadas*. *Jugos* are nothing more than the fruit liquidised with some sugar. *Batidos* feature crushed ice, whereas *merengadas* (milkshakes) are *batidos* but with the simple addition of milk.

Expect to find strawberries (*fresa*), pineapples (*piña*), apple (*manzana*), guava (*guayaba*) served with cinnamon in a *merengada*, papaya (*lechosa*), mango, watermelon (*patilla*), tamarind (*tamarindo*) and passion fruit (*parchita*). Invest in a blender, you won't regret it. From personal experience, *lechosa* is not recommended as the giant pale-green papaya produces a watery and nearly tasteless juice, unless made by experts.

> Freshly squeezed orange juice can be bought at roadside carts, although the taste of Venezuelan oranges may be somewhat sharper than you are used to.

Regional Drinks

Chicha is available in cartons in the city but is only really worth drinking in the country, preferably in the llanos, where it is made to perfection. With the severe heat of that region, you will be able to drink almost as much as you want, usually about your own body weight. It is a mixture of ground rice, salt, condensed milk, sugar, vanilla and ice. It is incredibly satisfying in the scorching heat of the plains.

Guarapita is a venomous mixture of fruit juices (commonly passion fruit) and *aguardiente*, which is a clear cane liquor, Venezuelan firewater! Be warned, it can be deceptively gentle on the palate. Don't end up like I did, chasing yelping hounds around dusty, deserted midnight villages.

Cocada is a liquidised mix of coconut, ice, milk, sugar and *canela* (cinnamon) and tastes just as good as it sounds.

Ponche crema is a sweet, smooth and creamy liquor that brings to mind both eggnog and Bailey's Irish Cream. Concocted from eggs, lime, condensed milk, evaporated milk, bitters and brandy or rum, it is a drink that Venezuelans are proud of and is celebrated in the sports commentators' "*suave y sabroso, dulce y cremoso, ponche!*" (*Ponche* also means 'out' in baseball parlance.)

WHERE TO EAT

There are a very wide variety of restaurants in Venezuela's cities. You can eat cheap and cheerfully, generally in Italian restaurants or in the ever-popular and typically Venezuelan *pollo en brasas* (grilled chicken) restaurants.

Many people are of the opinion that Venezuelan food is as hot as Latin blood is said to be. This is most definitely not the case. In Venezuelan restaurants, you will find on the table two silver bowls. One contains a thin red liquid and the other a thicker green sauce. The red liquid is made from chillies and is called *salsa picante* or just *picante*. Be careful as the red stuff has real chilli powder. The green stuff is a watery version of *guasacaca*, an avocado-based sauce which, at its best, is without parallel among all the sauces of the world. It is essential with *pollo en brasas*.

Also on the table you will find either a basket of cut bread or *arepitas*, which you slice open and fill with butter, or throw to the dogs, according to taste!

Venezuelan eating customs only depart from what you are used to in a few ways. This is still a macho country so men will probably insist on ordering and paying for their female companions. In Venezuela, napkins or serviettes are used frequently. As mentioned, bread or *arepas* are often served with the meal, and it is a major *faux pas* to use this to mop up gravy on your plate. Plates are not cleaned at all, although bread can be dipped into sauce during the meal.

In the cheaper Italian restaurants, the pasta is plentiful and the servings are large. *Pasticho* (lasagne) is always hearty and filling for the right price. Going upmarket, the finest of Venezuela's Italian restaurants are among the costliest in the country. The well-balanced, olive-oil rich food won't give you a coronary but the bill might!

What to Eat in Caracas

In Caracas, you can choose from a dizzying range that can't fail to whet the appetite—Spanish, Swiss, German, Hungarian, Japanese, Peruvian, Lebanese, Italian, French, Argentinean steak houses, ornate Chinese restaurants, fast food restaurants, and a couple of 'English' pubs. Caracas even boasts the self-advertised 'only Thai restaurant in South America'! The food is of the standard you pay for, although the local restaurants provide excellent fare at reasonable rates.

The restaurants themselves revel in the general Venezuelan showiness, which reveals itself in the life-size model dragons, giant painted Indian heads, fake Roman columns and theme restaurants, such as the one in Caracas seemingly set amidst a tropical jungle, complete with colourful, chattering parrots.

Shopping malls usually have *ferias* (food courts) which have been heavily infiltrated by foreign foods. Baskin Robbins, donut emporiums, pizza houses, Mexican fast food joints and the inevitable burger big boys are all present. If you want something in a bun, there's always McDonald's and Burger King, no different from those at home, unless you are a connoisseur. McDonald's in particular attracts the young, trendy and well-heeled. Prices are high by Venezuelan standards. There is also the Venezuelan alternative, Tropiburger, which has a reputation for being cheap and lacking in quality. Kentucky Fried Chicken outlets are spreading rapidly, news you will greet with joy or dismay. The Colonel's secret recipe may be intact, but Arturo's provides a fine alternative for crunchy deep-fried chicken aficionados.

For those Venezuelans who—God forbid!—missed breakfast or who are feeling a little peckish, the *panaderia* is the place to go. Running lunches are also eaten there. At lunchtime, you will find the counter crowded with workers enjoying a quick snack, napkin-wrapped pastry in one hand and tiny coffee in the other. *Panaderias* are bakeries-cum-mini cafeterias where you can munch on hot ham-and-cheese-filled *pasteles* while you sip your thimbleful of coffee. *Empanadas* are a greasy favourite, filled with ham and cheese, cheese, chicken, shark or minced meat. Venezuela's best *empanadas* are available at a *kiosko* in the coach park at Choroní, an unforgettable mix of chicken and coriander.

A wide variety of pastries, often filled with a gooey version of French crème patisserie, is also available. Others ooze with rich and sticky tamarind, definitely an acquired taste for most Westerners. Pizzas and *canillas* (short French sticks) are popular and can be bought with a variety of fillings; try *queso y jamón serrano*, said to be the world's finest ham. Hot rolls and croissants are also popular, as are the similar *cachitos de jamón*. Pastries filled with chocolate are delicious but extremely sweet.

EATING IN THE STREET

You probably already have a good idea of the strength of your stomach. Some people take the opportunity to indulge in roadside barbecues and the multitudinous burger carts—experiencing local fare is the whole point of being in another country. Those burgers are fabulous cholesterol bombs. The only disappointing part is the thin, nondescript burger. However, sat atop it is a fried egg, one or more large slices of avocado, two bacon slices, cheese, tiny crunchy potato chips and your choice of relish, from watery *guasacaca*, *salsa picante*, ketchup and mayonnaise. They are delicious. Less tasty but equally prevalent are hot dogs (*perros calientes*) sold from similar carts.

Churros are available at small roadside stalls. A *churro* machine produces long, serrated sweet lengths. They can be sprinkled with sugar or dunked in chocolate sauce. Fattening but well worth trying.

Ice creams and lollies can be bought from the little *Tio Rico* carts, preceded everywhere by the jingling of their bells. Venezuelan ice creams are the equal of any in the world and are cheap enough for you to indulge yourself whenever you like. Remember Pavlov's dogs and prepare to be conditioned! *Chupes* are the ice pops you get in little plastic sacs; they are tempting, especially after sport, but can be hazardous due to being made with low-quality water. Stomach bugs can easily be picked up from them.

> Snacks can be bought from roadside kiosks, as can cold drinks, which are kept in a metal icebox.

SHOPPING FOR FOOD

You can buy food at supermarkets or street markets, with no real difference in quality, although supermarkets tend to be more expensive. Supermarket displays will be familiar, but be prepared for the occasional unusual sight, skinned hares at the meat counter for example. In the tropics, food is harder to preserve and the quality of fruit and vegetables

You'll never go short of delicious fruits in Venezuela.

won't be up to the standards Westerners take for granted. You may often have to sift through over-ripe produce in order to find something edible. You also need to be careful with meat for the same reason. The heat means that smells are heightened, which isn't always pleasant. In a *panaderia*, I heard an American child asking loudly, "Mummy, why does it smell bad in here?"

Organisation is also lax and you may find that on some days something, sugar for example, just isn't available. Have a good look around at the prices, which, aside from changing more rapidly than at home, may mean that you will be better off eating more steak than chicken! Good prices can also be found at the membership wholesalers, such as Macro. Join through a friend.

In the bigger cities, delicatessens are common and it is here that you will find the largest range of familiar produce, if you are pining for anything from home. As in supermarkets, the high import prices might cool your enthusiasm. Britons desperate for Marmite will have to have it sent, or paddle their way through the swamps of the Orinoco delta to neighbouring Guyana. A couple of supermarkets rival North American ones for the lavish range of products on offer.

Small street markets are fun places to look for fruit and vegetables. When buying *yuca* (cassava) or avocados, always ask the vendor to cut them and show you the inside, to ensure fresh produce.

REGIONAL SPECIALITIES
The Llanos

Travelling through the great, flat sweeping plains of Venezuela, you see numerous thin, mournful-looking cattle wandering through the scrub. Many ranches own fatter animals that produce high-quality meat. A speciality of the region is almost-raw beef served in thinly cut strips—extremely tender and succulent.

Piranhas thrive in the wide, slow-moving Amazonian pools. They can easily be caught with a piece of meat on a line, tossed overboard from a small launch. They are thin and bony fish that offer only a small quantity of flesh. This doesn't detract from their value as a trump card in the 'strange things I've eaten' stakes.

Las Amazonas

While walking around your local supermarket, you may wonder what those flat white discs are for. This is *casabe* and it can be found all over Venezuela, although it originates from the Amazonas. It is eaten like a crisp, as a somewhat dry accompaniment to meals. It is formed by grating cassava, then pressing it to dry it, before finally cooking it on an instrument of native design called an *abudare*. Unfortunately it is far less interesting than the steaming tropics it comes from.

The Coast

Sancocho is a rich soup, usually of fish and other seafoods, featuring cassava, yam and plantain, sprinkled over with chopped coriander leaves. You squeeze quartered limes onto it. Be careful: lime juice in strong daylight can burn and leave a mark on skin that can take weeks to disappear.

Los Andes

Trucha (trout) is an Andean speciality. In the Andean town of Mérida, you can find *la pica Andina de Mérida*, a vegetable soup, as well as rainbow trout of the finest quality.

While waiting for your flight, try the mysterious 'Airport Cake', which never seems to be available. Watch carefully to see if the waiter sniggers when you order it. Mérida is also home to Helados Coromoto, a shop that stocks the strangest ice cream flavours in the world. The flavours change according to the eccentric imagination of owner Manuel Oliviera. Choose from among shrimp, tuna, fried pork and *pabellon criollo*, if you dare!

Coro

From the town famed for its breathtaking sand dunes comes *Chivo en coco*—goat cooked in coconut. *Sopas de morrocoy* (turtle soup) and *pastel de morrocoy* (turtle pie) are also regional specialities, although feasting on an endangered species may leave you with more than a full sensation in your stomach, especially if you ate the last one!

Cumana

The local speciality is *empanadas de cazon*. They are flavoursome but bitty and prone to containing the odd piece of shark cartilage.

Unusual Foods

- *Sopas de Mondongo*
  Soup featuring chunks of cow's stomach, which will weigh
  heavily in your own belly. Eat it only if you intend to dine out
  on the experience. On second thoughts, you had better save
  the story until after dinner...

- Lizard
  When ordering *sancocho* (soup, usually using fish), make sure
  you know exactly what type of *sancocho* it is, as *lagarto* (lizard)
  is an occasional variation.

- *Barbecued Intestine*
  Curly crispy chunks, quite delicious. As with *sopas de
  mondongo*, this is not available everywhere.

- *Hormigas Culonas*
  Ants with large abdomens, fried alive until crunchy.
  Unfortunately they have a taste that is negligible and so defies
  description.

- *Capybara*
  Capybara is eaten at Easter as it has cunningly been classified
  as a fish: it spends a fair part of its time in water. Catholics,
  of course, can't eat meat at Easter. It is dried and salted, then
  shredded and cooked in the same way fish is for Easter. It is a
  dry meat, not to everyone's taste.

SEASONAL FOOD

Hallacas, a Venezuelan speciality insanely eaten only at
Christmas, are one of the reasons the festive season is so
eagerly awaited. Oblong packets wrapped in palm leaves and
bound in string, *hallacas* are made by stewing a number of
ingredients, principally pork, beef and chicken, with olives,
capers and raisins, wrapping them in cornflour dough, then
boiling for two or more hours. Come Christmas, you will
doubtless be invited to try them at a friend's house. They can
also be bought on the street, although usually in the smaller
form of *hallacitas*. *Bolitas* are like *hallacas* but smaller, spicier
and cooked without meat.

Pan de jamón is another Christmas food that you really
should try, although it can be bought all year round. As the

name suggests, it features ham in bread as well as olives, raisins and capers.

Ensalada de Gallina is the traditional Christmas salad. *Gallinas* are a variety of hen said to have more flavour than other chickens. For this recipe, chicken breast is boiled with onion, coriander, cumin and salt. This is then shredded and served with peas, potatoes, white asparagus, apples and carrots. The dressing includes mustard, olive oil, mayonnaise, salt and sugar. It is rich and gives a wonderful contrast of consistency. It is also surprisingly filling for a salad.

WHAT TO BEWARE

Lettuce in Venezuela is believed to be covered with malignant microbes. In restaurants, it is not to be trusted, so do your utmost to resist the Caesar salads drowning in cream and smothered with Parmesan cheese! Most people go down at least once with enteritis; a two- or three-day spell in bed is not uncommon. For the main part, common sense is all you need to exercise. As a rule of thumb, the cheaper the joint the higher the danger, so avoid the very cheapest places.

Buen provecho!

ENJOYING THE CULTURE

CHAPTER 7

'Chess is a useful and honest game,
indispensable in the education of the young.'
—Símon Bolívar

Venezuelans adore their leisure time and are proud of their reputation for knowing how to enjoy themselves. In leisure, as in all other walks of life, traditional pursuits coexist with the modern. There are a great variety of ways to enjoy the weekend or the frequent and welcome public holidays. Whether alone, with friends or within a group or organisation, there are myriad ways to enjoy yourself in Venezuela. Naturally, the spectrum of possibilities is wider in the cities, and the countryside has a stronger representation of traditional Venezuelan activities.

SPORTS

Most sports have a following in Venezuela and places for practice; it is only for the more expensive hobbies that you might have any difficulty in fulfilling your needs. Small baseball courts and five-a-side football courts can be seen all over the country, in fact wherever there is a patch of spare ground. Sports are more participatory events than spectator ones in this country, with the exception of baseball, which is played often but also attracts a large (not to say fanatical) live and television audience. Dusty diamonds are also familiar sites in Venezuela's towns.

Baseball

Given the cultural dominance of the United States, the Venezuelan national sport is unsurprisingly baseball, at which

GRANDMA!

the Venezuelans do well, and sometimes excel. They send their fair share of players to the American major league, such as the 'big cat' Andrés Galarraga, Luis Sojo, Omar Vizquel, Luis Aparicio (the first Venezuelan to become an American Hall of Famer), David Concepción and Antonio Armas. These players are revered in their home country, where they often return to play in the Venezuelan league, which is possible as this is a winter league running from October to February. Some US up-and-coming stars also play in the Venezuelan league, which attracts a loyal following, both in the stadiums and for telecasts of games. Baseball is the arena in which the rivalries between different cities are played out and no other sport even comes close in this department.

Venezuelan baseball teams include the Leones de Caracas, the Magallanes of Valencia, the Zulia Eagles, the Aragua tigers and the Lara Cardinals. The biggest match is always the Leones against the Magallanes of Valencia, as the two big rivals were both originally from Caracas. See a game and burn your backside on the bleachers while guzzling yourself senseless on Polar. The crucial games towards the end of the season are almost impossible to get tickets for, such is the demand. Earlier games are extremely cheap. Baseball is a great way to improve your Spanish, as, if you are a fan, half the vocabulary you already know and the other half is entirely predictable.

Basketball

Basketball is coming up hard on the heels of baseball and courts are springing up in all localities. It is less popular as a spectator sport and a sell-out is rare in the stadiums. Both the local Venezuelan games and the NBA games from the United States are telecast, and there are strong financial backers who want to make this sport a success in the country, if only for the sponsorship opportunities. Basketball clothing is very popular among the young and American basketball heroes are also revered in Venezuela, as well as Venezuelan stars like Carl Herrera. Foreign stars play in the Venezuelan League of Professional Baseball and the national team has gone from strength to strength, winning the South American title in 1992 and beating the USA in the Americas Cup in 1997.

Boxing

Boxing has also grown in popularity as Venezuelan pugilists have followed in the steps of Carlos 'Morocho' Hernández, Venezuela's first title winner in 1965. There have been numerous titles since, most notably in the Olympics.

Football

In media terms, the game of the continent, football, is an irrelevance and the national team has been embarrassingly weak and subjected to routine humiliations such as the 7-1 defeat by Argentina in 1996. However, a recent upturn in fortunes, such as the near-qualification for the World Cup of 2006 and the under 21s reaching the final of the Juegos del Caribe in Cartagena, Colombia in 2007, means that Venezuela is no longer the walkover it once was. This has attracted more support for the national team and an upsurge in interest in football. It is also a popular sport in the parks of the country, played with an often surprising level of skill.

Of particular popularity is the game of *futbolito*, or salon soccer, which is played on a hard surface in teams of five, with a very small ball. It is fast and skilful, disdaining the more physical aspects of the European game. Traditional five-a-side is also popular, played on dusty, grassless fields under a blazing sun. You can easily walk up to a game and join in if a spare man is needed, or join one of the teams waiting for their turn—two goals wins the game, and the winners stay on. These games are more physical but not generally dangerous, despite the absence of referees.

One aspect of organised sports is that everything takes an extremely long time to organise, and you can expect to spend anything up to an hour debating the rules and formation of the teams. There are also organised leagues, each team having their own strip and the level of skill (or lack thereof) that you would expect to find in an English Sunday league team. To join one, you may have to go through a trial. Venezuelan league matches are very poorly attended and only the highlights are telecast. In contrast, full games from the Spanish, Italian and Portuguese leagues all get weekly airings on television, as do the finals of European Cups. The English language newspaper, the *Daily Journal*, publishes the scores and brief reports from European games, as well as sports from the United States.

American football can be seen, but only on the big screen in the more touristy bars of the cities. For ice hockey, the story is even sadder and aficionados must make do with reports in the *Daily Journal*.

Traditional Sports

Bullfights or *corridas* take place during the festivities to celebrate the *fiestas patronales* (patron saints' feast days), and in the *pueblos* even the untrained can try their luck against the poor bulls. The animals are killed in the course of this entertainment, so go only if your morals are untroubled by this prospect. Cockfighting is especially popular in the llanos, as much for the ferocity of the betting as for the talent of the sharp-spurred warriors. This sport even has its own small arena.

Bollas criollas is a traditional version of bowls featuring two contestants who take turns to lob a metal ball as close to a target ball as possible.

Chess tables where anyone can play: Sabana Grande, Caracas.

Gambling

Betting on cockfights is an integral part of the entertainment, but even more popular is betting on horse races. The bet called the *cinco y seis* (a daily double) has become so popular that it is used to describe any unlikely event. La Rinconada Hippodrome in Caracas has 2,000 stables and a swimming pool for the horses. The capacity is 20,000 and millions more watch the races on television or listen to the radio.

Walking and Other Exercises

Walking might not be a sport, but no matter where you are in the country, there is always somewhere worth walking around, and the perfect climate for this form of exercise is another persuasive argument for taking it up. If more strenuous exercise is your cup of tea, then all larger towns and cities have gyms where you can work out or join an aerobics class. In Caracas, several gyms cater for all budgets.

Surfing

Surfing is popular but many of the beaches on the Caribbean coast do not generate the right waves. Other watersports such as scuba diving, snorkeling, wateskiing and deep sea fishing are largely the preserve of the tourist industry. Joining a club

Venezuelans are proud of their reputation for knowing how to enjoy themselves. Here, hundreds of spectators cheer on an exciting bullfight.

SURF'S UP!

is the best option here, as it is for diving. The Caribbean coast is a diver's paradise, making this sport a tempting one for even complete novices to take up.

MUSIC

Salsa is the most popular music across the country. You will hear it everywhere, especially in the *por puestos* (small buses), where its rhythm brightens the ride immeasurably. *Merengue* is nearly as frequently heard and danced to as *salsa*. Do not be surprised to hear either, combined with a thunderous crashing, as of a trapped herd of caribou making a dash for freedom, emanating from your neighbour's flat on a Friday night. Do not fear, it is only those dance steps being given a turn, not some terrible domestic dispute.

Both of these are the sounds you will be dancing to if you venture into a Venezuelan nightclub. Nightclubs cater for all the music popular in Venezuela, but there are also places playing specific music genres catering for more specialised tastes. Of course these dark and often deafening places become less varied as the town gets smaller. In the smaller *pueblos*, discos for teenagers may be the best you can hope for.

Gaitas is popular, especially in the Christmas season, when the old favourites are dug out and the *gaitas* bands from Maracaibo can be found on all the park bandstands. Strangely *gaitas* has become the music of Christmas, although in its homeland of Maracaibo it is enjoyed all year round. **Aguinaldos** are Venezuelan Christmas carols, adapted and altered from the Spanish originals over the centuries.

Venezuela's King of Salsa is Oscar D'León, who achieved global superstar status after a string of hits in the 1970s and 1980s such as '*Lloraràs*'. He has had a huge string of hits down the decades and branched out into other musical styles from *merengue* to *reggaeton* and dueted with other greats such as Celia Cruz The energy of his live performances shows he is still going strong.

Joropo is the national music of Venezuela and involves an accordion called the *cuereta*, *maracas*, *bandolín*, acoustic guitars and the four-stringed guitar appropriately called the *cuatro*. The *joropo* dance is one of the most distinctive elements of Venezuelan culture. It includes a number of different phases, which may or may not be included in one dance, so each performance could be unique. There are regional variations, although the phase known as *zapateados*, with quick stamping moves, is distinctive. Indian music and Indian instruments have generally not been taken up by mainstream *criollo* society, just as the Indians do not use instruments brought by the conquistadors. In fact, instruments such as the *maremare* pipes can only be seen in museums, although the Indians still play them in some regions.

The *tono llanero* is typical of llanero culture in that it fuses African, native Indian and European influences. *Tonos* were sung during milking to soothe the cows. Simón Díaz has been the greatest champion of Llanero music, creating songs derived from the disappearing musical heritage of the plains. He has promoted Venezuelan music worldwide and turned his hand to comedy and starred in three plays and five films and produced and hosted 12 television shows that promoted Venezuelan folklore, as well as radio show on folklore and Venezuelan music that ran for 25 years. His works has been covered by many artists and his song '*Tonada*

Traditional European dances such as the mazurka, minuet, polka and walzes used to be popular in Colonial times. The *tanguito*, a Venezuelan version of the Argentine tango, formerly enjoyed great popularity in the 1930s, when an influx of music came from abroad, such as *merengue* from the Dominican Republic, *rumba, conga* and *son* from Cuba.

de la Luna Llena' was included on the soundtrack of the Pedro Amoldóvar film, *La Flor de Mi Secreto*. Other exponents of traditional Venezuelan music are Serenata Guayanesa (Guayanese Serenade), who have made over 40 albums of folk songs from different regions. Un Solo Pueblo (One People) interpret music from the mainly black Barlovento region, with songs that tell of the lives of the communities there.

Reggae is popular, the softer commercial kinds being favoured, especially the works of Bob Marley. Some dancehall sounds, especially those featuring Spanish music, are commonly heard. *Serenatas*, formerly extremely typical, have more or less disappeared from the scene, to be replaced at public functions by *mariachi* bands. Other music to have found its way from the Caribbean islands is the *rumba, bolero, conga, guaracha* and the Cuban *mambo*.

Tambores (drums) is the feverish dance of African descent. A lithe female takes the floor and undulates her body in a fast and enticing fashion. A solitary male approaches, shimmering backwards and forwards, bobbing up and down like a cockerel on heat. He approaches, but she spurns him as contact is about to be made, twisting away. He tries again, only to be rejected once more. Again and again he comes forward, only to be rebuffed each time. After a few minutes, he is unceremoniously shunted from the scene by a rival male, who is secure in the knowledge that he could not come to the same fate. Alas, try as they might, all the men are rejected, although the dance does not end when the lady tires, as she is quickly replaced by another keen to deflate the egos of the collective male population. Anyone from the circle of watchers can interrupt at any time, although you should give a dancer time enough for a fair shake. You will be invited to try your hand—well, your hips. Join in, but remember the rules and do not be disappointed when you are knocked vigorously aside. You can always return later for another bout.

Shown here are the four-stringed guitar known as the *cuatro, maracas, tambures* and *flautas* (flutes), near a *pila,* which is used to grind corn, and a stone *budare,* used to make *arepas.*

American rock music, particularly the more sentimental numbers, are played on the radio, while jazz has a firm following in Venezuela, as evidenced by the rather exclusive jazz clubs of the cities. Venezuela also produces rock in the best American traditions, the prime exponent being the enormously popular Franco da Vita, who is well worth a listen. The 1990s saw a boom in Venezuelan rock groups, such as Caramelos de Cianuro, who do soft rock with a punky edge, with songs like '*El Último Polvo*', one man's plea for one last night of passion with his ex. There is also Disorden Público, a Caracan ska, reggae and latin rock band who have carried on the tradition of UK eighties two-tone bands such as the Specials by writing songs of social commentary which advocate racial and social tolerance. *The Ska Album* (2004) has been released separately in the US and Europe and the band have toured Latin America, the USA and Europe. Los Amigos Invisibles are a disco, acid jazz, funk and latin outfit best known for their album, *The Venezuelan Zinga Son, Vol 1* (2003).

All forms of Latin music are enjoyed, but especially the music of artists who have achieved crossover success, such as Gloria Estefan and Jon Secada. Latin pop emanates from all the countries of Central and South America and the Spanish-speaking Caribbean islands. Venezuelan pop artists favour the ballad and smoother tunes, Ricardo Montaner and José Luis Rodríguez 'El Puma' are evergreen stars in the firmament of Venezuelan pop.

Cuba produces many popular artists, as does Colombia; *vallenato*, *porro* and *cumbia* are sounds from that country that are especially welcomed by the large expat contingents resident in Venezuela, both along the borders and in city centres. Mexico, though, produces the largest numbers of successful artists, and Mexican *mariachi* bands are popular, those in full costume being a familiar sight at private functions such as birthday parties. *Mariachi* came to Venezuela with the Mexican cinema that became popular during the 1930s. European singers who sing in Spanish are also big, such as Julio Iglesias and the Italian Eros Ramazotti.

Another popular area is *telenovela* (soap opera) soundtracks. The theme tune to the latest hit will be guaranteed huge national success, and be likely to propel the singer or group towards stardom, unless they are already there. In the towns, large stores sell CDs, but the easiest way to buy music across the country is on pirate CDs bought on any street corner. Although you can be sure pirate CDs will not last too long, they are still immensely popular.

TELEVISION

Television is important as a medium for conveying national identity and the sense of glamour and lavishness that pervades modern Venezuela. Television schedules can appear to be dominated by *telenovelas*, as there can be more than four or five on one channel in one day. Everyone talks about these *telenovelas*, which range from the insipid to the occasional socially realistic and politically challenging. *Telenovelas* have a limited lifespan of up to a year, and the best of them are still talked about years later.

They are produced in Venezuela, but are also bought in from Colombia, Brazil, Argentina and occasionally other Latin American countries. The plots are dramatic and complex and can include elements of fantasy. The actors are nearly always chosen for their looks as much as for their acting ability. There are now often stars from a number of countries in one *telenovela*, so one family may have a Mexican mother and Colombian father with Venezuelan and Argentinian children! As the *telenovelas* are not limitless, appearing in one is not the death of an acting career but very often the beginning.

Television provides the opportunity for the making of celebrities. The gossip itself is disseminated in society magazines, but television produces most of the material. Venezuelan TV has an abiding passion for the glamorous. Game shows feature not one but a bevy of beautiful assistants. The prime requisite for presenters is that they be female and usually blonde. *Espectaculos* are popular: these can be a whole afternoon or evening of variety entertainment featuring singing, choreographed dance, magic acts, comedy and other forms of entertainment. There are also children's programmes, comedy programmes (often slapstick), news and sports. A large number of international series and films take up a considerable portion of a station's output. English language series are dubbed, so you can expect your favourite hero to have a much deeper and more rugged voice.

There are four national channels, all of which are commercial: Venevisión, Venezolana de Televisión, Televén and ViVe. Radio Caracas Televisión (RCTV) had run since 1953 but did not have its licence renewed in 2007 after being openly critical of Hugo Chávez, but was reborn as a cable channel, RCTV International. There are about 100 regional networks and a yet greater variety of channels available on cable, reflecting the usual mix of news, sports, films and entertainment channels. A few are specifically Venezuelan, others have a Latin American and Caribbean focus and some, in Spanish, are from the United States.

NEWSPAPERS

There are a number of serious broadsheets and one paper devoted solely to Venezuelan sport (mostly the kind you can gamble on) but tabloids are virtually non-existent. Newspaper publishing is a serious business in this country. The journalistic style is instantly recognisable. The Venezuelan news section and the always expansive economy section (reflecting the readership) lean towards a plain representation of facts and a tendency to quote important figures. To balance this, there are usually a large number of commentaries by respected figures, as well as interviews with political movers and shakers. They reflect a respectful attitude to political figures and the absence of tabloid muck-raking and character assassinations. Whatever the public may think of top politicians, newspapers maintain a neutral position, except in the commentaries. Most papers carry supplements, especially at the weekend, although these are neither as large nor as glossy as you may be used to.

There is not the range of magazines you might expect, although the most popular genres are catered for, such as glossy society magazines and sports magazines. Many of these are produced for a Latin American market and so are not specifically Venezuelan. In 1990, there were roughly 67 provincial daily papers and 12 in Caracas. The best known Venezuelan newspapers are *El Universal* and *El Nacional*.

RADIO

Venezuelan radio is largely regional in focus, with most radio stations covering a state, or just one city. The stations offer variety in their programming although some may predominate in one kind of music. The many talk shows are excellent practice for tuning your ear to Venezuelan Spanish. There are hundreds of AM and FM channels in Venezuela, with familiar formats such as phone-in chat shows and competitions.

CINEMA

Venezuelan cinema gives you all the latest Hollywood films shortly after their release in the United States. English language films are all subtitled. On Monday nights, tickets are half-price and the cinemas are consequently packed. Even at the best of times, you can expect to face a long queue and possible disappointment. Venezuelan movies struggle to find sponsorship and you are more likely to see films made in other Latin American countries. You can buy and rent DVDs although going to the cinema is much more popular, possibly as it is cheap and more social than watching a DVD at home.

The Venezuelan film industry has a long history but it has been overshadowed by US imports and has struggled to find funding. The first Venezuelan films were short documentaries made in 1897 by Manuel Trujillo Duran. The first feature film was *El Fusilamiento de Pilar* (the Shooting of Pilar) but it was confiscated by government officials. The first Venezuelan film to be shown abroad was *La Trepadora* (The Climber) from 1925 directed by Edgar Anzola. It was based on a novel by Rómulo Gallegos and also claimed the distinction of being Venezuela's most successful silent film. Rómulo Gallegos himself attempted to grow the Venezuelan film industry, but his Estudios Ávila collapsed. Guillermo Villegas Blanco bought it out in 1942 and created Bolívar Films. Villegas Blanco succeeded in making Venezuelan film profitable and Bólivar Films made documentaries, news and information films, publicity shorts and eight feature films. These films were not notably Venezuelan in context and mainly featured directors, producers and actors from other Latin American countries whose film industries were more developed and stable. *La balandra Isabel llegó Esta Tarde* (The Yacht Isabel Arrived This Afternoon) was the best film of this era (made in 1950), a romantic interracial comedy which won a prize for photography at Cannes.

Margot Benacerraf was an important figure in the 1950s. She directed two important documentaries, *Reverón* (1952) dealt with the life of Venezuelan painter Armando Reverón and *Araya* (1958) about the lives of a coastal community surviving through fishing and working in a salt mine. Araya won an international prize at the Cannes film festival. César Enriquez Ludert explored the social themes of poverty and exploitation in *La escalinita* (The Stairway) in 1960.

Román Chalbaud is Venezuela's most notable director of the 20th century. He has won awards and international recognition for his many films. His first film was a play he had adapted for the cinema *Caín Adolescente* (Adolescent Cain) in 1959. It looked at the social phenomenon of urban migration that has transformed Latin America through the eyes of a poor family moving from the interior to Caracas.

In the 1960s, the era of democracy ushered in after the defeat of Marcos Peréz Jiménez in 1958 and the Cuban Revolution the year after stimulated the Left into producing many short films denouncing poverty and social inequality or in support of the guerilla movements active in Venezuela at the time. *La Paga* (the Wages) was directed by Ciro Durán and produced by a co-operative in 1962 about rural workers. It is seen as key in the development of the New Latin American Cinema that emerged at the end of the 1960s.

Other notable films from the 1960s were the romantic comedy *Loco por ellas* (Crazy about Them) from 1965 by Mauricio de la Pedrosa and the action film *Acción en Caracas* from Mueller y Xiol from 1966. In the same year, the documentary *La Cuidad Que Nos Ve* (The City that Watches Us) was produced from the Universidad Central de Caracas and directed by Jesús Enrique Guédez in the shantytowns surrounding Caracas. *Estudio 1* was the first film from Julio César Mármol.

Cuando Quiero Llorar No Puedo (When I Want To Cry, I Can't) was directed in 1973 by Mauricio Wallerstein and was based on a novel by Miguel Otero Silva. It follows the lives of three Venezuelans called Victorino who were all born on the same day and die on the same day. They are from different classes and therefore have very different experiences of life and death, which are contrasted to emphasis social inequalities.

In 1974, Román Chalbaud directed *La Quema de Judas* (The Burning of Judas) which told the stories of the daily struggles of the urban poor. This heralded a boom time through the rest of the 1970s and the 1980s as government funding backed Venezuelan cinema. Chalbaud directed *Sagrado y Obsceno* (Scared and Obscene) in 1976 and *El Pez Que Fuma* (The Smoking Fish) in 1977. Both films follow themes that run through Chalbaud's work such as urban poverty, violence and corruption intermingled with comedy and social commentary. Chalbaud reminded Venezuelans that despite the oil boom, there was always an underclass of prostitutes, *barrio* dwellers, criminals and the homeless who endure despite the many obstacles they face daily.

Mauricio Wallerstein has produced films on social issues such as class struggle (*La Empresa Perdona Un Momento de Locura*, 1978), women's rights (*Eva, Julia, Perla*, 1980), sexual freedom (*Máxima Felicidad*, 1983) and politics (*Crónica de un Subversivo Latinamericano*/Chronicle of a Latin American Subversive, 1975), based on the kidnapping of an American officer by political militants in Venezuela in 1964. Clement de la Cerda directed the hit *Soy Un Delicuente* (I'm a Delinquent) in 1977, which broke all box office records in Venezuela. Like all his work, it showed violence leading from class struggle when a young man falls into a world of crime and drugs in a Caracas shantytown.

Female directors began to have an impact during the 1980s. Fina Torres directed *Oriana* in 1985, which won a Cannes prize and deals with women's repressed sexual desires. It harks back to the oppressive social and sexual conventions of the past. Solveig Hoogesteijn directed *Macu, la Mujer del policía* (Macu, the Policeman's Wife) in 1987. It broke box office records at

In 1981, Luis Correa's Ledezma, *El Caso Mamero* (Ledezma, the Mamero Case) led to the director being jailed, but freed after a court case. The film was based on a case of police corruption and also showed the attempts of the authorities to stop the film's production.

the time and showed the abuse suffered by a young woman who enters a world of police corruption, brutality and hostile machismo. *Santera* from 1996 told the story of a black woman who gained supernatural powers through practicing Santeria. When accused of using her powers to kill, a white female doctor from Caracas attempts to prove her innocence. The very different lives of the two women are brought into sharp contrast.

Alejandro Saderman directed the comedy *Cien Años de Perdón* (One Hundred Years of Forgiveness) in 1998 wherein four middle-class friends decide to rob a bank in the face of Venezuela's economic crisis. Fernando Venturin directed the thriller *Tres Noches* (Three Nights) in 1998. 1999 saw the release of *Huelepega, Ley de la Calle* (Gluesniffing, the Law of the Street) by Elia Schneider which used genuine street kids to expose the world of drugs and violence of homeless street children.

LITERATURE

Independence is said to have sown the first flourishing of Venezuelan literature with very little pre-Colombian or colonial era literature extant. The oral tradition of some indigenous peoples, such as the Pemón, Warao and Guajiro, were translated into Spanish in the 20th century. *Historia de la conquista y población de la provincia de Venezuela* (History of the Conquest and Population of the Province of Venezuela, 1723) by José de Oviedo y Baños is a historical record written in a colourful and accessible style. Poets like José Antonio Martin and Abigaíl Lozano also gained popularity at this time.

Simón Bolívar (1783–1830) wrote letters of extreme historical and emotional impact such as the *Manifiesto de Cartagena* (1812) and the *Carta de Jamaica* (1815), written in periods of exile and defeat from his homeland of Venezuela, when re-asserting his arguments for the need to strive for independence. Simón Rodríguez was Bolívar's tutor for a time and a revolutionary thinker whose published work included *Sociedades Americanas* (American Societies, 1828) and *Defensa de Bolívar* (Defence of Bolívar, 1830).

Andrés Bello

Andrés Bello (1781–1865) was not only a famed poet and philosopher, but also a friend to other great figures of the era. He was a sometime tutor of Simón Bolivar, for a while the travelling companion of the German scientist Alexander von Humboldt, as well as a friend of Franciso de Miranda during his 19 years in London. Bello wrote the first book printed in Venezuela. He was the first and greatest of Venezuela's polymath intellectuals, writing on philosophy, science, art, history and politics. He was a law and linguistics expert, poet, journal editor, university rector, a senator and a founder and the rector of the national university in Santiago de Chile. His work is noted for a fusion of Romantic and Neoclassical styles, drawing inspiration from and bearing testament to the extraordinary natural beauty of the Americas. This is best exemplified by the poem *Silva a la agricultura de la zona tórrida* (Ode to the Agriculture of the Torrid Zone, 1826). His other greatest work is the *Gramátrica Castellana* (1847).

Fermín Toro (1806–1865) was another writer whose intellect ranged over the sciences, philosophy, history and linguistics. His most famous novel is *Los mártires* (The Martyrs, 1842). Toro also wrote in the form of the fictional sketches of daily life known as *costumbrismo*, as well as a number of poems. The oppressive regime of Juan Vicente Gómez (1908–1935) produced the short story writer Rufino Blanco, who was prolific in satirising the Gomez regime.

Teresa de la Parra (1889–1936) wrote *Ifigenia: Diario de una señorita que escribió porque se fastidiaba* (Iphigenia: Diary of a young lady who wrote because she was bored, 1924). The novel proved controversial as it included caricatures of Caracas society figures and immoral corrupt politicians. The novel deals with the struggle of a woman to find intellectual freedom when society attempts to pressure her into marriage and motherhood. Juan Vicente Gómez stopped the book being published in Venezuela but Teresa de la Parra travelled to Paris where it was published to acclaim.

Rómulo Gallegos (1884–1969) not only wrote Venezuela's most famous novel, *Doña Barbara* (1929), but also served briefly as Venezuela's president, as well as mayor of Caracas and director of the ministry of education and a member of the senate and house of deputies. Doña Barbara deals with Gallegos' recurring theme, the intellectual (landowner Santos Luzardo) who struggles to civilise corrupt and violent elements (rival landowner Doña Barabera herself) in Venezuelan society. Although the novel brought Gallegos fame, it also made him an enemy of Antonio Guzman Blanco as the novel was deemed to be a fierce critique of his regime.

Mariano Picón Salas (1901–1965) was another outstanding intellectual who authored works of fiction, biographies, literary criticism, essays and Latin American history, notably in *De la conquista a la independencia* (From the Conquest to Independence, 1944).

The Achievements of Arturo Uslar Pietri

Arturo Uslar Pietri (1906–2001) was a great Venezuelan figure who stamped his mark on the 20th century. He cast his influence over numerous fields, being a writer, politician, educator, journalist, diplomat, civil servant and intellectual. His achievements include the historical novel *Las Lanzas Coloradas* (The Red Lances, 1931) about the war of independence, the phrase *sembrar el petróleo*, 'sow the oil', meaning to be mindful to invest oil income wisely in the future of Venezuela. He served as minister of education, minister of the Interior, senator and presidential candidate, losing to Raúl Leoni. After the defeat, he moved away from politics and became director of the noted daily newspaper *El Nacional*. He then became Venezuelan ambassador to UNESCO and starred on television on *Valores Humanos*, a weekly arts and history programme. In total, he produced seven novels, along with numerous essays, plays, poems and short stories. His writing received numerous national and international awards.

Miguel Otero Silva (1908–1985) was an avant-garde poet, essayist, novelist and journalist who founded *El Nacional*. His novels deal with social issues in a modern literary style, within the context of recent history, such as *Oficina no.1* (Office No.1, 1961) about the social effects of oil exploitation. Francisco Herrera Luque (1927–1991) wrote about the heroes of independence. His most famous novel is *Boves el Urogallo*, about the Llanero leader José Tomas Boves, who played a pivotal role in the war of Independence. It is the best-selling novel in Venezuelan history.

VENEZUELAN ARTS

In the 18th century, the first portrait paintings appeared in Venezuela. Around 1784, the first theatre produced

Caracas' first plays. In the final days of Spanish colonial rule, Venezuelan was famed for the outstanding quality of its composers and musicians.

The dictator Antonio Guzman Blanco (who ruled from 1870 to 1888) proved a strong patron of the arts. He built the Municipal Theatre and the first Academy of Fine Arts. He appointed the French romantic painter Martín Tovar y Tovar (1827–1902) as the official artist. Tovar y Tovar produced the ceiling mural that can be seen in the Elliptical Salon in the Congress Building of the Battle of Carabobo. Also found in the Congress Building and the Pantheon are the monumental paintings of Tito Salas (1888–1974) which also helped build the legend of the Liberator, depicting scenes from his life.

The era of Independence led by Bolivar fired the national imagination and some of the art most revered today was produced at that time, or stimulated by it. Juan Lovera (1176–1841) was a self-taught artist famous for painting historical scenes, such as the signing of the Declaration of Independence.

Armando Reverón was Venezuela's leading Modernist painter in the late 19th and early 20th century. He painted models and landscapes in the coastal town of Macuto, using the unique features of the Caribbean light to illuminate his art, experimenting with subtle shades of light. He painted over 100 paintings of a small bay near his house, trying to capture the different shades of light produced at different times of the day.

THEATRE

Venezuelan theatre has been developed by many of the country's greatest writers in their guise of playwrights. Andrés Bello wrote Venezuela's first play, *Venezuela Consolada* (Venezuela Consoled) in 1804. Rómulo Gallegos wrote plays about how the country's social conflicts affected his principal characters. Arturo Uslar Pietri wrote two plays in the 1920s, experimenting with surrealism and futurism. In the 1940s, the government stimulated the growth of the theatre via subsidy. Luis Peraza (1908–1974) was a playwright who also directed the Teatro Obrero (Worker's Theatre) and founded the University Theatre at the Universidad Central de Caracas (Central University of Caracas). Román Chalbaud wrote plays that exposed Venezuela's underbelly, such as *Los Ángeles Terribles* in 1967 and *La Quema De Judas* (The Burning of Judas), which was later made into film to launch his filmmaking career. Nuevo Grupo (New Group) and Rajatabla were two highly successful theatre groups in the 1970s and 1980s. The economic woes of the 1990s meant that state funding largely dried up and Venezuelan theatre consequently went into decline.

BALLET

The Ballet Nena Coronil was Venezuela's first ballet company, founded in the 1940s. The National Ballet of Venezuela was founded in 1957, but ended in the 1970s, when the National Dance Company was formed. Choreographer Vicente Nebrada founded the Ballet Internacional de Caracas (International Ballet of Caracas), which toured Latin America and the USA in the late 1970s performing the *joropo*. They were accompanied by renowned pianist Teresa Carreño, after whom the Teatro Teresa Carreño in Caracas is named. Zhandra Rodríguez is Venezuela's most prominent ballerina. She performed with the American Ballet Company in the USA and was the prima ballerina with the International Ballet of Caracas.

ARCHITECTURE

Carlos Raúl Villanueva founded the college of architecture at the Central University of Caracas. He designed the layout of the campus with plazas, patios, gardens and canopied walkways and commissioned other artists such as Alexander Calder, Jean Arp and Fernand Léger to create murals and sculptures. He also designed the Olympic Stadium and Olympic Pool, the Museum of Fine Arts and the Maestranza César Girón bullring in Maracay.

The artist and sculptor Jesús Soto studied in Caracas and Paris and his abstract art was influenced by Piet Mondrian and Alexander Calder. His sculptures around Caracas take on different forms depending on the position of the viewer and some move independently. There is a Jesús Soto museum in his hometown of Cuidad Bolívar, which also showcases contemporary international artists. Alejandro Otero (1921–1990) was another great kinetic sculptor who experimented with massive steel and aluminium structures that move and change in response to wind and light. *Abra Solar* is a structure of poles and plates in Plaza Venezuela, Caracas. *Ala Solar*, in Bolívar state, is a 50-metre steel tower, surmounted by a wheel that reflects different colours as it moves in the wind.

Eloy Palacios (1847–1919) sculpted *La India del Paraíso* (The Indian Woman of Paradise) who stands atop a column in Caracas to symbolise the independence won at the Battle of Carabobo. The statue of Maria Lionza raising a jaw bone to the heavens atop a tapir was created by Alejandro Colina. Francisco Narváez (1905–1984) produced large neoclassical figures, which gradually became more abstract, reminiscent of the work of Henry Moore. He created *Las Toninas* in Plaza O'Leary in Caracas (1943), a fountain featuring reclining female figures and reliefs of waves and dolphins.

THE TOURIST INDUSTRY

Tourism is Venezuela's greatest underexploited resource and the country's major economic hope. New hotel complexes are continually going up and investors sought for further schemes. Venezuela is blessed with a fabulous range of environments and beautiful vistas. Fortunately, many of the richest areas come under national park boundaries and are therefore protected to a degree.

Considering the breathtaking beauty of the country, it is surprising that tourism has not been managed more efficiently. In many places, catering for tourists is at the level of what the local population has put together and guidance from the local government is poor or non-existent. Despite this, and the possible inconvenience, there are many places that you must visit if you are staying for a length of time in the country. The national parks of Venezuela as well as the other places worth seeing are given in Chapter Two.

VENEZUELA CELEBRATES

What you see of Venezuelan culture depends on where you are in the country. Some aspects are visible all over the country, such as Venezuelan food and music, but life in the cities tends to throw up a smokescreen of devotion to modern icons. The consumerist lifestyles pursued in cosmopolitan areas means that city culture does not look Venezuelan, from billboards advertising Scotch whisky to the dominance of Hollywood films in the cinemas and the love of baseball.

In the *pueblos*, Venezuela takes on a far more distinct character and this is never more clearly seen than during local festivals. This section will inform you about the unmissable town festivals. You can take part through eating the typical local food, sometimes eaten only at that time, drinking the alcohol, which is in bountiful supply then, especially the cane liquor *aguardiente*, joining the processions and entering the games or competitions that are part of the festivities. Catholics can also join the religious celebrations, including the midnight masses (*velorios*). The only obligation on your part is that you have a good time! Unfortunately you may have to take time off work for these festivals, but they will be worth it.

HOLIDAYS

Christmas and New Year

Christmas (Navidad) and New Year (Año Nuevo) are celebrated more or less as one ongoing holiday. Presents can be exchanged at either time, which depends on the preference of each family. In fact, New Year just about outdoes Christmas in terms of colour and festivities.

Christmas under a burning sun might seem strange, especially when there are plenty of familiar Christmas decorations imported from the United States available in the shops. You can even buy real pine trees (*pino navideño*), although the plastic versions are generally thought to be more sophisticated. Venezuelans even send each other Christmas cards featuring snowy scenes of tobogganing and other patently Nordic fun. Baby Jesus (*el niño Jesús*), the object of Christmastime adulation in times gone by, has now been largely supplanted by good old Santa Claus (*Papá Noel*).

Christmas in Venezuela is a family event, as it is the world over. This means that many people return to their hometowns to be with their families. The full Christmas dinner is served, including turkey and such Christmas food as *hallacas* and *pan de jamón*. A nativity scene (*Nacimiento*) is an almost essential household adornment, the bigger the better—big enough, in fact, to appear to be a shrine. This is a typically Venezuelan part of Christmas and families like to give it their own personal touch. You may even see large (possibly life-size) nativity scenes in the green spaces in your neighbourhood. Commercial centres display large-scale decorated models and are likely to have nativity plays going on in the build-up to Christmas. The country celebrates Las Misas de Aguinaldo from 16 December onwards, in some places with roller-skating (*patinatas Dicembrinas*) and afternoon strolls (*paseos matutinos*). Everyone is welcome to take part to burn off Christmastime excesses.

New Year's is when fireworks are set off (with little regard to safety) in the street and every house seems to have a party going on inside. On New Year's Eve, it is traditional in the hours leading up to midnight to visit all the parties in the neighbourhood to give best wishes for the new year, and of course to stop and have a drink or two.

At midnight, family members gather for the chiming of the 12 bells on the radio. At each chime, everyone consumes a grape from a cup filled with 12, each of which represents a New Year wish. At the stroke of midnight, there is a champagne toast, everyone embraces and wishes each other a Happy New Year—*Felíz Año Nuevo!*—and people take to the streets again until eventually driven home by exhaustion. People can be seen wandering the streets carrying suitcases, hoping for a journey in the new year, or money for prosperity. Yellow underpants are worn to bring good luck in the new year. Some people celebrate New Year in discos or even outside Venezuela, taking the opportunity of a winter holiday. Christmas decorations finally come down on 6 January (El Seis de Reyes).

Carnival

Two holidays that fall close to each other are Carnival (Carnaval) and Easter (Semana Santa or Las Pascuas). Carnival takes place in February, 40 days before Easter. Easter is probably the most religious time of year and Carnival is simply hedonistic.

Whenever there is a public holiday, Venezuelans look forward to getting a 'bridge' (*puente*) to the weekend. If the holiday falls on a Thursday, they will ask for Friday to be declared a holiday. The main reason for this is that city-dwellers like to travel during the holiday. This is no truer than at Carnival, when cities empty and people head for the pleasure spots along the Caribbean coast, or even go to Trinidad, famous for the splendour and extravagance of its carnivals. When that happens, the only remnants of Carnival spirit left in the cities are the extremely noisy fireworks set off by children and the waterbombs bombarding people foolhardy enough to walk the streets. The near-deserted cities can be dangerous places to be. Indeed, the murder rate rises at this time of year as the evacuations promote a greater sense of lawlessness.

There are several traditions that must be seen at Carnival, such as the whirling male dancers dressed as black women and the processions of drummers through towns along the Caribbean coast. The *tambores*, or drummers, are an important part of the celebrations at this time. El Callao

Carnival costumes in the town of Carúpano.

in Bolívar state is the town most famous for its Carnival celebrations. Carnival here has been influenced by the slaves and the descendants of French, English and American fortune hunters who once populated this town. Costumes include devils and traditional dresses from Guadeloupe and Martinique. In Carúpano (Sucre), the costumes for the Carnival parade are famed. Mythical and historical figures dance and play out ancient tales. There is dancing to live music, and the celebrations last for days.

Easter

Easter is the religious culmination of the holiday season that begins with Carnival, and the beaches are still extremely crowded. Easter is the only religious festival that has missed the Venezuelan touch. The religious ceremonies are well observed at this time, including processions and masses.

They begin with Palm Sunday (Domingo de Ramos), when palms are given out, to be formed into a cross and

Carnival at Carúpano: who says size doesn't matter?

placed within the home to give protection. Easter Monday (el Lunes Santo) commemorates the flagellation of Jesus and, following that, the humility and patience of Christ, the adoration of Christ, the day of the eucharist and the passion and crucifixion of Christ. Saturday is a time of reflection and silence for the death of Christ.

The biggest celebration is saved for Easter Sunday (el Domingo de Resurrección), ending in Hallelujah (Aleluya). On this day in parts of Venezuela, effigies of Judas are burned (La Quema de Judas). There is also the Día de Nazareno (Miércoles Santo) and El Santo Sepulcro (Viernes Santo). Those who are especially religious may undertake journeys to worship an especially venerated Jesus, such as the one in Achaguas in Apure state.

FESTIVALS

Each area of Venezuela has its own patron saint (*Santo Patrón*) and special feast days for patron saints are known as *fiestas patronales*. These festivals are usually religious in tone but besides processions, they also feature dances, bullfights, music and traditional touches unique to each festival.

There are also other celebrations in honour of religious and mythical events. If you want to experience Venezuelan traditions at first hand, then a visit to one or more of these festivals is essential. They are held on different dates, although each festival is usually celebrated in different towns on the same day. Some of the most popularly celebrated festivals are given below.

Fiesta del Día de los Comerciantes

This celebration features the parading of a man-sized rag doll (called Anacleto) on a donkey. Anacleto's followers sing and play traditional instruments such as the *cuatro*, *furruco*, *tambor* and *maracas*. Alcohol or money is given as the procession passes by. Some merchants close shop and dress in traditional garb—a straw hat with a black band, a smart waistcoat and a bow tie.

Festividad de Los Reyes Magos

Los Reyes Magos are the Three Wise Men. This festival celebrates their visit to baby Jesus with processions and traditional dances. In the town of Capacho, the whole story is played out in full costume, from their visit to baby Jesus to their capture and the death of Herod.

Fiesta de la Divina Pastora

The image of the Divina Pastora has been kept in the town of Santa Rosa since 1736. The procession towards Barquisimeto has taken place every year since 1855, when cholera ravaged the country. People come from all over the state of Lara to join in the procession.

Nuestra Señora de Coromoto

This festival celebrates the vision of the Virgin Mary to Coromoto, an Indian after whom a tribe was then named, the Coromotanos. People dress as Indians and reenact the sighting of the apparition.

Fiesta de San Pedro

This festival originates from a legend concerning a slave, María Ignacia, whose daughter Rosa Ignacia was dying. María promised the image of San Pedro that she would dance and sing all day if he cured her daughter. The cure was effected and today the scene is reenacted with music and dancing. A man in drag plays María Ignacia and carries a rag doll representing Rosa. San Pedro, the carrier of his image and the devil also take part in the dance. The dancers go from house to house, receiving money. When the dance ends, the dancers eat a special meal called *tropezón*, made with white beans and casabe. In the morning, there is a mass honouring San Pedro.

Nuestra Señora de la Candelaria

This festival ends Christmas in the central and eastern states. It is celebrated differently in different areas. In Caracas, it is celebrated in La Iglesia de la Candelaria with hymns and worship. In La Parroquia (Mérida), people dress in the costumes of Los Vasallos de la Candelaria and enact choreographed dances to music specific to the occasion.

Nuestra Señora de la Paz

This is a time of religious activity with baptisms, masses and processions.

Paradura del Niño

Jesus is presented to the temple. In the Andean states of Trujillo, Mérida and Táchira, there may also be the stealing and finding of Jesus (El Robo y Búsqueda del Niño). Jesus is stolen from one of the cribs in a nativity scene in people's houses and the owners go searching from house to house. When it is found, the town's people gather to celebrate with food, drink and worship of baby Jesus, who is then placed on a large handkerchief and taken around town by candle-holding worshippers. As the procession stops at houses, drinks are offered.

San Antonio de Padua

In Lara, this festival is celebrated with a complex dance known as *el Tamunangue*. It has various parts with their own meaning: *la salve*, *la batalla*, *la bella*, *el chichivamos*, *la juruminga*, *le perrendenga*, *el poco a poco*, *el galerón* and *el seis figurao*. It finishes with a prayer to the Virgin Mary.

San Sebastián

The fiesta of the patron saint of San Cristóbal attracts thousands of visitors. There is dancing, bullfights, horse races, an international bike race and other sporting events. This fiesta also features traditional dances and agricultural and industrial fairs.

Fiesta de Corpus Christi

San Francisco de Yare is home to Venezuela's most renowned devil dancers, who wear incredible black and red costumes and grotesque giant papier-mâché masks. The dance is a ritual battle between good and evil and is performed at a level of skill expected of the continent's oldest devil-dancing society.

San José

In some areas, this is a *fiesta patronal*. It features a procession of floats and antique cars, expositions, bullfights, beauty contests, cockfights, dances and fairs. The fiesta in Maracay attracts world-famous bullfighters and also features an agricultural exposition.

San Juan Bautista

This festival in June is celebrated in two ways. In Aragua, Carabobo, the Distrito Federal and Miranda, it is associated with the *tambores* of Barlovento, a region in Miranda state that comprises Curiepe, Higuerote, Caucagua and other smaller towns. The population is largely descended from black slaves who worked on the extensive coffee and banana plantations of the area in colonial times.

The celebrations are based around the most mesmeric of drumming. The villagers are faced by three or more drummers who pound on hollow logs in sublime harmony, producing a stunning effect. The audience, caught up in the rhythm, sit enraptured and chant the odd word or phrase as the song demands. It is a deeply moving and spiritual experience, even for confirmed atheists.

On 24 June, the statue of San Juan is paraded by worshippers dressed in his colour, red. Libations of rum are drunk and sprinkled on the statue. It is placed on an altar, around which the dancing begins. Dancing continues throughout the shortest night of the year.

In other parts of the country, there are songs, nocturnal prayers (*velorios*), dances and religious celebrations such as ritual cleansing by groups of women bathing in the sea. The celebrations can last all through June. In Amazonas and Portuguesa, it is not celebrated at all.

Velorios de la Cruz de Mayo

The crosses found in squares in towns and villages are decorated with wreaths of flowers. Celebrants stay awake throughout the night, singing to the cross in a candlelit ceremony. The tunes played in the central states are *fulías* and *décimas*. In the east, they play the melodies known as *galerones* and *décimas*. In the llanos, they sing the *Tonos de Velorio*.

In Cumaná, altars are built on seven levels to represent Christ's Calvary. Near each altar, they build shelters and decorate them with bouquets of flowers. The decorations sometimes include candles placed inside bamboo tubes. The men pay for the altars and the women bring flowers. *Padrinos* (godparents) are chosen for the cross and they have the coveted task of placing it on the altar. This act is

Saints are feted at this celebration.

accompanied by traditional *joropo* songs and dancing. Rum plays a not insignificant part.

Virgen de Chiquinquirá

Mainly celebrated in Zulia, it honours La Chinita, the patron saint of the area. There are fairs, processions, songs and dances. It also marks the beginning of the *gaitas* season in Zulia.

Virgen del Carmen

In El Carmen in Caracas, there are sack races, egg-and-spoon races, races with lit candles and other games. At Margarita, there are regattas and all along the coast processions make pilgrimages in boats. In the nine days before the festival, hymns are sung, *aguardiente* is drunk and special dishes eaten.

Virgen del Valle

This is an eastern festival and it may include a pilgrimage in boats. There are fairs, dances and expositions. The most important fiesta is held at El Valle de Espíritu Santo (in Nueva Esparta) in honour of their *patrona*.

Calendar of Festivals

If you are interested in Venezuelan traditions or just in having a good time, a state by state calendar will help you plan your visits. It includes religious and secular festivals. For public holidays, see page 189.

Amazonas
- San Fernando de Atabapo: Virgen del Carmen (16 July)

Anzoátegui
- Anaco: Virgen del Valle (8 September)
- Aragua de Barcelona: San Juan Bautista (23–25 June)
- Cantaura: Nuestra Señora de la Candelaria (2 February)
- Clarines: Velorios de la Cruz de Mayo (3 May)
- El Tigre: Virgen del Valle (8 September)
- Mapire: Virgen del Carmen (16 July)
- Pariaguán: Velorios de la Cruz de Mayo (3 May), Virgen del Carmen (16 July)

Venezuelans come together to celebrate Carnival.

- Puerto La Cruz: Velorios de la Cruz de Mayo (3 May), Virgen del Carmen (16 July)

Apure
- Guasdualito: Velorios de la Cruz de Mayo (in May)
- Achaguas: Día del Nazareno and Cristo Negro de Achaguas (Miércoles Santo, two days after Easter Monday)

Aragua
- Maracay: San José (12–19 March), San Juan Bautista (24 June)
- Ocumare de la Costa: Feria de San Sebastián (20 January), Día de Corpus Cristi (May)
- San Casimiro: Virgen del Carmen (16 July)
- Turmero: Nuestra Señora de la Candelaria (2 February)

Barinas
- Cuidad Bolívar: Virgen del Carmen (16 July)
- Various towns: Virgen de Chiquinquirá (18 November)

Bolívar
- Upata: San Antonio de Padua (13 June)

Carabobo
- Puerto Cabello: San Juan Bautista (24 June)

Cojedes
- Cojedes: Nuestra Señora de la Candelaria
  (2 February)
- El Baúl: Nuestra Señora de la Candelaria (2 February)
- El Pao: San Juan Bautista (24 June)

Distrito Federal
- Carabellada: Nuestra Señora de la Candelaria (2 February),
  San Juan Bautista (24 June)
- Caracas: Día del Nazareno (Miércoles Santo, Easter week)
- Carayaca: San José (15 March)
- Naiguatá: Día de Corpus Cristi Diablos Danzantes de
  Naiguatá (May)
- Various towns: Nuestra Señora de Coromoto (5 September),
  Día de los Santos Inocentes and El Gobierno y la Revolución
  (28 December)

Falcón
- Coro and nearby towns: Fiesta del Día de los Comerciantes
  (2 January)
- Capatarida: Velorios de la Cruz de Mayo (3 May)
- La Vela: Virgen del Carmen (16 July)
- Pedregal: Virgen del Carmen (16 July)
- Pueblo Nuevo: Virgen del Carmen (16 July)
- Puerto Cumarebo: Nuestra Señora de la Candelaria
  (2 February)
- Tucacas: Virgen del Carmen (16 July)

Guárico
- Altagracia de Orituco: Virgen del Carmen (16 July)
- Calabozo: Virgen del Carmen (16 July)
- San Juan de los Morros: San Juan Bautista
  (23–26 June)
- Valle de la Pascua: Nuestra Señora de la Candelaria
  (1–3 February)

The Venezuelan flag is proudly hoisted in front of the Municipal Palace in Nueva Esparta. Venezuela has fought hard for its independence and success and the people take great pride in their country.

An overview of Caracas at dusk. The most modern city in Venezuela, it has something to offer everyone and Caraqueños are generally hospitable and friendly.

Water cascading down steep rocks at Kavak, an Indian village near Angel Falls.
Opposite page: The economy in the country is growing steadily and modern offices and international institutions flourish in the cities.

Canaima lagoon and falls at Canaima National Park. It is the second largest park in Venezuela and is a worthy UNESCO World Heritage Site, with breathtaking views and the unique *tepuis* (table-top mountains) that are characteristic of the area.

Festivals are lively and colourful affairs. They are often religious and feature dances, bullfights, music and elaborate costumes.

Lara

- Barquisimeto: La Divina Pastora (14 January)
- Cabudare: San Antonio de Padua (13 June)
- Curarigua: San Antonio de Padua (13 June)
- Duaca: San Juan Bautista (23–26 June)
- El Tocuyo: San Antonio de Padua (13 June), Día de los Inocentes and La Zaragoza (28 December)
- Sanare: San Antonio de Padua (13 June), Día de los Inocentes and La Zaragoza (28 December)
- Siquisique: San José (19 March)
- Various towns: Virgen de Chiquinquirá (18 November)

Mérida

- Bailadores: Nuestra Señora de la Candelaria (2 February)
- Ejido: Virgen del Carmen (14–17 July)
- Mérida: La Paradura del Niño (1–2 January), Feria del Sol (during Carnival, a festival that includes bullfights, beauty queen contests and a float procession)
- Pueblo Llano: La Paradura del Niño (1–2 January)
- Various towns: Día de los Santos Inocentes and Locos y Locainas (28 December)

Miranda

- Barlovento: Día de los Santos Inocentes and Los Boleros (28 December)
- Curiepe: San Juan Bautista and Tambores de San Juan (24–25 June)
- Guatire: Fiesta de San Pedro (29 June)
- Higuerote: Los Reyes Magos (5 January), Virgen del Carmen (16 July)
- Ocumare del Tuy: Nuestra Señora de Coromoto (11 September)
- San Francisco de Yare: Día de Corpus Cristi, Diablos Danzantes de Yare (May)

Monagas

- Caicara de Maturín: Día de los Santos Inocentes and El Mono (28 December)
- Maturín: Virgen del Carmen (16 July)

Nueva Esparta

- El Valle del Espíritu Santo: Virgen del Valle (8 September)
- Juangriego: Velorios de la Cruz de Mayo (May)
- San Juan Bautista: San Juan Bautista (24 June–1 July)

Portuguesa

- Guanare: Nuestra Señora de la Candelaria (1–3 February), Nuestra Señora de Coromoto (7–9 September), Coronación de la Virgen de Coromoto (11 September)
- Guanarito: Nuestra Señora de la Paz (22 January)

Sucre

- Cariaco: Velorios de la Cruz de Mayo (3 May)
- Carúpano: Velorios de la Cruz de Mayo (3 May), Día de Corpus Christi (May), San Juan Bautista (24 June)
- Guiria: Virgen del Carmen (14–16 July)
- Irapa: San José (19 March)
- San Antonio del Golfo: Velorios de la Cruz de Mayo (May), San Antonio de Padua (13 June)

Táchira

- Capacho: Los Reyes Magos (6 January)
- Pregonero: La Paradura del Niño (1–2 January)
- San Antonio: San Antonio de Padua (13 June)
- San Cristóbal: Feria de San Sebastián (20 January)
- San Juan de Colón: San Juan Bautista (23–30 June)
- Various towns: Virgen de Chiquinquirá (18 November)

Trujillo

- Betijoque: San Juan Bautista (20–24 June)
- Boconó: Virgen del Carmen (15–17 July)
- Carache: San Juan Bautista (20–24 June)
- Escuque: El Santo Niño de Escuque (13 January)
- La Puerta: Nuestra Señora de la Paz (24 January)
- Mesa de Esnujaque: Nuestra Señora de la Candelaria (2 February), Velorios de la Cruz de Mayo (May), San Juan Bautista (20–24 June)
- Trujillo: Virgen del Carmen (15–17 July)
- Valera: San Juan Bautista (20–24 June)

- Various towns: Día de los Santos Inocentes and Locos y Locainas (28 December)

Yaracuy
- Nirgua: Velorios de la Cruz de Mayo (3 May)
- Urariche: San Juan Bautista (24–30 June)

Zulia
- Bobures: Virgen del Carmen (14–17 July)
- Machiques: San José (19 March), Virgen del Carmen (14–17 July)
- Maracaibo and other towns: Virgen de Chiquinquirá (18 November)
- San Carlos de Zulia: Virgen del Carmen (14–17 July)

Public Holidays: Días Nacionales
Venezuelans do not celebrate their national days with any gusto. If the day falls on a Friday or Monday, then the opportunity will be taken to spend a long weekend at the beach or visiting relatives in another part of the country. These public holidays are enjoyed on full pay. To know when you can expect a day off (or more, if you can get a *puente*!) and find the shops shut, here are the dates.

- 1 January: New Year's Day is a day of tranquillity as people recover from New Year's Eve celebrations.

- Variable, April–May: Carnival. The public holidays during Carnival fall in the week preceding Lent. Monday and Tuesday of that week are holidays. Semana Santa starts on the Wednesday of Easter week.

- 1 May: International Workers' Day (Día Internacional de los Trabajadores). There are workers' meetings, largely to discuss pay deals.

- 24 June: Anniversary of the Battle of Carabobo. To commemorate the final decisive battle of the War of Independence, the Venezuelan flag is displayed outside houses and street parades, which may attract crowds, are telecast.

- 5 July: Independence Day. On this day, too, the Venezuelan flag is displayed outside houses and street parades are telecast. Government and military ceremonies take place in Caracas.

- 24 July: The birthday of Simón Bolívar. The Venezuelan flag is displayed outside houses and street parades are telecast.

- 12 October: Día de la Raza. The Venezuelan flag is displayed outside houses and street parades are telecast.

- 25 December: Christmas Day begins early. Festivities start on Christmas Eve and most workers take two weeks off over this period.

Public Holidays in Venezuela		
Date	Name	Comments
1 January	New Year's Day / Día de Año Nuevo	
6 January	Epiphany / Día de Reyes	Feast to celebrate the three magi visiting Jesús.
Mon / Tues before Ash Wednesday	Carnival / Carnaval	
From Palm Sunday to Easter	Easter Holy Week / Semana Santa	Commemoration of the Passion and Adoration of Christ
19 March	Saint Joseph's Day / Día de San José	

Public Holidays in Venezuela

19 April	Beginning of the Independence Movement / 19 de Abril	Remembering the 1810 coup and start of Venezuelan independence
1 May	Labour Day / Workers' Day / Día de Trabajador	
24 June	Battle of Carabobo / Battala de Carabobo	Celebration of the battle to secure Venezuelan independence. Also Army Day
5 July	Independence Day	Signing of Venezuela's Declaration of Indepedence
24 July	Birth of Símon Bolívar / Natalicio Del Libertador	Also Navy Day
12 October	Day of Indigenous Resistance / Día de la Resistencia Indigena	Previously Día de la Raza and commemorated the arrival of Christopher Columbus
1 November	All Saints' Day / Día de Todos los Santos	
17–19 November	Festival of La Chinita / Feria de la Chinita	In Zulia state, the festival celebrates the miracle of Our Lady of Rosario of Chinquinquirá
17 December	Death of Símon Bolívar	

Public Holidays in Venezuela

24 December	Christmas Eve / Noche-buena	Birth of Jesus (el Dvino Niño)
25 December	Christmas Day	
31 December	New Year's Eve / Nochevieja	

LEARNING THE LANGUAGE

CHAPTER 8

'He who reads much and travels much,
sees much and knows much.'
—Miguel de Cervantes

As Venezuela has absorbed enormous cultural influence from the United States and, to a much lesser extent, Europe, you will see a great deal of English on the streets. English language newspapers and magazines such as *Time* and *Newsweek* are readily available and most billboards are splashed with advertisements for products bearing English names. This may lead you to the expectation that most Venezuelans have a good grasp of the language. Unfortunately this is not the case.

WHO SPEAKS ENGLISH?

English is the second language of choice and is taught in schools. However, Venezuelans learn English at school only to a rudimentary level. By the time they leave school, all that remains of this education is the ability to say "How are you?" and respond "Fine." Those who study at private language schools go immediately into the lower levels, indicating that the amount of English taught in schools is actually minimal. Many students do go on to study more English at a university, but this tends to concentrate more on grammar than on communication.

On the other hand, there are many people who have spent some time in the United States visiting relatives or for business, study or pleasure. Such people will be more than happy to practise their English with you. You can meet them just about anywhere in the cities, hopefully when you most need them. There is another category of English speakers, who need English for their work: English is the only language used in the literature of some professions, such as medicine, computing and aviation. These people will have a good understanding of the vocabulary required in their working lives, but may not have spoken fluency.

Those most likely to speak good English are richer Venezuelans and those in the upper echelons of companies, or those who are self-employed in the export/import business. Anyone who works in a multinational company, if they attend meetings with the top brass, will need to speak English well enough to survive in a business environment.

In general, most people you will meet will have little or no understanding of English, certainly not enough to conduct a normal conversation. This means that in order to go about your daily business effectively, a certain amount of Spanish is required. You will meet English speakers in bars and clubs, riding buses and in hospitals and clinics—but unfortunately not working in shops.

LEARNING SPANISH

You can live exclusively with English speakers and frequent the places English speakers like to go. This is a mistake. You will learn Spanish, but slowly and in a fragmented fashion. The only way to really learn Spanish is to push yourself wholeheartedly into a Spanish-speaking environment. This means doing absolutely everything you can in the language, which may be exhausting and frustrating but is enormously beneficial both to your language skills and your social life.

Learning the language is essential in enabling you to feel like a fully functioning human being. It can be mortifying to realise that a five-year-old child is a more adept social being than you are. More than just the language, however, you must learn how the people use it and how it expresses your personality. You need to use the right intonation, stress and vocabulary to get yourself across, as well as observe the appropriate social conventions of conversation. All of these will be explained in due course.

With No Spanish

If your Spanish is non-existent, make sure you take a course before going to Venezuela. Ideally you should join a class, as at a basic level it is vital for survival in the unavoidable social situations. Learning from books and tapes can help, but you really need to experience successful social encounters. At first, basic conversation and the ability to order cheese will be more important than grammatical accuracy. The friendly Venezuelans will readily tolerate your errors without ridiculing you, but will demand that you speak, so be prepared to loosen your tongue! Being in Venezuela will stretch whatever language capability you have. People will be naturally curious and will bombard you with questions, usually without any sympathy for your position as a language learner.

With Some Spanish

Clearly, Venezuelans who want to progress in English cannot rely on the school system but must pursue the subject at university, through private lessons with a tutor, or in a private language school. This means that although you might come across some excellent English speakers, most people you will talk to have little idea of what trying to pick up a foreign language is like, because they have not experienced it. Venezuelans will often greatly overestimate your ability in the language and mistake your silence for unfriendliness, when all you are doing is trying to grope for the word for 'sharp'.

At an intermediate level, when you can converse but frequently find your vocabulary insufficient to express your ideas, it is vital that you be flexible and use other words when you cannot find the one you are looking for. Or you can simply ask "what's the word for…" and give a description of the object. Venezuelans will be unfailingly helpful as long as they can see that you are trying. Attempting to speak the language will endear you to them more than any other thing you could do. This can be a bit disconcerting, as you will be expected to pitch in with gusto into any and every conversation. As people get used to you, they will slow down, allow you the time you need and fill in the words you don't have. Remember that when you are asking for some form of service, patience is rare, so you must be able to communicate your needs clearly and fairly quickly.

Opportunities to Pick Up More Spanish

The media is an excellent aid to language learning. Television presents you with language in a controlled environment that is clearer than normal (the news, cartoons) or that is repetitive and predictable (soap operas, dramas). Listening to the radio attunes your ear to the rhythm and stress patterns of spoken Spanish. With daily practice, the incomprehensible soon becomes clear. Newspapers, books and magazines are helpful, not only for vocabulary and expressions, but also for learning phrases and how sentences are put together and improving your pronunciation and mastery of stress by reading to yourself.

Learning By Doing

When I arrived in Caracas, I managed to avoid learning much Spanish by the simple expedient of living with Americans and working in an environment where people either spoke

English or were learning how to do so. This meant that virtually the only point of contact with the language was shopping. In supermarkets, you can put most things straight into the trolley, leaving only the delicatessen counters to deal with. My essential vocabulary was therefore composed of weights and measures and gave me my first taste of some of the problems of learning a language.

Learning from Experience

I learnt much of my vocabulary by trial and error. For example, I learnt the meaning of *rallado* when the man serving me in a panaderia used it in a one-word question, "*¿Rebanado?*" in reference to some cheese I was buying. Unable to guess from the context, I said, "*Si*" and he quickly ran it over a cheese slicer. I did not want my cheese sliced. The next time I was asked, memory failed me and once again I came away with unwanted sliced cheese. By the third time, I had remembered and my cheese remained whole.

Hearing a word used within its context helped me to remember it, even if I could not translate it into English. This meant that television, especially soap operas, was very important for me, as the context was frequently predictable and clear. This way I learnt when words and phrases were used, so when the right moment came I could use them myself. A friend took a pocket translator with him wherever he went so whenever he heard a new word he would whip it out and find the translation. You will have to find out by trial and error which ways of learning best suit you.

The Value of Lessons

It is also a good idea to take classes in Spanish, if only for the grammar. I knew a number of people who had spent a few years in the country without any formal study of the language and they all showed the same type of speech. They had great fluency and excellent use of idioms and other expressions. On the other hand they would pepper their conversation with an impressive array of grammatical errors. If they tried, they would find them very hard to correct as they have been so used to making these mistakes and had no trouble communicating—people understood what they meant despite their mistakes.

PRONUNCIATION

One of the joys of Spanish is that it is a relatively phonetic language. This means that once you have seen how words are pronounced, you can pick up anything written in Spanish and read it out loud, getting the pronunciation largely correct. So with only a little study, you can amaze your friends and family with your command of the language. But this is not a good thing to do with Venezuelans, as they will then talk to you as if you were a native speaker.

A few hints to aid your pronunciation of Spanish may be helpful. Say the word *amigo* and you have already mastered most of the vowels, as they are unchanging wherever you may find them. 'A' is *ah*; the 'i' in Spanish is always long, forming almost an *ee* sound; 'o' is the *Oh!* used when expressing surprise, spoken with a rounded mouth.

Spanish is a syllable-timed language. Each syllable is pronounced with full emphasis, unlike English where syllables are squeezed to fit a stress pattern. This means that Spanish seems to exercise the facial muscles more than English, making it difficult to speak when tired. 'E' is a short vowel like the *e* in bed, and so Pedro is not *Peedro* or *Paydro* but *Pehdro*. 'U' is *ooh*, like the sound in 'you'.

Other differences to English are the notoriously tricky 'rr', which is easy if you can do a Scottish 'r'. Try saying 'great' in a heavy Scottish accent, and roll that 'r' as hard as you can. The 'll' is pronounced somewhere between a 'y' and a 'j' so 'chicken' becomes *por-yo* with a hint of the vibration a 'j' would give it. 'Ñ' is an 'n' followed by a 'y' as in 'onion'.

'J' (always) and 'h' (before 'i' or 'e') are hard but not guttural. 'H' is usually silent. 'Z' is pronounced as an 's'.

A 'u' after a 'g' shows that the 'g' should be pronounced normally, like the English 'g' in 'great'. A 'u' with two points over it (an umlaut—ü) is pronounced with a 'w' sound.

MAKE YOUR OWN WORDS

There are some words, known as false friends, which can cause confusion, as they seem very similar to words in Spanish but do not share the same meaning. *Embarazada* does not mean 'embarrassed' but 'pregnant'. *Fastidioso* does not mean fussy, like 'fastidious', but 'boring'. I always took a delight in getting similar words right. My major triumph was in successfully buying mosquito repellent by walking into a shop and asking for *repellente*. 'Mosquito' itself is a Spanish word meaning small fly. Another delight of the language lies in discovering the Spanish words that you already knew with a light bulb-like flash of understanding. "I should have known that *ecuador* means 'equator' in Spanish!" is an example.

There are some words that are analogous with English but with one systematic change. This makes them easy to learn but also tricky to spell as the English version interferes with correct pronunciation. Most English words with *-tion* or *-sion* endings are the same in Spanish but with *-ción* or *-sión* endings. *Conversión* and *misión* are two examples. English words that end in *-ity* nearly always end in *-idad* in Spanish, such as *identidad*. There are some words of Greek origin that are common to both languages. In English they end in *-em* or *-ama* and in Spanish *-ema* or *-ama*. Examples are *sistema* and *problema*. These words are also exceptions to the rule that nouns ending in 'o' are masculine and nouns ending in 'a' are feminine, as they are all masculine (*el problema*).

> This masculine/feminine distinction can be hell to remember, but mistakes in this area are unimportant, although noticeable. Just remember that good language learners make mistakes.

HOW TO TALK TO LANGUAGE LEARNERS

The most important point to remember is that the largest barriers to comprehension are the speed at which you talk and the vocabulary you use. Strong accents also present problems. When speaking to people without much practice with English, it is important to speak clearly and fairly slowly, but not exaggeratedly slowly. Concentrate on the person you are speaking to, so that you know they are following you. If they cannot understand something, do not just repeat it but try to say the same thing in simpler language.

It is important to establish early on which language you intend to use. It is a shame to listen to someone struggle with English when they would have greatly appreciated your attempts at Spanish. It can also be excruciating when you know your Spanish is better than their English, as I found out with a 'helpful' bank clerk who ignored my attempts to change our conversation into quicker and more convenient Spanish.

VENEZUELAN SPANISH

Venezuelan Spanish is a rich dialect that reveals some truly Venezuelan characteristics such as irreverence, sense of humour and warmth. This last is especially reflected in greetings, of which there are many. After the greeting, there is often nothing left to be said, so it is important that the greeting be effusive and protracted.

Venezuelan Spanish is not as rude as the Spanish of Spain, although it of course has its own fair share of swear words. Everybody swears, using all but the most profane language. *Coño* is equivalent to English's worst word, but not as strong. It is often softened to *conchale*. People of all ages and at all levels of society swear. I once passed an elegant, obviously wealthy, middle-aged lady stepping out of a car. She stumbled slightly and uttered *coño* loudly and without shame. Every Spanish-speaking country seems to have a favourite word for 'fuck' and in Venezuela this is *joder*. *No joda!* means 'No shit' and *No me jodes* is 'Don't fuck me around.'

Venezuelan Spanish naturally includes a number of words that are exclusive to the country. Some of these are *lechosa* for 'papaya', and *carro* or *auto*—not *coche*—for 'car'. 'Passion fruit' is *parchita*, not *maracuya*. *Parchita* means 'homosexual', as does *mariposa* (butterfly). *Pavo*, as well as meaning 'turkey', also means 'young person'.

VENEZUELAN EXPRESSIONS

There are, of course, a huge number of *criollo* idioms that give Venezuelan Spanish its own distinctive flavour. These often reflect the light-hearted, joke-loving Venezuelan nature or the national love of gossip. There are many ways to greet someone, indicative of the importance of keeping in touch, but the frequent lack of any words after this initial stage hints at the lack of depth of many social contacts.

¿Cómo estás?	How are you?
¿Cómo está la cosa?	How is everything?
¿Cuéntame de tu vida	Tell me something about your life.
¿Cómo lo pasaste?	How was it?—referring to the weekend, a party or other event.
¿Cómo está la vaina?	How's things? (*vaina* is a slang expression for stuff)
¿Cómo te va?	How's everything?

These are all popular, informal ways of keeping up acquaintance. There are also words that have been picked up from other Spanish-speaking countries, most of them popular slang words. *Chevere*, meaning 'lovely' or 'great', comes from Cuba. *Vaya!* indicates admiration and is a Caribbean word. *Chamo/a* is Mexican, from *chamaco*, and it signifies 'friend'. It has even been corrupted further to *zamo/a* and is much in vogue among teenagers.

REGIONAL VARIATIONS

The language in each area of Venezuela has its own accent and regional colour. In the Andes, the Spanish is more sibilant, like Argentinean Spanish, and uses *Vos*, an alternative to *tú*. It is the only part of Venezuela to do so. *Ustedes*, the formal variant, is always used in its place. Spanish here is smooth and song-like and is also more refined.

In the llanos the Spanish is harsher and more guttural. It is filled with words and expressions of African and Indian origins, making it hard for even other Venezuelans to follow.

In the capital, speech tends to run words together, especially as 's' is frequently omitted. Words are often contracted, for example, *para adelante* (ahead) becomes *pa'lante* and *me entendiste?* (Did you understand me?) becomes *mentendiste?* This creates a distinctive *caraqueño* accent. It can cause problems if you do not consider the possibility of having to break down the words being strung together and instead believed them to be one word.

> We were having breakfast in a café in Apure when a grizzled llanero (plainsman) walked in and gave a bass rumble of *Buena* (for Buenos *dias*). We all returned with incomprehensible growls of our own, much to the surprise of a good Spanish speaker recently arrived in the country.

A common *caraqueño* phrase is *ete* (*este*), drawn out to give a pause for thought and often repeated—*este, este, este. Ustéd* is used for elder family members or other people in positions that demand a little respect. The harsh, guttural sounds prevalent in Spanish Spanish are not used and 'c' and 'z' are not given the 'th' sound, as in Spain.

SIMPLER SPANISH

Phrasebook Spanish is fine for most social situations but too formal for casual chat among friends, when you will find that people will say *damelo* (give it to me) instead of the formal *Me puede pasar el libro, por favor?* and *pasamelo* (pass it to me) and *dime* (tell me).

Besides this use of the imperative, there are other ways of simplifying your use of Spanish grammar. The present simple tense can be used to refer to the present, the immediate past and the future, such as *ya vengo* (I'm coming). In Venezuela, the present perfect is used in the same way as in British English, for example *he terminado* is 'I have finished'.

Some grammar is simple to learn, such as the suffixes for adjectives *-ado* and the continuous participle *-iendo*. If you focus on the grammar that has a direct parallel in English, your life will be made easier. At the same time, noting where the differences are is also vital. The various changes to the verb mean that the subject is redundant and is only used for emphasis. *Quiero un helado* (I want an ice-cream) is said instead of *yo quiero un helado*. On the other hand, reflexive pronouns are much more frequently used: 'I like it' is *me gusta*. Adjectives are different in that they change to reflect the number and gender of the noun. They also follow a noun that they describe. Thus three changes to the adjective *linda* are: *chicas lindas* (pretty girls), *chicos lindos* (handsome boys) and *una mujer linda*. As you can see, some nouns also change form to be both masculine and feminine (*chico/chica*).

SPANGLISH

There exists a shady middle ground between the two languages, known as Spanglish. Spanglish occurs when an attempt at translation is made and fails, or when an English word is appropriated and 'Spanglicised'. There are many examples of this, such as *molestar*, a verb meaning to be annoyed in Spanish, whereas in English being molested is obviously more serious. *Estoy molesto*—'I am molested' —is a possible mistranslation that you will do well to be wary of.

On the other hand, many words of English origin are directly translated. Two examples are hot dog, which is *perro caliente*, and screensaver, which is *salvapantallas*.

Understanding Spanglish

A friend never seemed to get hold of anyone when she called, as whenever she asked for someone the reply was *"de parte?"* Without paying too much attention to the intonation, she thought that this meant they had departed. Eventually it dawned on her that a better translation would be "Who's calling?" and instead of hanging up she gave her name.

SPANISH YOU ALREADY KNOW

Helpfully, there are many English words in use in Venezuela, although you may not recognise either the pronunciation or the spelling. Here are a chosen few, to give you a handle on the language and a sense of familiarity. You will also need to know which words you can use and those you cannot. 'OK' is well known in its usual context but is also used to mean 'goodbye'. 'Yes' or 'yeah' are strangely unknown. As the people in my local *panaderia* clearly understood the meaning of 'OK', I thought they would also understand 'yeah', so I would reply to the proffered lump of cheese and the query of "*¿Está bien?*" (Is this OK?) with "yeah." The question would be repeated and so would my answer. Finally I would grow angry and say "OK, OK!" This had the desired result.

Broadly speaking, there are three categories of English words. Firstly there are those that have been absorbed into Spanish and which most Spanish speakers consider to be Spanish. Secondly there are words that are more or less universally known, and thirdly those that are known by some but are generally corrupted and mispronounced. You are perfectly safe with the first two categories and you can pepper your conversation with them as liberally as you wish. The third category is inadvisable and mentioned here only so that you may recognise them. You may experience an aural double take when a Venezuelan uses one of these words, due to the omission of letters or Spanish pronunciation.

There are many English words in the area of food and drink. Whisky (often pronounced *whikey*) is the drink of choice, sandwiches are familiar but not so popular. Other food words are pub, grill, beef steak (*bifstek*), roast beef (*rosbif*), on the rocks, Bloody Mary, Manhattan, Gin Tonic and Gin Fizz (*Geen Feez*). There are also many English words on products themselves, such as country crackers, although their meaning would be lost to most Venezuelans if they did not sit alongside the Spanish words (a useful way of picking up vocabulary).

In sports, all the terminology for baseball, the national sport, has been taken directly from the English and is usually recognisable, *jonron* (homerun) being the most Spanish example. Other games have their names untouched—golf, volleyball, bowling, tennis, basketball (usually abbreviated to basket); soccer is *futbol*. Soccer vocabulary that has survived translation includes corner, penalty, shoot (*chutalo*—shoot it!—the fans shout) and of course, goal (*gol*). *Box* (boxing) also has some English vocabulary—ring, knock down/out, round, ranking and referee.

In the worlds of business, entertainment and home, you have jet set, rock, jazz, look, in and super (a popular adjective applicable to everything). Other words are charter, boarding pass, motor home, taxi, feeling, stress (*estres*), club, hobby, off the record, leader (*líder*), a political meeting (*mitin*), chance (pronounced *chan-say*), background, office boy, dry cleaning, real estate, penthouse, hall, water closet, resort, townhouse, store, fashion, staff, dollar (*dolar*), camping, tour, picnic and ticket. You will wear *blue jean* (not jeans), *chort* (shorts), *esmoking* (dinner jacket), brassiere, panties (which are tights), tanga and bikini. Some holidays are recognised, such as Thanksgiving Day, Halloween, weekend and, of course, Happy Birthday (with the 'th' omitted).

FRIENDLY TONGUES

One linguistically fortunate fact is the Norman Conquest of Britain. A legacy of that era is the French influence in English, which means that there are many words common to English and the Latin languages. If you speak French,

Italian, Portuguese or even Romanian, learning Spanish, particularly in a Spanish-speaking environment, should be simplicity itself. My own grasp of French is rudimentary but when I had my first Spanish lessons, I found myself using a flood of French that had been long forgotten.

French Spanish

There are some words in French that are used in English and are also in common use in Venezuela. French was considered the language of style and sophistication, so was once much in use in Venezuela. Happily for many of us, English has now supplanted it as the second language of choice, but many words remain from those halcyon days. Caution is advised, as some words have been transformed into Spanish and some do not have the same meaning as they do in English.

Monsieur and *madam* have been Spanglicised to *Musiú* (which is now applied to all foreigners) and *madama*. 'Chauffeur' does not just mean someone who is paid to drive someone else, but any car driver. It is the commonest Venezuelan word for 'driver'. Other familiar French words are restaurant, paté (*de fois*), petis pois, fondue, crépe, menu, bidet, chalet, parquet, boulevard, souvenir, premier, matinee, rendezvous, cachet, dossier, champagne, cabaret, glamour, and boutique.

French words are spoken and rarely written, so pronunciation may have evolved into something slightly different from the original, hard to catch on first hearing, with possibly a mistake on a sound or two. However, it is usually clear from the context what the word means so an educated guess will be enough to grasp it.

Spanish and Other Languages

Latin has been long taught in Venezuela as in other countries. Some examples of Latin that are also familiar to English speakers are *habeas corpus*, *erga omnes*, *alma mater*, *te deum*, *ad hoc*, *pro forma*, *in memoriam*, *opus*, *curriculum vitae*, *post mortem*, *modus vivendi*, *ipso facto*, *per se*, *vox populi* and *modus operandi*.

Italian words mainly concern food, for example pizza, spaghetti (*espageuti* in Spanish), macaroni, risotto and calzone. *Ciao* is a word for 'goodbye', not both 'goodbye' and 'hello' as in Italian. It is spelt as it is pronounced—*chau*.

BODY LANGUAGE

In general, Venezuelans are demonstrative people, possibly using much more expressive body language than you are used to. You may easily find yourself reading their signals wrongly. Several times I saw scenes where I was sure that a fight was going to break out but it never did.

There are some gestures peculiar to the country that may cause you embarrassment or surprise if you are not prepared. Pointing, as in many cultures, is considered rude, and there is a possibly comical alternative: purse the lips and thrust them in the direction of what you wish to point out. Heads will turn to see what you are 'pointing' at. A way of catching attention is to hiss. You will hear this on the streets although it is generally pretty ineffective. It is especially used to gain the attention of women, and will be accompanied by the obligatory repartee.

A forefinger placed under the eye so that it draws down the lower eyelid is used to indicate that the speaker is telling a tall tale. The OK sign is not used, and indeed a smaller version, usually held close to the hip, is extremely offensive. A small wave of the hand near the hip signals a thief. The hand waved towards the mouth is not 'boring' but 'food'. A small wave of a horizontal hand means 'finished'. The reversed victory V, with the same meaning as a single extended forefinger, is unknown. You may be flicked an unintentional V-sign if someone is indicating two of something, so don't take it personally! A hand waved furiously as if burnt, accompanied by a pained expression, indicates that someone is in deep trouble.

WORKING IN THE COUNTRY

CHAPTER 9

'Find happiness in work, or you will not be happy.'
—Christopher Colombus

BUSINESS ETIQUETTE

Venezuelans like to know and be able to trust the person they are dealing with, so it is important to establish a relationship with your Venezuelan counterpart. This may indicate why it is so difficult to do any meaningful business over the phone, by written forms such as email or any other remote method, as these are too impersonal and do not help build a relationship. Networking is vital as Venezuela is still a country in which who you know is of paramount importance. Younger business people and those used to dealing with Westerners will focus more on business matters and place less importance on establishing trusting relationships. Local contacts can be vital to initiating business meetings.

In business, a certain level of formality and respect is important. It is respectful to call people by their titles: *Doctor(a)* for those with an MD or PhD, *arquitecto* for architects, *abogado* for lawyers and *profesor* for teachers; *Señor* for Mr, *Señora* for a married woman and *Señorita* for an unmarried woman. Formalities are also important, such as clothing, cleanliness, working hours, respect for the boss and so on. In the morning, you will recognise who is going to work and in what kind of place because of the clothing the person is wearing.

Business Attire

In Venezuela, appearance is extremely important and what you wear will be noticed. Dress to impress and don't be afraid to wear expensive watches, jewellery and use brand named accessories like pens. Men should wear dark suits of natural fibres, light wool for the tropical heat is recommended. In Venezuelan culture, status is highly important and, at least in business, those who show their success are admired rather than resented, although showing a casual disregard for money will obviously not impress. In a similar vein, it is important to stay in a hotel with an excellent reputation. People working in offices in Venezuela still wear a tie and jacket to go to work, which is a way to say 'I am working and I am serious'.

Meetings

Appointments should ideally be set up at least two weeks in advance. This can be done via fax, email or phone. They should then be confirmed in Spanish (for clarity) by fax or email about a week before the meeting. All written correspondence should be followed up by a phone call. Morning appointments are preferable and can be followed up by an invitation to lunch. Fridays should be avoided as Venezuelans tend to extend the weekend as far as is feasible and Friday afternoon is considered to be the start of the weekend.

Venezuelans are punctual for business meetings, although the meeting itself is for discussion rather than decision making. Greet colleagues with a firm handshake. Venezuelan women may give one kiss on the cheek to people they do not know well and two kisses for those they do. Business cards should be in English on one side and Spanish on the obverse, with the title and position clear to see. Cards should be presented after introductions have been made. There is not usually much small talk at meetings; lunch will be more relaxed and easy-going. The first meeting will be formal, as relationships begin to be established. Written material should be made available in English and Spanish. During meetings, the two most senior executives should sit opposite

Avoid trying to do business around the holiday periods, especially two weeks before and after Christmas, Carnival and three weeks before and after Easter.

each other. Venezuelans like to be in control and have matters proceed at their own pace. After the meeting, a thank you note should be sent to the most senior executive present.

It is normally very difficult to avoid discussing Venezuelan politics, as it is such a polarizing issue and vital in establishing identities. However, bringing up politics, the country's wealth disparities and economic woes should be avoided. When you know a Venezuelan's family members personally, it is good to enquire about them, but when the family background is unknown, this could be awkward. Venezuela is a very macho society, where men traditionally have one or more mistresses and this has been accepted, but now the divorce rate is one of the highest in South America and the marital situation can be nebulous.

> It is impossible to say too much about your positive impressions of Venezuela, so feel free to range over history, the arts, music, food, sports and of course, Venezuelans themselves.

The best restaurants in the city and country clubs are the best places to entertain, but remember that dinner is for socialising and lunch is for business.

Business Gifts

Business gifts should be given after a relationship has been established, unless a situation that calls for a gift has arisen, such as an invitation to a private home for dinner. Gifts are best given during the more relaxed context of a lunch meeting, not during business hours. Good gifts are something for the office such as a high quality pen, or good quality whisky, colognes and perfumes or even just chocolates. Remember that Venezuelans have access within Venezuela to almost any product that they might want to purchase. Businesswomen should be aware that giving gifts to male businessmen and / or going out alone with them could easily be misconstrued. Women in Venezuela will attract looks and comments that are intended to be flattering, rather than abusive.

INTERNATIONAL TRADE

The Venezuelan government has been working towards expanding trade cooperation in the region. It is a member

Los Torres de Parque Central. the two tallest towers in Venezuela and a hive of offices.

of the Andean Community (CAN) with Bolivia, Ecuador, Colombia and Peru, the Latin American Association for Integration (Aladi) with Argentina, Bolivia, Brazil, Chile, Colombia, Ecuador, Mexico, Paraguay, Peru and Uruguay, the Group of Three (G-3) with Colombia and Mexico, and the Southern Common Market (MERCOSUR). Venezuela also has a trade and investment agreement with the Caribbean Community (CARICOM), and its exports have preferential treatment with the European Union. Venezuela's main trading partners are the USA, Colombia, Mexico and Brazil. The main exports are metals, minerals and chemicals. Venezuela imports 80 per cent of its food, as well as electrical and chemical goods and transportation products.

THE VENEZUELAN AT WORK

Venezuelans that you meet in the street are unfailingly helpful and courteous, so it can be a shock to encounter some Venezuelans at work. The general Venezuelan attitude to work is likely to have you believing that most people consider their job their own personal fiefdom. Rules are less important than the interpretation given to them by the person who happens to be doing a particular job at the time.

The Flexibility of Rules

I once purchased a set of student rate Metro tickets without any difficulty. The next time I returned for more, the man at the counter said that what I had done was impossible. Despite showing him proof in the form of the student travel card I had spent hours queuing for, he denied the possibility of my actions, claiming that I needed a Venezuelan ID card (a *cédula*). I produced my passport, but nothing could shake him from his belief that, as I had been there a year, I had to have a *cédula*. I returned another day in the hope that I would be attended to by someone who did not deny reality or applied the rules less stringently.

Venezuelans who are extremely generous with their time outside of work may suddenly acquire a lack of patience. I was once told over the phone by a taxi company employee that I should learn to speak Spanish before I called the next time! If you do not show a sufficient level of respect to the person you are dealing with, you may find that the rules have suddenly changed.

People ignore or misrepresent rules to suit themselves. This makes the system vulnerable to open bribery. Someone might tell you that there is a certain fee for a particular service, and for all you know, there is. The only truth you can be certain of is that if you pay the 'charge', your business will move ahead much more speedily.

One important point to remember is that there is no institutionalised service ethic in the country—Venezuelan employees may never have been told that 'the customer comes first'. This means customers must be quite clear and assertive about their needs. In a restaurant, I once waited for over half an hour before being brought my bill despite frequent plaintive cries of "*Señor*!" We were only able to pay by walking out of the restaurant.

Venezuelans are accustomed to starting early (8:00 am usually, and 7:00 am is not unknown) and finishing late (6:00 pm or 7:00 pm), so they think that 9-to-5 Europeans are lazy. The working day can be a leisurely one. Given the lack of emphasis on service, you can set your own pace and even take your time when serving customers.

Another feature of Venezuela is an apparent tendency towards over-employment. This affects all sectors of society. On game shows, you will see an unnecessarily large number of glamorous assistants, whereas back home two would suffice. A small roadworks that could apparently be done by four men will have those four men working away in the hole and another six outside watching the four and drinking coffee. In stores, if you go in at a slow hour, you will see a reasonable number of people inside the shop. After a while, you will be surprised to see that they are all employees of the shop. Encountering the Venezuelan at work is just about the only time you will have complaints about the people, so do not be put off by this, just expect a different type of service.

It is true to say that when you have a question, you will get a different answer from each person you ask. Information gathering is a problem here. The only way to get accurate information is by talking to all the people concerned face to face, at the same meeting. This means that it is preferable to organise large numbers of meetings than try to gain information by other means. Another reason in favour of meetings is that Venezuelans always appreciate the personal touch and they will be much more responsive in a personal meeting. Although there is the technological background to send faxes and email (not, however, as extensively as you might be used to), faxes can easily drift into a void and telephones calls can experience problems, especially when calling out of Venezuela.

It is easy to drift into the misconception that Venezuelans are inefficient. You have to understand the business culture operating in the country. Personal contacts are the way in which most business transactions occur, so getting to meet people is vital. The entire culture operates around the principle that people are more important than rules. In practice this means that friends are offered contracts and relatives are given jobs. Friends will bend the rules for you when they can, so the cultivation of friendships is vital.

It is also true that it is important for favours to be eventually returned: *una mano lava la otra* (one hand washes the other), the expression runs tellingly. Offers of introductions should always be taken up, especially in informal situations such as parties, where rapport can be built up. When invited to lunch or dinner, allow the small talk to go on for as long as possible.

Do not worry if you do not get to the heart of the matter at the first meeting. If it went well, there will be other occasions. The important thing is to have patience and introduce business matters when you feel that the relationship has begun to flourish. The promises you receive may well be forgotten the very next day. Keep the dialogue ongoing, prodding gently in the right direction. Of course if you are dealing with your direct subordinates, you can impose demands, but try to draw the line at giving stress to your employees as they will then lose confidence and become more inefficient.

You will probably be referred to with *tú* so avoid using *Usted* unless you are clearly in the presence of a superior.

BANKING

By far the easiest way to open a bank account in Venezuela is to have your company do it for you. Any company with legal status in Venezuela can do this without running into difficulties. For a foreign company, you may need to produce a translation of the company's registration document. Individuals, on the other hand, are generally asked to show a *cédula* or an in-transit visa as proof of identity. A passport is not sufficient. You also need to show bank references from your country. If you are setting up your own business, you will find that dealings with banks can be as lengthy and protracted as with government agencies unless your company has legal status in Venezuela.

The larger banks have cash machines with a familiar variety of functions. One difference that you may encounter is that cheques can be cashed simply with proof of identity (a passport will do) at the bank of the cheque issuer. This is in fact more common than depositing cheques into an account. It is also easy to draw money from a credit card account by presenting the card and proof of identity. All major credit cards are accepted for purchases and cash withdrawal in Venezuela.

Websites of Banks

Banco Union: http://www.bancunion.com

Banesco: http://www.banesco.com

Banco de Venezuela: http://www.bcv.org.ve

Banks are nearly always busy places and long queues are inevitable, especially early in the morning and at around lunchtime.

SETTING UP A BUSINESS IN VENEZUELA

The Venezuelan government has created programmes designed to open up the country to foreign investment. The most successful of these have been in the fields of manufacturing, telecommunications and banking. Countries that have invested the most are the USA. Japan, Spain, Holland, France, Italy and Colombia. The incentives for investment by foreign companies include a maximum income tax rate of 34 per cent and a tax rebate of 20 per cent for industries, including tourism-related business and tax-free dividends. Venezuela has treaties or agreements with a number of countries to avoid double taxation. Foreign companies are allowed to repatriate 100 per cent of their profits and capital. All sectors of the economy are open to full investment, with the exception of radio broadcasting, television and Spanish-language newspapers. Maximum investment allowed in these media areas is 19.9 per cent.

Companies qualify as a Venezuelan national company (with less than 20 per cent foreign capital), a joint venture company (between 20 per cent and 49 per cent foreign capital) and a foreign company (with over 49 per cent foreign capital). Companies must be registered in a particular form. Those possibilities are:

- Corporation (*Sociedad Anónima S.A.* or *Compañia Anónima C.A.*)—with a determined capital and shareholders involved according to the value of shares held. It is the most popular form for a foreign company to take.
- Limited Liability Company (*Sociedad de Responsabilidad Limitada S.R.L.*)—the capital is divided into shares or negotiable titles. This form is mainly taken where the share capital is less than 2,000,000 bolívares.
- Limited Partnership (*Sociedad en Comandita Simple, Sociedad en Comandita por Acciones*)—silent partners are liable up to the value of their shares and general partners have unlimited liability.
- General Partnership (*Sociedad en Nombre Colectivo/ Sociedad Civil*)—all partners are equally liable. It has less tax benefits and is rarely used. A *Sociedad Civil* is a

professional partnership used by lawyers, accountants and other professionals.

- An Unincorporated Joint Venture (*Consorcio, Asociación de Cuentas de Participación*)—the joining of companies under common rules and leadership for a specific project. It does not have to be registered as a separate entity.
- A Foundation or Association has philanthropic aims and is ruled by the will of the founder/s.
- There are also Independent Companies, Subsidiary Companies, Branches and Representations.

The company must be registered with the Registrar of Commerce (*Registro Mercantil*) and shareholders must sign the Memorandum of Association and Articles of Association (*Documento Constitutivo y Estatutos Sociales*). Directors (*Administradores* or *Directores*) are appointed to control the running of the company and internal auditors (*Comisarios*) are appointed to protect shareholders' rights. Directors are required to file the *Documento Constitutivo* with the Registrar of Commerce within 15 days of incorporation. The document must also be published in a local newspaper.

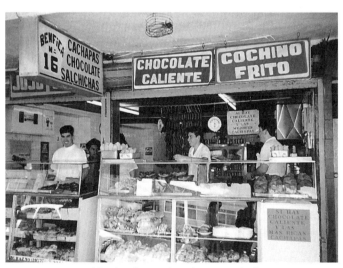

A Portuguese-owned food stall. Note the reference to the famous football team.

Upon incorporation (*constitución*), a stamp duty of 1 per cent is paid. An account must be maintained at a local bank, and payment into this is made of 20 per cent of the subscribed share capital (in cash); 50 per cent of capital to be issued in other forms must also be paid into an account. A reserve fund must be set up to contain 10 per cent of the subscribed capital (paid in 5 per cent of liquid assets yearly).

The company must register with the Superintendency of Foreign Investments (SIEX) within 60 days of being inscribed in the Registrar of Commerce. SIEX has the following functions: as the Registry of Foreign Investments, Registry of Technology Importation Contracts, Use and Exploitation of Patents and Brands, Granting Company Qualification Certificates and Granting National Investor Certificates. The Central Bank of Venezuela (BCV) holds a record of investment which is all-inclusive, so therefore covers cash, physical assets, loans, commercial credit, funds transferred and profits. Some areas are overseen by Superintendencies, such as the Superintendency of Banks and other Financial Institutions (*Sudeban*).

Registration with SIEX demands certified copies of the Memorandum of Association (*Documento Constitutivo*) and Articles of Association. Another copy is required and this must be translated into Spanish by a public translator, authenticated and certified by the Venezuelan consulate of the company's country of origin. A power of attorney has to be decided in favour of the investor. An application for the status of the company as national, joint venture or foreign has to be made. Incorporation with the Municipal Tax Administration and registration with the Tax Information Registry (RIF) and the Tax Administration (SENIAT) are also required.

Books and records that must be kept are a shareholder register, minutes of board meetings, minutes of shareholders' meetings, a journal (*Libro Diario*), a general ledger (*Libro Mayor*), an inventory (*Libro de Inventario*) and a wholesale tax registry book. Hydrocarbons, mines, banking and insurance are not covered by SIEX but by the Energy and

Mining Ministry, the Insurance Superintendency and the Bank Superintendency, respectively.

CONAPRI (the National Council for the Promotion of Investment in Venezuela, website: http://www.conapri. org) produces some useful publications including *A Guide for the Investor*, *Investment Opportunities*, *Legal Framework for Foreign Investment in Venezuela*, *Invest in Venezuela Handbook*, *Legal Bulletins* (law updates) and *PULSE Venezuela* (a monthly magazine).

THE BUREAUCRATIC MACHINE

There is a large amount of bureaucracy involved in processing documents. DEX (*Direccion de Extranjera*), the department that deals with visa applications, is a modern-day Tower of Babel constantly filled with visa supplicants. You will require several visits in order to see applications processed. The address is Edificio 1000, 2nd Floor, Calle 1000, Esquina San Pablo, El Silencio, Caracas.

As an example of what is required, for a work transient visa (an alternative is a non-resident business visa), you need to produce an Entry Request (*Solicitud de Ingreso*), two photocopies of the Mercantile Registry inscription, two *cédula* copies (one from the contractor and one from the agent authorised by DEX), a photocopy of the company's authorisation to process income, work authorisation from the Labour Ministry (*Ministerio de Trabajo*), a description of purposes, passport photocopy, photo, the latest tax return, a 60 bolívares fiscal stamp and a 10,800 bolívares stamp upon approval. The visa is valid for a year, with multiple entries into Venezuela permitted. For technical or professional posts, you can apply for visas for your family.

All projects that will involve over two million bolívares must be registered with the Industry and Commerce Ministry (*Ministerio de Industria y Comercio*). All companies must register their fiscal information with the Finance Ministry (*Ministerio de Hacienda*).

Helpful Websites

The following websites are helpful to newcomers and those already established.

- CONAPRI (National Council for the Promotion of Investment in Venezuela): http://www.conapri.org
- British Chamber of Commerce (Camara Venezolano Britanica de Comercio): http://www.britcham.com
- Embassy of the Republic of Venezuela in the United States: http://www.embavenez-us.org. Here you can find a wide range of information, from business links and visa information to the history of the Venezuelan flag and the lyrics of the Venezuelan national anthem! There is also cultural information, for example, on Venezuelan writers and artists.
- Ministry of Trade and Industry: http://www.mic.gov.ve
- Caracas Chamber of Commerce: http://www.ccc.com.ve
- The tax agency SENIAT: http://www.seniat.gov.ve
- Venezuelan Central Bank: http://www.bcv.org.ve
- Venezuelan-American Chamber of Commerce: http://www.venamcham.org

---

TAX

All non-residents and corporations are taxed at the top rate of 34 per cent. Residents (those actually in the country for more than 180 days in one year) pay between 6 per cent and 34 per cent tax, depending on income and possible tax relief. In practice, tax collection has long been a huge problem for the Venezuelan government, and may be as low as 60 per cent.

Businesses are subject to income tax (*Impuesto sobre la Renta*), business assets tax (*Impuesto a los Activos Empresariales*) and wholesale tax (*Impuesto a las Ventas al Mayor*).

Wholesale tax is equivalent to VAT, is payable monthly and is charged on self-consumption of goods and services, imports of goods and services, rendering services and sale of personal property. It is currently at 16.5 per cent. Wholesale tax is reflected in the ticket price of goods. Banks, insurance and temporary imports are exempt from this tax. Tax credits are available against the import and sale of basic goods.

Business assets tax is 1 per cent of the value of assets. Income tax paid is deducted from the amount payable of the business assets tax.

Besides a general sales tax, there is also a luxury consumption tax, which imposes a high tax rate on some items (including flights) that significantly raises the cost.

Payable municipal taxes are industry and trade license tax (*Impuesto sobre Patente de Industria y Comercio*) and urban real estate tax (*Impuesto Inmobiliario Urbano*).

SOCIAL SECURITY

The social security system provides for pensions on a pay-as-you-earn basis. Employers must pay a percentage of social security payments (around 7–9 per cent), as well as a percentage of unemployment insurance, as do workers (around 4 per cent). Employers must also pay small percentages to cover the Lay-Off Regulations and to the Housing Plan.

WORKERS AND LABOUR LAWS

All companies with over ten workers must employ Venezuelans as 90 per cent of the workforce. Salaries paid to foreign workers must be less than 20 per cent of the total.

Workers have important rights under Venezuelan law. After one months' employment, they cannot be dismissed arbitrarily and are entitled to a period of notice. After one month's work, this is one week's notice, after six months it is 15 days, after one year one month in advance, and so on. This payment is equal to ten days' salary for the first six months of employment, and one month per year thereafter. Union workers, pregnant workers and striking workers cannot be dismissed, thus eliminating the danger of reprisals for industrial action. If company ownership changes, its workers are guaranteed the maintenance of their old working relationship for one year.

A minimum wage is in effect, which is currently equivalent to 238 USD per month, one of the highest in Latin America. Companies pay a Christmas bonus equivalent to 15 per cent of their liquid profits divided among all workers. The minimum is the equivalent of 15 days' pay and the maximum is four months' pay. Vacations are controlled: 15 days after one year's service and an extra day per year of service thereafter (with a maximum of 15 extra days). There is a vacation bonus of seven days' salary, one day's salary added per year of service, up to 21 days.

The day shift is a maximum of eight hours and the night shift a maximum of seven hours. There is a maximum of 44 hours per week allowed for day work, 40 for night work and 42 for mixed shifts. Overtime is paid at an extra 50 per cent in the day and more at night. Women are entitled to six weeks' prenatal leave and 12 weeks' postnatal leave on full pay.

FAST FACTS

CHAPTER 10

'An ignorant nation is the blind
instrument of its own destruction.'
Símon Bolívar

Official Name
Conventional long form: Bolivarian Republic of Venezuela
Conventional short form: Venezuela

Capital
Caracas

Flag
Three equal horizontal bands of yellow (top), blue, and red with the coat of arms on the hoist side of the yellow band and an arc of eight white five-pointed stars centered in the blue band

National Anthem
Gloria al Bravo Pueblo (Glory to the Brave People)

Time
GMT (UTC) −4.5

Telephone Country Code
58

Internet Country Code
.ve

Area
Total: 912,050 sq km
Land: 882,050 sq km
Water: 30,000 sq km

Highest and Lowest Point
Lowest point: Caribbean Sea (0 m)
Highest point: Pico Bolivar / La Columna (5,007 m)

Climate
Tropical; hot, humid; more moderate in highlands

Population
26,414,815 (June 2008 est.)

Ethnic Groups
Spanish, Italian, Portuguese, Arab, German, African, indigenous people

Religion
Roman Catholic 96 percent, Protestant 2 percent, others 2 per cent

Language
Spanish (official), numerous indigenous dialects

Government
Federal republic

National Holiday
Independence Day, 5 July

Administrative Divisions
Twenty-two states and a Distrito Federal. The states are: Amazonas, Anzoátegui, Apure, Aragua, Barinas, Bolívar, Carabobo, Cojedes, Delta Amacuro, Falcón, Guárico, Lara, Mérida, Miranda, Monagas, Nueva Esparta, Portuguesa, Sucre, Táchira, Trujillo, Yaracuy and Zulia

Currency
Bolívar (VEB)

Gross Domestic Profit (GDP)
$334.6 billion (2007 est.)

Agricultural Products
Corn, sorghum, sugarcane, rice, bananas, vegetables, coffee; beef, pork, milk, eggs; fish

Industries
Petroleum, construction materials, food processing, textiles; iron ore mining, steel, aluminum; motor vehicle assembly

Exports
Petroleum, bauxite and aluminum, steel, chemicals, agricultural products, basic manufactures

Imports
Raw materials, machinery and equipment, transport equipment, construction materials

Natural Resources
Petroleum, natural gas, iron ore, gold, bauxite, other minerals, hydropower, diamonds

Airports
Total: 390 (2007)

Railways
Total: 682 km

FAMOUS PEOPLE
Francisco de Miranda
The 'Precursor' to Simón Bolívar, the greatest pre-revolutionary leader. His revolutionary attempts were foiled but his life's work, including his diplomatic efforts in New York and London, paved the way for liberation.

Simón Bolívar

El Libertador freed his homeland from Spanish rule but his superhuman efforts could not make his dream of a united Gran Colombia (spanning Venezuela, Ecuador, Panama and Colombia) come to fruition. His deeds and words have almost as much resonance today as when he wrote them.

Antonio José de Sucre

The heir apparent to Simón Bolívar, he was Galahad to Bolívar's Lancelot and carried the hopes of Bolívarianism with him until the dream died with his early death.

Luisa Cáceres de Arismendi

A tragic and heroic figure of the struggle for Independence, she refused to succumb to torture and thus betray her general husband and her country, she nows adorns the 20 Bolívar Fuerte note.

Rómulo Gallegos

Author of Venezuela's most famous novel *Doña Barbera*, mayor of Caracas and reformist president in 1948, a giant in Venezuela's more recent history.

Teresa Carreño

An internationally-renowned pianist, singer, composer and conductor who toured the world in the latter half of the 18th century and early 20th century. She gave her name to the Teresa Carreño Cultural Complex in Caracas.

Arturo Uslar Pietri

A polymath whose abilities were legion. Like Rómulo Gallegos, he was a successful 20th century politician as well as an award-winning author. He achieved more than seems possible for just one lifetime.

Andrés Bello

Tutor to Simón Bolívar, friend of Alexander von Humboldt and Francisco de Miranda, Bello was a great poet and philosopher, whose writing influenced many fields of Venezuelan thought.

Oscar D'León

A truly international Venezuelan star who personifies the spirit of salsa and bestrides the stage like a colossus. The King of Salsa has made a giant contribution to Latin music since the 1980s.

Irene Sáez

From Miss Venezuela and Miss Universe in 1981 to major of Chacao in Caracas in the 1990s and presidential hopeful in 1998, the route of beauty queen to politician is so far a unique one among the many Miss Venezuela success stories.

Hugo Chávez Frias

The list would not be complete without Venezuela's controversial president, whose Bolívarian reform has wrought fundamental change in Venezuela, politically and socially.

CULTURE QUIZ

SITUATION 1

You have arranged to meet some people for dinner. You are at the appointed meeting place but they are over half an hour late. Do you:

A Leave immediately. Nobody so irresponsible can be worth any more of your time.

B Try to call them before leaving.

C Think nothing of waiting for a further half an hour.

D Give them ten more minutes—maximum.

Comments

Any response other than **C** may lead you to feel rueful after they have proffered their perfectly reasonable explanation (as they will do).

SITUATION 2

You, a man, are about to get into a car that already holds a male driver and a female passenger in the back. Another female passenger is waiting to get in.

Ⓐ You get into the front seat.
Ⓑ You sit in the back.
Ⓒ You hold the front door open for the lady.
Ⓓ You hold the back door open for the lady.

Comments

Ⓐ and **Ⓓ** would be greeted with laughter. **Ⓑ** is fine and **Ⓒ** would be excite a cry of "*Que cabellero*!" (What a gentleman!) Anything other than this seating arrangement would be viewed with surprise. A couple in a taxi would sit in the back. Women must be accompanied by a man, whether you are their other half or not.

SITUATION 3

Some documents must be processed by a government agency and the official you deal with asks for a payment to 'make it go quicker'.

Ⓐ You agree and pay up.
Ⓑ You wait until you have found out if this is an officially sanctioned payment.
Ⓒ You angrily refuse and mutter something about bribery.
Ⓓ You try to deal with someone else in the same department.

Comments

Ⓐ will probably have the promised result and you can salve your conscience with the thought that this is standard practice. **Ⓑ** sounds good, if you can find the official literature; it may prove difficult. **Ⓒ** risks a shouting match and the chance they will never deal with you again. **Ⓓ** is a good idea, but you may well find that everyone will say only that person can help you, which is why **Ⓒ** is a bad idea. You can come back another day and hope that official will not be there.

SITUATION 4

You have been introduced to a prospective business partner and want to discuss a business proposition.

Ⓐ You call to discuss business over the phone.

Ⓑ You call to make an appointment.

Ⓒ You go to his office unannounced.

Ⓓ You send a fax suggesting that you meet.

Comments

Ⓐ is doomed, for he will have no time to go into detail on the phone. **Ⓑ** is good and **Ⓒ** is likely to be even more effective. Refusal to see you is unlikely, and the personal contact will be appreciated. **Ⓓ** is not recommended, as faxes can very easily fall into a vacuum.

SITUATION 5

You have been invited to a party where you only know a couple of people. You feel your Spanish is not good enough to enable you to hold conversations with strangers.

Ⓐ You speak only to your friends.

Ⓑ You ask people if they speak English and say you don't speak Spanish.

Ⓒ You try to talk and get people to help you fill in the gaps by explaining in other words what you want to say.

Ⓓ You co-opt a friend into being a translator for the night.

Comments

Ⓒ is the best option and you will find your efforts genuinely appreciated. In **Ⓓ**, you lag behind the conversation and may feel left out. **Ⓑ** will probably only allow you to talk to a few people and you will disappoint others. **Ⓐ** will win you no friends.

SITUATION 6

A friend invites you to dinner and then insists on paying, saying that as they invited you, they must pay.

Ⓐ You accept and make a mental note to invite them the next time.

Ⓑ You offer a token protest and then accept.

☉ You insist on paying your share.
☉ You decide to show your generosity and absolutely insist you pay.

Comments

☉ and **☉** are rather rude. Custom dictates that if someone invites, they pay. **☉** is good and **☉** is, of course, the best answer—unless you do not like them! Men can also be expected to pay for women. I was once unwittingly landed with half a bill as my friend had invited me and two girls to dinner. I could have insisted he pay, but I didn't.

SITUATION 7

In a *panaderia*, you want a *café con leche* and a *pan de chocolate*.

☉ You wait diligently in a line, moving forward as the people in front are served.
☉ You shout your order from where you are standing.
☉ You muscle your way to the front and shout your order.
☉ You push to the front and attempt to make eye contact.

Comments

☉ is normal behaviour and therefore your best bet, as you jockey for position surreptitiously, without too much open aggression. **☉** and **☉** are far too timid and you may have to wait an eternity. **☉** is unlikely to work unless you are a known client, and you will have to get to the front to pick up your order anyway.

SITUATION 8

You rent a flat and Venezuelan friends recommend the services of their maid.

☉ You ask what she can do, how much she costs and when she is free.
☉ You ask to interview the maid yourself.
☉ You refuse, saying you're not comfortable with hiring a servant.

D You refuse, saying you're more than capable of looking after yourself.

Comments

A or **B** are fine. Despite the mutterings of some folk, a recommended maid is usually reliable. **C** will make you look like a crazy foreigner and **D** exposes your cultural preconceptions. If you really feel you would be exploiting someone, either pay them really well (but make it a secret) or just say you will think about it. Having a maid is normal for many Venezuelans, not just the rich. A recommendation is not a slur on your housekeeping skills!

SITUATION 9

You are a woman. While walking in the street, you find yourself face to face with a man making suggestive comments (*tirando piropos*) at you.

A You ignore him completely.
B You throw a choice insult at him.
C You smile and walk on.
D You ask him to repeat what he said and speak more slowly so that you can understand.

Comments

The best choice is **A**. If the guy looks drunk, **A** is the only choice. **C** and **D** are asking for more amorous entreaties, which will definitely happen if his friends are around to encourage him. **B** is likely to elicit an insult in turn.

SITUATION 10

You, a man, are enjoying your bus ride when an attractive girl asks you your name and starts talking.

A You end the conversation as quickly as possible. You are not interested in someone who would be so forward.
B You ask her for her phone number.
C You wait until she asks you for your phone number.
D You ask her if she is free now, for coffee perhaps.

Comments

Venezuelan women have plenty of romantic initiative, so do not be put off by this. **B** is not too peremptory, although a phone number is not quite the promise of a date. **C** is also possible and might well work. **D** is a good option. It might be rebuffed, but you could still try **B** or **C** afterwards.

DO'S AND DON'TS

DO'S

- Flirt if you feel like it.
- Bring a gift when invited to a Venezuelan home.
- Be complimentary about Venezuela and the Venezuelans.
- Show your enjoyment of hospitality, food and drink.
- Join in with any dancing.
- Send a personal note after invitations.
- Follow up an agreement to meet with a phone call a couple of days later.
- Feel free to chat to strangers wherever you are.
- Be scrupulous about your personal appearance.
- Be on your guard when out on the streets and keep moving.
- Accept invitations without being 10 per cent sure if you can go.

DON'TS

- Wear revealing clothing (women, obviously) or flirt (men or women) if don't want to be propositioned.
- Unfavourably compare Venezuela or Venezuelans with other countries or nationalities.
- Wear sandals or shorts anywhere but the beach.
- Expect punctuality for any situation other than at business meetings.
- Avoid physical contact e.g. kissing on the cheeks or close physical proximity or eye contact.
- Expect every invitation to a party, the beach and so on to come to fruition.
- Go out at night alone.
- Shop at street markets.
- Try to dominate a conversation.
- Slouch or put feet on furniture.
- Discuss politics or poverty.
- Decline an offer of coffee (it means coffee, not sex!).
- Refer to the USA as 'America' or maintain that South America is not a separate continent.
- Be negative about Simon Bolívar.

GLOSSARY

STARTER KIT OF WORDS AND PHRASES

Abrazo	An embrace between Venezuelans when they meet
Aguinaldo	Traditional Christmas song
Arepa	A thick cornmeal disc with the filling of your choice
Barrio	Working class neighbourhood
Bolo	A Bolívar (currency)
Bonche	A party
Cachapa	A sweet cornflour pancake
Caraqueño	A resident of Caracas
Cédula	The identity card that Venezuelans carry
Chavisto/a	A supporter of Chavez
Chicha	Sweet drink of rice and milk
Chiguire	Venezuelan term for a capybara
Chévere	An exclamation of approval
Chimbo	Something of poor quality, rubbish
Chisme	Gossip
Colina	Neighbourhood of high-quality housing
Compadrazgo	The ties created through being godparents
Compadre	Godfather
Conuco	Farming system with small plots used in rotation
Criollo	Creole. Originally used to describe someone of Spanish ancestry, now describes anything typically Venezuelan
Cuatro	A small four-stringed guitar

Echón	A lazy and wasteful person
Encomienda	The system wherein the Spanish *encomendero* permitted Indian farmers to work the land in return for a tribute. They also received protection, housing, clothing, food and medicine
Farándula	Gossip about show business and celebrities
Franela	T-shirt
Hacienda	A large plantation or estate
Hamaca	A woven hammock
Hato	A hacienda where raising livestock is the principal activity
Joropo	The traditional dance generally seen as the national dance
Liqui-liqui	The traditional cotton suit still worn by many Venezuelans
Llanero	Someone or something from Los Llanos, the plains, usually the saddle-hardened cowboys
Llanos	The central plains of Venezuela and also Colombia
Manta	An intricately woven shawl wore by Spanish and Latin American women, notably in Venezuela by Guajiro Indians
Malandro	A small-time criminal
Mestizo	Someone of mixed ethnicity, originally specifically Spanish-Indian
Pabellón criollo	The national dish
Palafito	The palm leaf huts built over water on stilts by the Parajuano Indians
Palo	Stick or alcoholic drink (colloquial)
Pan de jamon	Bread with olives and ham
Pana	A friend, pal, mate

Papelón con limon	Cane sugar and lemon juice drink
Pardo	A person of mixed Spanish and Indian ancestry
Pasapalos	Snacks served as a starter or at parties
Piñata	Often the centrepiece of a child's birthday party. A brightly coloured model of an animal or cartoon figure commonly made from paper or papier-mache. It can be hit with sticks until it breaks and the contents fall out, to be fought over by children. These may include sweets and small toys and glitter
Quinceañera	A girl's coming-of-age celebration on her 15th birthday
Quinta	Luxurious detached house
Rancho	A makeshift shanty house built on atop another on the outskirts of cities and towns
Ratón	A mouse or hangover (colloquial)
Repartimiento	The system of allocating land to the *conquistadores* and of forcing Indians to spend their income at the official Spanish store
Sifrino	A snob
Telenovela	TV soap opera
Tepui	A flat-topped mountain symbolic of the Guiana Highlands
Vaina	An expression used as a filler to mean stuff
Venezolano	A Venezuelan
Zanahoria	A carrot or someone very boring
Zancudo	A mosquito

RESOURCE GUIDE

EMERGENCIES AND HEALTH
Hospitals
Public hospitals are generally underfunded and overcrowded, so private clinics—which are expensive—are preferable.

- **Clínica el Avila**
  Avenida San Juan Bosco con 6a Transversal, Altamira, Caracas
  Tel: (212) 276-1111/1052
  Fax: (212) 276-1035
  Website: http://www.clinicaelavila.com
- **Policlínica Metropolitana**
  Calle A con Avenida Principal de Caurimare, Caracas
  Tel: (212) 908-0100 / 908-0229
  Website: http://www.policlinicametropolitana.com.ve/
- **Nuestra Señora del Carmen Centro Clinico** (Trujillo State)
  e/Carreras 21 y 22, C. C. Cosmo, P-6
  Tel: 253-4956; (0416) 750-8750
- **Centro Clínico la Isabelica (Valencia)**
  Avenida 2, Este-Oeste Urbanización La Isabelica
  Tel: (0241) 832-3264
- **Centro Clínico Nardulli I C.A.** (Cuidad Ojeda, Zulia State)
  Tel: (0265) 662-6865
- **Centro Clínico Padre Pío** (San Bernadino)
  Sn Bernardino Caracas, La Gran Caracas, Venezuela
  Tel: (02) 552-9502
- **Centro Medico de Ojos** (Maracaibo)
  Av.8 (Santa Rita), Esquina con Calle 83, Maracaibo-Edo. Zulia.
  Tel: (0261) 797-4375 / 797-4523 / 797-4548 / 798-0349
  Fax: (0261) 798-6736.
- **Hospital de Clínicas Caracas**
  Av. Panteón con Av. Alameda San Bernardino, Hospital de Clínicas Caracas. Apartado Postal 1011, Caracas-Venezuela
  Tel: (0212) 508-6111
  Website: http://www.clinicaracas.com

- **Hospital Clínico el Rosario (Cabimas)**
  Website: http://www.hospitalelrosario.com
- **Hospital Metropolitano del Norte (Valencia)**
  Website: http://www.hospital metropolitano.com
  Tel: (0241) 700-7000
- **Centro Médico Maracay (Maracay)**
  Av. Las Delicias, Urb. El Bosque, Edf Centro Médico Maracay
  Tel: (243) 232-3324 / 232-0545
  Website: http://www.centromedicomaracay.com
- **Clínica Félix Boada (Caracas)**
  Calle Bolívar De Baruta
  Tel: 903-02-000-501-Clinica (0-501-254-6422)
  Website: http://www.clinicafelixboada.com
- **Centro Médico Cagua C.A.**
  C/Pichincha Este, Frente Carretera Nacional Cagua
  Tel: (0244) 395-4265 / 395-4673 / 395-4218
  Email: centromedcagua@cantv.net
- **Centro Médico Paso Real**
  Autopista Charallave-Ocumare Del Tuy, Ubicación Charallave Urbanización Paso Real, Parcela 3-C
  Tel: (0239) 220-9500

Medical Services
- **Rescarven**
  Website: http://www.rescarven.com/index_2.htm
- **Sanitas**
  Tel: (0212) 206-5800
  Website: http://www.sanitasvenezuela.com

FITNESS CENTRES
- **Action Club**
  San Benito, Maracaibo
  Tel: (261) 793-2937
- **Activa C.A**
  Tierra Negra, Maracaibo
  Tel: (261) 793-1495
- **Aerobic's Leidy Gym**
  La Victoria, Maracaibo

Tel: (261) 753-0911

- **Areostep**
  Av 74 entre 3G y 3H, Maracaibo
  Tel: (261) 792-9184
- **American City**
  San Blas, Valencia
  Tel: (241) 859-1979
- **Body Line**
  Las Delicias, Maracaibo
  Tel: (261) 741-3114
- **Body Spa Fitness Centre C.A.**
  Zona Industrial Municipal Sur, Valencia
  Tel: (241) 832-0374
- **Corpus Spa Gimnasio**
  1era Transversal Edif. Don Pedro, P. B., Loc-B, Los Platos
  Grandes, Caracas
  Tel: (212) 283-8334
- **Down Town Gym**
  Circunvalacion 2, Maracaibo
  Tel: (261) 786-5389
- **Gimnasio Cosmos**
  S.R.L. Av Ppal El Bosque, Edif. Pichincha Ofic. 81, Chacaito,
  Caracas
  Tel: (212) 952-1483
- **Gimnasio Domeni's Gym**
  Los Haticos, Maracaibo
  Tel: (261) 764-3225
- **Gimnasio Golden Gym**
  Av Bolívar Sur, Valencia
  Tel: (241) 853-3089
- **Gimnasio Gustavo Cuba**
  Primero de Mayo, Maracaibo
  Tel: (261) 752-7851
- **Gimnasio Henry's Gym Unisex**
  Calle 69A, No.79-216, Los Aceitunos, Maracaibo
  Tel: (261) 754-5560
- **Gimnasio JKA**
  Av Fco de Loreto, La Victoria, Aragua
  Tel: (244) 322-8053

- **Gimnasio Levi Paez**
  Tierra Negra, Maracaibo
  Tel: (261) 798-2819
- **Gimnasio Maracuay Fitness Centre**
  Av Mara, Urb, Maracuay, Ctro Com. Maracuay Plaza, NvC2,
  Loc-2, Caracas
  Tel: (212) 258-0060
- **Gimnasio Santa Monica**
  Av Rufino Blanco Fombona, Quinta La Corteza, Caracas
  Tel: (212) 661-6232
- **Gimnasio Yinzentai Calle Mariño**
  Entre Carabobo y Santa Barbara, Puerto Cabello
  Tel: (242) 361-0774
- **Ginger's Gym**
  Av Las Delicias, La Floresta, Maracay
  Tel: (243) 242-5091
- **Gimnasio Mr America**
  Calle Mariño C/Cl Bolívar, Edif. Centro Royal, Maracay
  Tel: (243) 246-2503
- **Imagen Gym**
  La Isabelica, Valencia
  Tel: (241) 834-5270
- **Jorge Gym**
  Los Haticos, Maracaibo
  Tel: (261) 765-1120
- **Lubrigim Canta Claro**
  Maracaibo
  Tel: (261) 742-5272
- **Millenium Gym**
  Sabaneta Larga, Maracaibo
  Tel: (261) 787-5729
- **Olympia Gym Unisex**
  Indio Mara, Maracaibo
  Tel: (261) 752-4607
- **Power House Gym**
  Ctro Com. Caracas, P-4, 2da Av, Montalban III
  Tel: (212) 443-4304
- **Street Muscle Gym**
  Av Paez con Cl Los Estadios, 3er Piso, El Paraiso, Caracas

Tel: (212) 451-2590

- **Struktura**
  C.A. Av Universidad, La Granja, Naguanagua
  Tel: (58-241) 867-1313e

HOME AND FAMILY
Estate Agents (Bienes Raíces)

Here is a selection of estate agents with English websites.
Many others can be found through webguides like http://
www.auyantepui.com.

- **Administradora Yuruary c.a.**
  Tel: (212) 573-0122
  Website: http://www.yuruary.com
- **Betty Vielman Bienes Raíces**
  Tel: (001) 305-273-8093 (Miami office)
- **Century 21**
  Website: http://www.century21venezuela.com/newsite/
- **Mi Casa International Centro**
  Integral Santa Rosa, Planta Superior, Local 1 Urbanización
  Santa Rosa de Lima.
  Tel: (02) 991-0022; Fax: (02) 993-78-04.
  Email: Micasa@cantv.net
- **Valencia**
  C.C. Siglo XXI (Frente al Hotel Inter-Continental), nivel
  Boyacá.
  Tel: (241) 822-7194; Fax: (241) 822-9555
- **Puerto La Cruz**
  Av. Principal de Lecherías, C. Comercial Forum Plaza.
  Tel: (081) 811-670; Fax: (081) 819-686
  Website: http://www.micasa.com.ve
- **Organización Rent-A-House**
  (Caracas, Maracaibo, Puerto la Cruz)
  Website: http://www.rentahouse.com.ve
- **Direccion**
  CCCT, Torre D, Piso 1, Oficina D-101, Ave. La Estancia,
  Urb. Chuao, Caracas 1064
  Tel: (212) 959-0511
- **Concorde Bienes Raíces**
  C.A. Ciudad Guayana Avenida Estados Unidos, Centro

Comercial Villa Alianza, Urbanización Villa Alianza II, Nivel 1, Local 40 (Referencia: Redoma Chilemex, de la Ave. La Americas) Puerto Ordaz Bolivar
Tel: (286) 923-2364

- **Servicios InmoSoft**
  C.A. (Rif. J-30494154-4)
  Av. José María Vargas, Edif. Artico, Piso 2, Ofi. 23-A, Urb. Santa Fe Norte, Caracas
  Tel: (212) 975-4860

- **C.C. La Viña**
  Nivel 1. Valencia, Edo.Carabobo. Llámenos por los
  Tel: (241) 824-1446

Websites

- http://www.Inmobiliarios.com.ve
- http://www.tualiado.com
- http://www.tuinmueble.com
- http://www.tupromotor.com/
- http://www.nuevohabitat.com/
- http://www.inmobilia.com
- http://www.caracasinmuebles.com/
- http://www.consorciocsi.com
- http://www.habitable.com.ve
- http://www.inmueblesgrancaracas.com
- http://www.megainmueble.com/index2.htm
- http://www.tucasa.com.ve
- http://www.tusmetros.com
- http://www.vargasypinilla.com
- http://www.unocasa2.com.ve

International Schools

- **Colegio Internacional de Caracas**
  PO Box 025323, Miami, FL 33102, USA

- **Escuela Campo Alegre**
  Jet Cargo International M314, P.O. Box 02-5255, Miami, FL, 33 102 0010, USA

- **International School of Carabobo**
  BAMCO-VLN 001200, PO Box 522237, Miami, FL 33102-2237, USA

- **International School of Caracas**
  POBA International #233, PO Box 02-5255, Miami, FL 33102-5255
- **S.A. Escuela Bella Vista**
  Buzoom C-MAR-P1815, PO Box 02-8537, USA

University Websites

- **Universidad Católica Andrés Bello**
  Website: http://www.ucab.edu.ve
- **Universidad Central de Venezuela**
  Website: http://www.ucv.ve
- **Universidad Bicentenaria de Aragua**
  Website: http://www.uba.edu.ve
- **Universidad Centrooccidental Lisandro Alvarado (UCLA) (Barquisimeto)**
  Website: http://www.ucla.edu.ve
- **Universidad de Carabobo (UC)**
  Website: http://www.uc.edu.ve
- **Universidad de Los Andes (ULA)**
  Website: http://www.ula.ve
- **Universidad de Oriente (UDO)**
  Website: http://www.monagas.udo.edu.ve
- **Universidad del Zulia (LUZ)**
  Website: http://www.luz.ve
- **Universidad Metropolitana (UNIMET)**
  Website: http://www.unimet.edu.ve
- **Universidad Nac. Exp. de los Llanos Ezequiel Zamora (UNELLEZ)**
  Website: http://www.geocities.com/CollegePark/Classroom/9356
- **Universidad Nacional Abierta**
  Website: http://www.una.edu.ve
- **Universidad Nacional Experimental del Táchira (UNET)**
  Website: http://www.unet.edu.ve
- **Universidad Nacional Experimental Politécnica (UNEXPO)**
  Website: http://www.unexpo.edu.ve
- **Universidad Nueva Esparta (UNE)**

Website: http://www.une.edu.ve/administracion
- **Universidad Santa María (USM)**
  Website: http://www.welcome.to/industrial
- **Universidad Simón Bolívar (USB)**
  Website: http://www.usb.ve
- **Universidad José María Vargas**
  Website: http://www.ujmv.edu

MANAGING YOUR MONEY
Bank Websites
- **Banco Latino**
  Website: http://www.banco-latino.com
- **Banco Mercantil**
  Website: http://www.bancomercantil.com
- **Banco Noroco**
  Website: http://www.noroco.com
- **Banco Provincial**
  Website: http://www.provincial.com
- **Banesco**
  Website: http://www.banesco.com
- **Interbank**
  Website: http://www.interbank.com.ve

Law Offices (Bufetes)
These have websites in Spanish and English:
- **Anzola Raffalli Y Rodríguez**
  Torre Centuria, Piso 8, Av Venezuela, El Rosal, Caracas 1060
  Tel: (212) 952-0995
  Website: http://www.arr.com.ve/english.index.htm
- **Badell Y Grau**
  Edf Seguros Mercantil, Piso 5, Av Las Acacias, Francisco Solano López, Urb Sabana Grande, Caracas 1050
  Tel: (582) 582-763-0994
  Website: http://www.badellgrau.com
- **Espiñeira, Sheldon & Asociados**
  Av. Ppal. De Chuao, Ed. Del Rio. Estado Miranda, Caracas
  Tel: (582) 918-111; Fax: (582) 915-210
  Contact: Dr Jesús Alemán

- **Perez Mena Everts, Báez, Marales & Asociados**
  Multicentro Empresarial Del Este, Edf. Libertador Núcleo
  A Piso 12. Of. 121-A Caracas, Edo Miranda
  Tel: (582) 285-2434; Fax: (582) 261-4830
  Contact: José Laría
- **Perez Porta, Cachafei Y Asociados**
  Edf. Mene Grande Ii Piso , Of. 26 Av. Francisco De Miranda,
  Los Palos Grandes, Caracas
  Tel: (582) 285-2168 / 283-9712; Fax: (582) 285-3014
  Contact: Salvador Porta Ferré
- **Lara Rodriguez, Marambio Y Asociados**
  1a Transversal , Multicentro Los Palos Grandes , Piso
  9 Apdo Postal 6365 Los Palos Grandes, Edo Miranda,
  Caracas
  Tel: (582) 285-3923; Fax: (582) 285-6960
  Contact: Emilio López Quiroga
- **Sarmiento Nuñez, Brillembourg Y Asociados**
  Av. Francisco De Miranda, Edf. Easo, Piso 5 Ofc. 5b - Apdo.
  Postal 63194 Chacaito, Dtto. Federal
  Fax: (582) 953-7096
  Contact: Carlos Jose SarmieNto Sosa
- **Dempaire Reyna Bermúdez & Asociados**
  Edif. Bancaracas, P.H., Plaza La Castellana, Caracas
  Tel: (582) 264-6244; Fax: (582) 264-7543 / 264-7743
  Contact: Director Dr Faustino Flamarique
- **Klahr Zighelboim, Colmenares & Trivella**
  Multicentro Empresarial Del Este, Torre Miranda A, Piso
  7, Of 76 Y 77, Av Libert, Caracas
  Tel: (582) 266-0862 / 2005 / 0497 / 7 ; Fax: (582) 262-
  1085
  Contact: Dr Marcos Colmenares
- **Bentata Hoet & Asociados**
  Av. Fco. De Miranda, Torre Europa, P.H., Caracas
  Tel: (582) 951-2067; Fax: (582) 951-3067
  Contact: Dr Franklin Hoet
- **Torres Plaz & Araujo**
  Edif. Polar,Torre Oeste,Paseo Colon, Urb. Los Caobos,Plaza
  Venezuela, Caracas
  Tel: (582) 709-5311; Fax: (582) 709-5300 / 01 / 03

Contact: Dr Adolfo Plaza

- **González De La Vega Abogados**
  Av Libertador, Chacao, Centro Parima, Piso 8, Of. 801,
  Caracas
  Tel: (582) 267-6518 / 6601 / 6719; Fax: (582) 261-0077
  Contact: Dr Eugenio González De La Vega
- **Aparicio, Varela Y Asociados**
  C/ Villa Flor, Esq. Boulevard De Sabana Grande, Edif
  Asuncion, Piso 5, Of. 502, Caracas
  Tel: (582) 762-0576; Fax: (582) 762-0576
  Contact: Dr Alejandro Nine Aparicio
- **Borjas, Pelayo & Salvuchi Abogados Consultores**
  Avda. Fco. De Mirnada, Edif. Roraima, Piso 4, Of. 4-G,
  Campo Alegre, Caracas
  Tel: (582) 953-5970 / 4468 / 95127; Fax: (582) 953-4638
- **International Law Practice**
  Edif. Torreon, Piso 10, C/ Veracruz, Las Mercedes,
  Caracas
  Tel: (582) 912-751 / 2853 / 920723; Fax: (5820 921-252
  Contact: Heraclio Atencio Bello
- **Escritorio Jurídico M & P Asociados**
  Av. Francisco De Miranda, Torre Cemica, Piso 8, Ofc. C,
  Chacao, Caracas
  Tel: (582) 263-4195; Fax: (582) 263-4195
  Contact: Dr Marco Tulio Moreno
- **Barreto, Oteyza, Romero, Trejo, Matthies & Azpurua**
  Ernesto Blohm, Torre Diamen, Ph, Chuao, Caracas
  Tel: (582) 993-5650 / 8364 / 8428 / 9; Fax: (582) 927-389
  Contact: Dr Jose Angel Trejo / Dr F Roland Matthies
- **Sandoval & Associates** (immigration law specialists)
  Website: http://www.sandovalassociates.com/index.html
- **Index Of Venezuelan Law**
  Website: http://www.derecho.org/comunidad/
  bufetesvenezolanos

LEISURE AND ENTERTAINMENT
Among the very many restaurants and cafés in Caracas, here
are native Caraqueño Francisco's choices:

Restaurants

- **Bellevue** (Venezuelan meat grills with great views)
  Sector Canta Rana, Alto Hatillo
- **Casa Urrutia**
  Calle Madrid and Calle Monterrey, Las Mercedes
- **Catay**
  Centro Comercial las Cupulas, Los Palos Grandes
- **Chez Wong** (Chinese)
  Av Francisco Solano, La Castellana
- **Doña Caraotica** (typical Venezuelan)
  Av Principal Las Mercedes
- **El Tizón** (Peruvian / Mexican)
  Centro Comercial Bello Campo (basement)
- **El Tizoncito** (Mexican)
  Centro Comercial Paseo Las Mercedes
- **L'Attico** (TexMex; very popular with young Norteamericanos.)
  Av Luis Roche, 2a Transversal, Altamira
- **La Cita**
  Esq de Alcabala, La Candelaria
- **La Empalizada** (Venezuelan grilled meats)
  Carretera de Baruta, Sector Hoyo de la Puerta
- **La Strega** (Italian)
  Av los Chaguaramos, La Castellana
- **La Tertulia**
  Alcabala a Urapal, La Candelaria
- **Lasserre** (French)
  3a Av, between 2a and 3a Transversal, Los Palos Grandes
- **Lee Hamilton** (international meat dishes)
  Av San Felipe, Esq el Bosque, La Castellana
- **Sakura** (Japanese)
  1a Av Los Palos Grandes
- **Samui**
  Av Andrés Bello and 1a Transversal, Los Palos Grandes
- **Spizico** (Italian)
  Av Principal la Castellana

Cafés

- **Art Café**
  Los Palos Grandes

- **Café Olé**
  Las Mercedes
- **Citron**
  Centro Comercial Sambil
- **Collins Avenue**
  La CasTel:lana
- **Ibiza**
  Las Mercedes
- **Houlihan's** (upmarket attempt at an Irish pub)
  Centro Comercial Ciudad Tamanaco
- **News Café**
  Los Palos Grandes
- **Top's**
  Centro Comercial Sambil

Internet Cafés and Facilities

- **CopyNet**
  Avenida Universidad Esquina Sociedad & Camejo, Centro
  Comercial Galerías, Caracas
  Tel: (484) 0574-484-1629
  Website: http://www.copynetjl.com.ve
- **Cyber Café 2000**
  Boulevard de Sabana Grande, Edf Galerías Bolivar, Caracas
  Website: http://www.cybercafe2000.com
- **Cyber Café la Mac@rena**
  Centro Comercial la Macarena, La Macarena Sur, Carretera
  Panamerica, Km 24, Piso 1, Local 14, Los Teques,
  Miranda State
- **Cyberclub Porlamar**
  4 de Mayo Porlamar Porlamar calle fermin edif. la torre
  ofic.#232, Porlamar-Nueva Espaarta, 606301
  Website: http://www.go.to
- **North American Connection**
  Carabobo Street, C.C. Paseo Plaza #5 Puerto La Cruz,
  Anzoategui 6023
- **CafeSuite**
  Maturín-Monagas
  Tel : (291) 644-025
  Website: http://www.cafesuite.net.ve

Shopping Malls (Caracas)

- **Ciudad Tamanaco**
- **Galerias**
- **Lido**
- **Plaza Las Américas**
- **Sambil**

Nightspots

- **Al Trote** (a gay club)
  Los Palos Grandes
- **El Maní es así** (Latin music)
  Sabana Grande
- **Le Club** (members only)
  Centro Comercial Chacaito
- **Mazai**
  Centro Comercial San Ignacio
- **Pals**
  Centro Comercial Cuidad Tamanaco

Museums

- **Galeria de Arte Nacional**
  Website: http://www.gan.org.ve
- **Museo de Arte Colonial**
  Website: http://www.quintadeanauco.org.ve
- **Museo de Arte Contemporáneo de Caracas Sofía Imber**
  Website: http://www.maccsi.org
- **Museo de Arte de Coro**
- **Museo de Barquisimeto**
- **Museo de Bellas Artes** (Caracas Fine Arts Museum)
- **Museo de Ciencias Naturales** (Caracas Natural History Museum)
- **Museo de los Niños de Caracas**
  Website: http://www.maravillosarealidad.com
- **Museo del Táchira**
  Website: http://www.museodeltachira.gov.ve
- **Museo Sacro de Caracas**
  Website: http://www.cibernetic.com/sacro

Theatres

- **Ateneo de Caracas**
  Website: http://www.ateneodecaracas.org/
- **Ateneo de Carúpano**
- **Ateneo de Valencia**
  Website: http://www.ateneodevalencia.org/
- **Ballet Contemporaneo de Caracas**
  Website: http://www.caracasballet.com/
- **CELARG**
  Website: http://www.celarg.org.ve
- **Grupo Teatral Sábado**
- **Teatro Baralt de Maracaibo**
  Website: http://www.teatrobaralt.org

Cinemas

Caracas has multiscreen cinemas in some shopping malls.

Cultural and Social Organisations

- **Cámara de la Cultura de Nueva Esparta**
  Cultural organisation for Margarita and Coche
  Website: http://www.geocities.com/camaradelacultura
- **Centro Cultural Eladio Alemán Sucre**
  Carabobo State cultural organisation
  Website: http://www.el-carabobeno.com
- **Fundación Bigott**
  Cultural organisation with an excellent magazine on culture, heritage and history
  Website: http://www.fundacionbigott.com
- **Fundación de Etnomusicología y Folklore (FUNDEF)**
  Latin American / Caribbean traditional cultural organisation
  Website: http://www.ivic.ve/

Bookstores and Libraries

- **Books for Kids**
  Website: http://www.farmavitaca.com/booksforkids.htm
- **Las Novedades**
  In all shopping malls
- **Librería del Ateneo**
  Ateneo de Caracas

- **Mundoalegre** (Amazon.com associate)
  Website: http://www.mundoalegre.com
- **Tecni Ciencia Libros**
  Centro Comercial Ciudad Tamanaco, Centro Comercial Sambil

Beaches and Parks

- **Inparques**
  The national park authority.
  Av. Rómulo Gallegos, con 2da Av. de Sta. Eduvigis, al lado de la estación del Metro Parque del Este.
  Tel: (212) 273-2860; Fax: (212) 273-2862.
  Website: http://www.inparques.gob.ve/

TRANSPORT AND COMMUNICATIONS

Taxis

There are a number of smart taxi services in Caracas, including:

- **MóvilEnlace**
  Tel: (212) 577-3344
- **Taxitur**
  Tel: (212) 794-1264
- **Teletaxi**
  Tel: (212) 753-4155

Telephone

The country code is 0058. State codes are:

Amazonas	048
Anzoategui	Barcelona 281
Apure	047
Aragua	Barinas 073; Cata, Choroní, Maracay 243; Colonia Tovar 033
Bolivar	Ciudad Bolívar 085; Ciudad Guayana (Puerto Ordaz–San Felix) 086; El Callao 088
Carabobo	Delta Amacuro 087; Puerto Cabello 042; Valencia 041

Caracas	212
Falcón	Chichiriviche 042; Coro 068; Punto Fijo 069; San Juan de los Morros 046
Lara	Barquisimeto 051; El Tocuyo 053
Mérida	074
Miranda	Guarenas, Guatire 036; Higuerote 034; Los Teques 0323; San Francisco de Yare 039
Monagas	Caripe 092; Maturín 091
Nueva Esparta	Isla Cubagua, Isla de Coche, Margarita 095
Portuguesa	Acarigua, Aruare 055; Guanare 057
Sucre	Cumaná, Cumanacoa 093; Carúpano 094
Tachira	La Fría 077; San Antonio de Táchira, San Cristóbal, Rubio 076
Trujillo	Trujillo 72; Valera 071
Vargas	El Hatillo 02; El Junquito 033; La Guaira 031; Maiquetía 212
Yaracuy	Chivacoa 051; San Felipe 054
Zulia	Cabimas 064; Ciudad Ojeda 065; Maracaibo 061; San Carlos del Zulia, Santa Bárbara 075; San Rafael del Moján 062

MEDIA
Newspapers and magazines

- **Economía Hoy**
  Website: http://www.economiahoy.com
- **El Nacional**
  Website: http://www.el-nacional.com
- **El Universal**
  Website: http://www.el-universal.com
- **El Venezolano**
  Website: http://www.elvenezolano.com
- **La Hora**
  Website: http://www.lahora.com
- **La Nación**
  Website: http://www.lanacion.com.ve

- **Meridiano**
  Website: http://www.meridiano.com.ve
- **Venezuela Analítica** (Spanish business magazine)
  Website: http://www.analitica.com
- **Dinero** (Spanish business magazine)
  Website: http://www.dinero.com.ve

Radio

91.1 FM Avil, 94.1 FM Hot 94, 94.3 FM Gente, 101.5 FM KISS, 104.5 FM Capital Fun, 105.3 FM Planeta, 107.3 FM La Mega Estación, 710 AM Radio Capital, 970 AM Radio Continente, 1590 AM Radio Deporte

- **Radionet**
  Website: http://www.radionet.com.ve

Television

- **Radio Caracas**
  Website: http://www.rctv.net
- **Televen**
  Website: http://www.televen.com
- **Venevisión**
  Website: http://www.venevision.com
- **Venezolana de Televisión**
  Website: http://www.vtv.gob.ve

Internet

- **ENIAC (Internet for Companies)**
  Website: http://www.eniac.com
- **Internet Communicaciones**
  Website: http://www.internet.ve
- **Telcel**
  Website: http://www.Telcel.net.ve

Search Sites

- Website: http://www.yellowpages-caribbean.com
- Website: http://buscador.infoguia.net
- Website: http://www.paginasamarillas.com.ve
- Website: http://www.venezuelasite.com
- Website: http://www.latinworld.com

- Website: http://www.venezuelatuya.com
- Website: http://www.mipunto.com
- Website: http://www.thinkvenezuela.net
- Website: http://www.caracasvirtual.com
- Website: http://www.rumbacaracas.com

LANGUAGE INSTITUTES AND CLASSES

- **Centro Venezolano Americano (CVA)**
  Avenida Principal José Martí,
  Edificio Centro Venezolano Americano
  Urbanización Las Mercedes
  Caracas 1060-A
  Tel: (212) 993-7911 / 993-8422
  Website: http://www.cva.org.ve
- **Centro Venezolano de Español**
  PO Box 54583, 1050 Caracas
  Caracas: Avenida Francisco de Miranda, Centro Empresarial
  Del Este, Torre Miranda Caracas
  Puerto La Cruz: Calle Simón Rodriguez, Puerto La Cruz
  Tel: (212) 771-9294
  Email: info@ceves.org.ve
  Website: http://www.ceves.org.ve
- **Centro Electrónico de Idiomas y Computación**
  Avendia 11 con Calle 78, Edificio C.E.I., Maracaibo, Zulia
  Tel: (261)797-4161 / 797-6089 / 798-6130
  Email: info@centroelectronico.com
  Website: http://www.centroelectronico.com
- **Iowa Institute**
  Avenida 4 con calle 18Mérida. Edo. MéridaVenezuela
  Website: http://www.iowainstitute.com
- **VEN-USA** (U.S. Contact Office)
  6542 Hypoluxo Rd #324, Lake Worth, FL 33467
  Tel: (561) 357-8802; Fax: (561) 357-9199
  Email: venusa@earthlink.net
  Website: http://www.venusacollege.org
- **CELA Spanish School**
  Calle Corocoro Qta. CELA Urb. Playa El Angel Pampatar
  Isla de Margarita Venezuela, South America
  Tel and Fax: (0058) 295-262-8198, (0058) 295-808-8411

Email: info@cela-ve.com
Website: http://cela-ve.com
- **VEN-USA College** (Venezuela Study Abroad Site)
  49-49 Avenida Urdaneta, Edificio Guilam, Mérida
  Tel: (274) 263-763; Fax: (274) 263-3525
  Email: venusa@earthlink.net

EMBASSIES
Venezuelan Embassies
- **Australia**
  7 Culgoa Circuit, O'Malley, Canberra, ACT 2606
  Tel: (02) 6290-2900
- **Belgium**
  10 Avenue Franklin Roosevelt, 1050 Brussels
  Tel: 228-7284
- **Canada**
  32 Range Rd, Ottawa, Ontario, K1N 8J4
  Tel: 613-235-5697
- **France**
  11 Rue Copernic, 75116 Paris
  Tel: 14-553-2998
- **Germany**
  Schillstrasse 9-10, 10785 Berlin
  Tel: 030-832-2400
- **Italy**
  Via Nicolo Tartalgia 11, 00197 Rome
  Tel: 06-807-9797
- **Netherlands**
  Nassaulaan 2, 2514 JS The Hague
  Tel: 70-352-3851
- **Sweden**
  Engelbrektsgatan 35-0B,11432 Stockholm
  Tel: 8-411-0996
- **Switzerland**
  Morillonstrasse 9, 3007 Bern
  Tel: 31-371-3282
- **UK**
  1 Cromwell Rd, London, SW7 2HW
  Tel: 020-7581-2776

- **USA**
  1099 30th St, NW, Washington DC 20007
  Tel: 202-342-2214

Embassies in Venezuela

- **British Embassy**
  Torre La Castellana, Av Principal de la Castellana, La Castellana, Caracas
  Tel: (582) 993-4111
  Website: http://www.britain.org.ve
- **Canadian Embassy**
  Av Francisco de Miranda con Sur Altamira, Caracas
  Tel: (212) 264-0833 / 266-7176
  Email: crcas@dfait-maeci.gc.ca
- **French Embassy**
  Edificio Embajada de Francia, Calle Madrid con Trinidad, Las Mercedes, Caracas
  Tel: (212) 909-6500
  Website: http://www.francia.org.ve
- **Italian Embassy**
  Edf Atrium, Calle Sorocaima entre Avenidas Tamanaco y Venezuela, El Rosal, Caracas
  Tel: (212) 952-7311
  Email: ambcara@italamb.org.ve
- **US Embassy**
  Calle F con Calle Suapure, Colinas del Valle Arriba, Caracas
  Tel: (212) 975-6411 / 975-7811
  Website: http://www.embajadausa.org.ve
- **German Embassy**
  Torre La Castellana, Av Principal de Castellana, La Castellana, Caracas
  Tel: (212) 261-0181
  Email: diplogermacara@cantv.net
- **Spanish Embassy**
  Quinta Marmolejo, Av Mohedano entre 1a & 2a Transversal, La Castellana, Caracas
  Tel: (212) 263-2855
  Email: espanve@cantv.net

BUSINESS ORGANISATIONS

- **Trade Venezuela**
  Website: http://www.trade-venezuela.com
- **Caracas Stock Exchange**
  Website: http://www.caracasstock.com
- **Organisation for the Promotion of Investment (CONAPRI)**
  Website: http://www.conapri.org

COUNTRY INFORMATION
Weights and Measures
Venezuela uses the metric system.

Necessities and Documents to Bring
You will need a passport in good condition with six months' validity. Most Western nationals do not need visas, as airlines and cruise ships issue 90-day tourist cards (*tarjeta de turismo*). Your passport and tourist card will be stamped. Keep the yellow copy. Overland entry is also possible with a tourist card for most Western nationals; the cards are issued free-of-charge at Venezuelan consulates and border crossings.

To be safe, however, get a tourist visa before leaving your country, as Venezuelan immigration officials may ask for it for land entry. A one-year visa is valid for multiple entries. Requirements are: a bank statement or letter, a passport valid for at least a year, an employer's letter, a photograph and a return ticket.

You can extend your tourist card for three months at the Oficina Nacional de Identificación y Extranjería (ONIDEX). The Caracas office has been in chaos for years, but the brave and patient can visit it at Departamento de Turismo, 2nd Floor (east stairs), Av Baralt and Este 8, Plaza Miranda, El Silencio, Caracas. Requirements are: two photographs, a letter on legal paper (*papel sellado*) giving the reason for the extension, a photocopy of your plane ticket and an identity card (*cédula*) from your travel agent/representative. It is a very good idea to take a DEX veteran with you, especially since DEX is in the busy and potentially dangerous Capitolio markets.

Pre-Entry Vaccinations

There are not required by law. Jabs are really needed only when travelling deep into the interior. Those staying within the big cities are unlikely to need vaccinations. But to be safe, it is worth consulting your doctor for a course of anti-malarial tablets and these vaccinations:

- Tetanus-Diptheria: a ten-year booster to defend against typhoid.
- Polio: also lasts ten years.
- Hepatitis A: Havrix 1440 and/or Avaxim last ten years. Expensive.
- Hepatitis B: three doses over six months.
- Typhoid: lasts three years but is only 60 per cent effective.
- Yellow fever: lasts ten years. Expensive but well worth the money.
- Rabies: three doses over 3–4 weeks.

FURTHER READING

Unfortunately very little has been written on Venezuela in English that is neither academic nor a travel guide. For accessible and useful information on contemporary Venezuela, the Internet is far more rewarding than a trawl through a library would be.

For the media, there are the newspapers *El Universal* at http://www.eud.com and *El Nacional* at http://www.el-nacional.com, both in Spanish. *Yahoo!* has up-to-date news under 'World News-Countries-Venezuela' and the magazine *Venezuela Analitica* covers a range of topics in Spanish at http://www.analitica.com.

The best site for food is *La Cocina Venezolana* where you can find many authentic Venezuelan recipes in English and Spanish. You can find it at http://members.tripod. com/ ~ cocinavzla.

A large amount of information is available from the Library of Congress's Federal Research Division at http://cweb2. locgov/frd/cs/venezuela, together with a fairly exhaustive bibliography which contains many works on politics and economics.

For history, Benjamin Keen's *A History of Latin America* (published by Houghton Mifflin) contains interesting information on the continent that goes beyond a mere retelling. In Spanish, most authoritative work tends to be dense and overdetailed. For an introduction to some of Venezuela's most influential contemporary writers in this area, the two-volume *Venezuela: 500 Años* (published by the oil company Lagoven) is an interesting and informative read.

Mount Roraima may have been the inspiration behind Sir Arthur Conan Doyle's *The Lost World*, but Venezuela is not otherwise well represented in fiction in English. However, the final days of Símon Bolívar are brilliantly interpreted in Gabriel Garcia Marquez's *The General in His Labyrinth*.

For Venezuelan writers writing in Spanish, Rómulo Gallegos is the nation's greatest. His best work is *Doña Barbara*, which gives some insight into the country, even though the story itself does not stand up well to contemporary scrutiny. His work, alongside that of the best of the rest of Venezuela, can be found in *Coleccíon El Dorado*, published by Monte Avila. To find more information on Venezuela's poets and novelists, take a look at the website of the Venezuelan Embassy in Washington at http://www.embavenez-us.org.

- *The Man of Gold*. Fombona Rufino Blanco. Brentano's, 1920.

- *Doña Barbara*. Rómulo Gallegos. Peter Smith, 1948.

- *Canaima*. Rómulo Gallegos. University of Oklahoma Press, 1988.

- *Mama Blanca's Memoirs*. Teresa de la Parra. 1993.

- *Iphigenia: The Diary of a Young Lady Who Wrote Because She Is Bored*. Teresa de la Parra. University of Texas Press, 1993.

- *The Red Lances*. Arturo Uslar Pietro. Alfred A Knopf, 1963.

- *Venezuelan Short Stories*. Lyda Aponte de Zacklin (ed). Monte Ávila, 1992.

- *The Four Voyages*. Christopher Columbus. Penguin Classics 1969.

- *The Liberators: Latin America's Struggle for Independence*. Robert Harvey. Robinson Publishing, 2002.

- *Café con Leche: Race, Class and National Image in Venezuela*. Winthrop R Wright. University of Texas Press, 1990.

- *Hugo Chavez and the Bolivarian Revolution: And the Bolvarian Revolution in Venezuela*. Verso Books, 2005.

- *In Defense of the Indians*. Bartolomé de las Casas. Northern Illinois University Press, 1992.

- *Culture and Customs of Venezuela*. Mark Dinneen. Greenwood Press, 2001.

- *The General in His Labyrinth*. Gabriel Garcia Marquez. Penguin Books Ltd, 1995.

- *In the Shadow of the Liberator: Hugo Chávez and the Transformation of Venezuela*. Richard Gott. Verso, 2000.

ABOUT THE AUTHOR

Kitt was born in Torquay in 1969 and grew up in South Devon. He has been an English teacher since he graduated from university, where he studied psychology.

He lived in Venezuela for over two years, teaching English and studying Spanish. He has travelled extensively around Venezuela and has returned numerous times to visit old friends and visit parts of the country. While in Venezuela, he married a Colombian, Sofia, and they maintain close contact with family and friends in both countries.

He has developed a love of South America, especially the food, and his main ambition is to show his two children, James and Gabriela, all the places he has been to and fallen in love with and explore new places together. His other ambition is to escape teaching and management and write full-time.

INDEX

Titles in the CultureShock! series:

Argentina	Hawaii	Paris
Australia	Hong Kong	Philippines
Austria	Hungary	Portugal
Bahrain	India	Russia
Barcelona	Indonesia	San Francisco
Beijing	Iran	Saudi Arabia
Belgium	Ireland	Scotland
Bolivia	Israel	Sri Lanka
Borneo	Italy	Shanghai
Brazil	Jakarta	Singapore
Britain	Japan	South Africa
Bulgaria	Korea	Spain
Cambodia	Laos	Sweden
Canada	London	Switzerland
Chicago	Malaysia	Syria
Chile	Mauritius	Taiwan
China	Mexico	Thailand
Costa Rica	Morocco	Tokyo
Cuba	Moscow	Turkey
Czech Republic	Munich	Ukraine
Denmark	Myanmar	United Arab
Ecuador	Nepal	Emirates
Egypt	Netherlands	USA
Finland	New York	Vancouver
France	New Zealand	Venezuela
Germany	Norway	Vietnam
Greece	Pakistan	

For more information about any of these titles, please contact any of our Marshall Cavendish offices around the world (listed on page ii) or visit our website at:

www.marshallcavendish.com/genref